D1409947

Imperfect Institutions

This series provides a forum for theoretical and empirical investigations of social phenomena. It promotes works that focus on the interactions among cognitive processes, individual behavior, and social outcomes. It is especially open to interdisciplinary books that are genuinely integrative.

Editor: Timur Kuran

Editorial Board: Tyler Cowen   Avner Greif

                         Diego Gambetta   Viktor Vanberg

Titles in the Series

Tyler Cowen. *Markets and Cultural Voices: Liberty vs. Power in the Lives of Mexican Amate Painters*

Thráinn Eggertsson. *Imperfect Institutions: Possibilities and Limits of Reform*

Vernon W. Ruttan. *Social Science Knowledge and Economic Development: An Institutional Design Perspective*

Phillip J. Nelson and Kenneth V. Greene. *Signaling Goodness: Social Rules and Public Choice*

Stephen Knack, Editor. *Democracy, Governance, and Growth*

Omar Azfar and Charles A. Cadwell, Editors. *Market-Augmenting Government: The Institutional Foundations for Prosperity*

Randall G. Holcombe. *From Liberty to Democracy: The Transformation of American Government*

David T. Beito, Peter Gordon, and Alexander Tabarrok, Editors. *The Voluntary City: Choice, Community, and Civil Society*

Alexander J. Field. *Altruistically Inclined? The Behavioral Sciences, Evolutionary Theory, and the Origins of Reciprocity*

David George. *Preference Pollution: How Markets Create the Desires We Dislike*

Julian L. Simon. *The Great Breakthrough and Its Cause*

E. L. Jones. *Growth Recurring: Economic Change in World History*

Rosemary L. Hopcroft. *Regions, Institutions, and Agrarian Change in European History*

Lee J. Alston, Gary D. Libecap, and Bernardo Mueller. *Titles, Conflict, and Land Use: The Development of Property Rights and Land Reform on the Brazilian Amazon Frontier*

Eirik G. Furubotn and Rudolf Richter. *Institutions and Economic Theory: The Contribution of the New Institutional Economics*

Daniel B. Klein, Editor. *Reputation: Studies in the Voluntary Elicitation of Good Conduct*

Richard A. Easterlin. *Growth Triumphant: The Twenty-first Century in Historical Perspective*

Imperfect Institutions

Possibilities and Limits of Reform

Thráinn Eggertsson

University of Michigan Press
Ann Arbor

Copyright © by the University of Michigan 2005
All rights reserved
Published in the United States of America by
The University of Michigan Press
Manufactured in the United States of America
♾ Printed on acid-free paper

2008   2007   2006   2005   4   3   2   1

A CIP catalog record for this book is available from the British Library.

Thráinn Eggertsson, 1941–
   Imperfect institutions : possibilities and limits of reform
Thráinn Eggertsson.
       p.   cm. — (Economics, cognition, and society)
   Includes bibliographical references and index.
   ISBN 0-472-11456-5 (cloth : alk. paper) — ISBN 0-472-03039-6
(pbk. : alk. paper)
   1. Institutional economics.   2. Right of property.   I. Title.
II. Series.
HB99.5.T485   2004
330.1—dc22   2004017530

Acknowledgments

For more than twenty years I have found inspiration and motivation in the work of Douglass North, who is always years ahead of me in his ideas. Doug is an intrepid thinker and a true friend. It is to him that I dedicate this book.

I see *Imperfect Institutions* as an extension of my previous book, *Economic Behavior and Institutions,* which aimed at synthesizing emerging contributions to the new institutionalism in economics. The new book explores the implications for policy of new institutional economics, while reflecting on recent developments in the field as well as in my own thinking.

Colleagues at home and abroad have given me invaluable help in writing this book. They all have my thanks, but their number is large and only a few are mentioned below. Recently I have spent much time away from my roots at the University of Iceland. Initially, my friends at Washington University in St. Louis put me on the institutional path. Two years with Lin and Vincent Ostrom and their team at Indiana University's Workshop in Political Theory and Policy Analysis were invaluable, both intellectually and emotionally. Similarly two years at Stanford University's Hoover Institution were important and delightful. Of the outstanding people at Stanford University, I owe special intellectual debts to Barry Weingast and Avner Greif. One semester with Steven N. S. Cheung at the University of Hong Kong's School of Economics and Finance opened my window to the Far East. Two semesters at the Max Planck Institute for Research into Economic Systems in Jena opened a door to German institutionalism and modern Germany. Unfortunately, my association with the Jena Institute was cut short by the untimely and tragic illness of its director and esteemed colleague, Manfred E. Streit.

In recent years, I have spent the fall in Iceland and the spring term in New York, initially as Olin Fellow at Columbia University's School of Law. The opportunity to learn more about legal aspects of institutions and enjoy the superb intellectual company of the professors and students at the law school was a wonderful experience. The same is true of my contact with the political science department. For all this I thank Victor Goldberg, Richard Nelson, and many other friends at Columbia. My current home away from home is New York University's Politics Department, where I am part-time professor, enjoying a great intellectual environment and generous, supportive colleagues. I am particularly indebted to the department chair, Bruce Bueno de Mesquita.

The University of Iceland has treated its wayward son with patience and generosity. I mention particularly former university president Sveinbjörn Björnsson, and former dean Ágúst Einarsson. Several of my colleagues in Iceland have read individual chapters of the manuscript: Ásgeir Jónsson, Thorvaldur Gylfason, and Tryggvi Thór Herbertsson. Gylfi Zoega read the entire manuscript. I thank them for valuable suggestions. I also thank innumerable professors, graduate students, and conference participants in various countries who have assisted me with this book.

The editor of the series, Timur Kuran, has critically examined virtually every paragraph of my text, as well as its overall structure and logic. The book has benefited enormously from his suggestions. I am also thankful for thoughtful comments by two anonymous readers. The staff at the University of Michigan Press has been exceptionally efficient, helpful, and encouraging. I thank my initial in-house editor, Ellen M. McCarthy, and her successor, Raphael Allen. Marcia LaBrenz was in charge of copyediting and did a fine job. I also thank Kelly O'Connor, editorial assistant, for her help.

Finally, warm thanks go to personal friends and family members who have supported me in various ways.

Contents

Introduction
Opportunities Lost

In the last two and a half centuries, a scientific and technological revolution has created astounding opportunities for humanity, but the benefits have accrued primarily to people in the industrial countries. The majority of the human race lives in the so-called developing countries that enjoy few of these opportunities; even economically advanced countries have regions and industries that lag behind. In this book I am concerned with opportunities lost: the question of why most nations have not enjoyed the full benefits of the technological revolution. Imperfect social institutions, I propose, are at the root of the problem.

This volume continues and extends the work that I began with *Economic Behavior and Institutions* (1990), which tried to order and synthesize various contributions to the study of social institutions. The multidisciplinary line of research that I reviewed in 1990 had come of age in the 1980s, and I limited my survey to studies that modified neoclassical economics while leaving its core methods intact. The new institutional economics sets out to explain how institutions coordinate behavior, affect transaction costs, and enable or block economic activity. My 1990 book toured their landscape, so to speak, from the valleys to the mountaintops, beginning by examining economic results that flow from different kinds of property rights institutions; then moving up to explore the organization of exchange, including contracts, firms, and market practices; and finally looking at the social and political framework that envelops the economy. Focusing on (voluntary and involuntary) transactions and transaction costs has proved to be a fruitful method for analyzing the organization of both economic and noneconomic activity.

Many people seem to think that inherent in the new institutional economics is an assumption or claim that the world is always efficient. Although mistaken, this view is understandable because a segment of the literature asks the following questions: Does the structure of efficient economic (and social) organization differ from one type of activity or exchange environment to another? If differences exist, do they arise because different measurement, monitoring, and enforcement problems require different solutions? These studies attempt to test the logic of the transaction-costs approach and, for example, to explain differences in the structure of firms and contractual arrangements in competitive markets as solutions to various transaction problems. The underlying assumption of these works is that market competition selects effective arrangements and weeds out more costly ones. Other studies even portray the institutions of tribal societies as effective solutions to transaction problems in a world of limited knowledge and primitive technology. Without efficient organization, primitive societies will not survive the forces of nature, it is assumed.

Mechanisms for filtering social arrangements, when they exist, will select only from the available (and often imperfect) structures, and the selection criterion is not always economic efficiency. When efficiency bias contaminates the literature, it reflects not the basic methods of the new institutional economics but the mind-sets of individual scholars. In fact, the transaction-costs approach is an effective way of analyzing wasteful social arrangements that has helped us to better understand the problems of open access, perverse regulatory regimes, and destructive economic systems.

When social structures are stable and social systems yield expected and desirable results, there is relatively little demand for new knowledge about the deeper logic and inner mechanisms of such structures and systems. The authorities, it is thought, know how to operate their systems, and that is sufficient. The surge of interest in institutional analysis at the end of the 1980s should be understood in this context. At that time, institutions and economic systems had come under close scrutiny. In Europe and Central Asia, the Soviet states and their economies had collapsed; in the developing world, certain economies were in steep decline while others were producing economic miracles; several industrial economies seemed to suffer from economic sclerosis; a new ecological movement was afoot, proclaiming disastrous side effects of industrialization; and finally, advances in computer science and biotechnology were creating hitherto unknown problems of ownership and property rights.

The new institutional economics was of immediate interest to scholars and reformers throughout the world by offering a fresh way of thinking about economic organization and its broader social context. Yet, as it turned out, the field did not fully satisfy reformers' expectations—or my own. The new institutional economics surveyed in my 1990 book is essentially a static theory that analyzes the logic of particular institutions and the social outcomes that they yield but does so without offering a policy perspective. Banerjee (2002), in an essay on the "uses of economic theory," arrives at a similar conclusion. Discussing the old question of whether economics is a positive or normative discipline, he states that each subdiscipline within economics has made its own choice: "For example, the related sub-fields of positive political economy and institutional analysis are explicitly focused towards interpreting the world" (2). And in a footnote, he adds, "Canonical examples of this style of research include Stigler (1986), Olson (1965), and North (1981)" (2). We are, therefore, left with the interesting question of why the new institutional economics did not give more weight to the policy implications of its contributions.

Imperfect Institutions branches as an outgrowth of *Economic Behavior and Institutions* in two directions. Part I and part II (a case study) explore institutional failure; part III seeks ways to think systematically about institutional policy. I will now briefly summarize the main features of my approach in this book.

Modern growth theory in economics is my starting point for studying why some countries are relatively poor. Growth theory has gone through three phases in the last half century, but it has unwaveringly emphasized technological change as the engine that drives sustained economic growth. Economists like to think of technologies as public goods that are nonrival in consumption and available to all, after they have been invented, yet developing countries clearly have not installed modern technologies. My approach to this puzzle, described in chapters 1 and 2, is to divide technologies into production technologies and social technologies. I argue that analytically it is essential to make such a distinction because production technologies have characteristics of public goods, whereas social technologies do not travel well. For example, it is far easier for a poor country to effectively appropriate or re-create the production technologies used by aluminum smelters than to appropriate the social technologies represented by the U.S. Constitution or Western contract law. Modern production technologies, however, are not effective unless complemented by social technologies of minimal quality. Reasoning along these lines, I conclude (as others have done) that financial and engineering issues are not the ultimate cause of poverty in developing countries but that social and political factors associated with imperfect institutions are. The concept of social technology may remind some readers of social engineering or large-scale social planning, but that is not my intention. As I use the term, *social technologies* describes the mechanism or the decentralized process whereby social institutions produce particular social outcomes (see especially the third section of chapter 2). I argue that imperfect institutions provide by far the most significant explanation for the relative poverty of nations.

My focus in this book, therefore, is on institutions that generate poverty and backwardness. It may appear that institutional pathology is a topic without much general interest. I believe, however, that close examination of institutional maladies will yield insights and knowledge not only about the nature of sound institutions but also about cures.

In chapters 2 and 3, I modify standard rational-choice methods by inserting what I call social models into the decision process. My argument is that both ordinary people and policymakers behave like social scientists when they strive to understand social structures and make decisions in a social environment: they compress complexity into simple social models. Social models specially structured for policymaking (by actors of one type or another) I call policy models. Although it is assumed that actors behave rationally in terms of their policy models, the complexity of their choices depends on the complexity of the models. The approach does not exclude the possibility that actors sometimes follow routines. I am particularly interested in ideological drift—correlated movement of social models of distinct groups in comparable directions, such as toward a more religious (secular) state or toward centralization (decentralization) of economic activity.

Chapters 4–7 explore various aspects of poverty traps and search the literature for explanations. Poverty traps, which usually involve political, economic, and cultural elements, are social equilibria with low levels of technology and income. The chapters discuss, for example, the political logic of imperfect economic institutions; the role of inefficient social norms; and how traditional institutions can both be efficient in the usual static sense and have inefficient dynamics that block structural reform. To supplement the book's theoretical section and to climax the discussion of poverty traps, I include a case study, "Why Iceland Starved." The country's deadly poverty trap had both foreign and domestic elements, and my analysis centers on the mystery of a missing industry—a full-scale fishing industry, which emerged only toward the end of the nineteenth century.

In part III, I turn to the problem of institutional policy and how to approach it. I begin this exploration in chapter 8 by turning for guidance to the theory of economic policy, which emerged after the Second

World War to support macroeconomic policy and planning. Actually, the theory of economic policy is an application of mathematical decision theory and advises policymakers about how to use policy models to reach the best available macroeconomic outcomes. Although the approach is independent of any particular economic theories, the pioneers illustrated their method with traditional Keynesian macroeconomics, which was in vogue at the time. I briefly trace how rational-expectations macroeconomics transformed our thinking about policy by assigning policy models to representative economic actors and by assuming that private actors are capable of counterpolicy. I also discuss bounded-rationality macroeconomics, which studies how the various actors form, adjust, and coordinate their policy models—a requirement before rational-expectations equilibrium is reached. Finally, I suggest several lessons for institutional policy from more than a half century of thinking about macroeconomic policy.

Chapter 9 discusses how endogenous policy limits feasible institutional reform and even precludes reform, if the logic of standard rational-choice theories is taken literally. When social structures are completely known, the Bhagwati paradox tells us that in social equilibrium there are no actors who are willing and able to reform social institutions (beyond what already has been done or planned). Limited knowledge and incomplete policy models provide some relief from Bhagwati's paradox by creating opportunities for advice and persuasion (especially in times of heightened uncertainty) that may lead to revision of policies. Yet one of my main conclusions is that economists are prone to underestimating the importance of endogenous policy and the limits for reform.

Following a discussion of various shocks that sometimes make poverty traps loosen their hold, chapter 10 argues that a country's history affects both the success of reforms and the directions they take. When economists look at an economy in isolation from the rest of society, they are sometimes tempted to claim that a country, such as China, is mistaken in following its particular path instead of choosing some other economic reform strategy that apparently has much greater payoff. Such arguments are often flawed because the reform path was not freely chosen from a large set of alternatives but grew out of bargaining and clashes among social groups with conflicting interests. Reform paths are slippery, reversals are common, and history casts a long shadow, influencing how nations handle institutional reforms. I use three cases to illustrate this viewpoint: China, the USSR, and Botswana.

Chapter 11 examines why transplanting or otherwise introducing new social technologies (for example, a modern law code) is a delicate task with uncertain results. We need to know more about the causes of large negative transplant effects, the minimum levels of legality required to sustain economic growth, and the least-cost strategies that poor countries could follow to reach the required level. I argue that the failures of new institutions often have fairly straightforward causes that need not involve irreconcilable conflict between traditional social models and modern institutions. Governments may simply invest too little in the infrastructure and the operations of modern social systems, such as legal systems. Moreover, although the central government is willing, traditional (often local) centers of power can act to sabotage new systems that directly challenge traditional authority.

There are other considerations. The evidence suggests that the feasible road to progress, the available opening, varies for historical and political reasons from one country to another. There is no single method for a transition to a modern economy. With incomplete policy models, furthermore, the policy process involves bargaining under uncertainty as well as learning with sequential updates of public and private policy models. Little is known about the direction that such dynamics may take. Economic systems often perform well for a considerable period of time, only later to become sclerotic and slump, but social scientists are better at explaining these turning points ex post facto than at predicting them. Finally, I conclude with an empirical case that illustrates the subtle art of major institutional reform—attempts by the Icelandic government toward the end of the twentieth century to introduce elements of exclusive property rights in the country's 200-mile fisheries zone.

PART I

Imperfect Institutions—Theory

CHAPTER I

Imperfect Institutions and Growth Theory in Modern Economics

Introduction: The Dependent Variable

In this study, economic growth is the dependent variable of primary interest, but that is not the whole story because my chief concern is with the social causes of economic failure—in particular, with the role of institutions in the pathology of economic stagnation and decline. In medicine, pathology is a discipline that studies the nature of diseases, their causes, processes, development, and consequences. The main goal of research in pathology, however, is not to study functional manifestations of diseases for their own sake but rather to find cures and develop preventive medicine. My motivation for studying economic decline is similar: the belief that knowledge of economic regress will improve our understanding of economic progress.

To assess the economic health of a nation I use a conventional but imperfect indicator, the country's national income (or product) per capita. Official national product and income statistics are incomplete solutions to the formidable task of summarizing in one figure the net output of all producers in a country.[1] Yet data from national income accounts, adjusted for distortions caused by exchange rates, permit us with tolerable accuracy to rank countries according their output per capita and to track their performance through time. It is unlikely that future advances in measuring economic performance will significantly change the ranking of nations in terms of their prosperity or alter our ideas about the social causes of relative economic backwardness.[2]

In the twentieth century, the distribution of national economic performance measured by average output per person has become more unequal than at any previous time in history (DeLong 2000, 17–20). I focus on the low end of this unequal distribution, but domestic inequality I consider only for its possible role as an independent variable in the growth equation—the argument being that economic inequality may be related to behavior that undermines economic growth.[3]

Redistribution within a country from rich to poor households obviously improves the living standards of the poor, but sustained economic growth is of a different magnitude. The historical increase in income and output per person in the United States illustrates the overwhelming importance of economic growth relative to redistribution. Best estimates show that on the eve of the American Revolution (1775–83), gross domestic product per capita amounted to $765 in 1992 dollars but by 1997 gross domestic product per capita (also in 1992 dollars) was $26,847, about thirty-five times greater (Hulten 2000, 1). The various errors in these estimates partly cancel out, and the residual bias is unlikely substantially to distort the true picture.[4]

In the vocabulary of economics, growth of per capita output (or per capita income) is known as intensive growth, and growth in the total output of an economy is known as extensive growth. In the beginning, extensive growth allowed the human species to multiply, spill out of Africa, and populate the various continents (Roberts 1997, chapter 1). Prior to the modern era, nearly all workers everywhere were primarily occupied in farming and hunting, but extraordinary sustained intensive growth, originating some 250 years ago in Western Europe, has revolutionized economic performance and daily life in the industrial and postindustrial economies. The economic revolution was fueled by technological change, yet at the beginning of the twenty-first century, the so-called developing countries in many parts of the world have not been able significantly to upgrade their methods of production and therefore have fallen behind (Jovannovic 2000, 6–7). In 2000, average income levels in the world's poorest and the world's richest nations differed by a factor of more than 100.[5]

The modern growth experience presents us with these two basic puzzles. First there is the phenomenon of growth leaders. Why do some countries for a period of time lead the rest of the world in developing and applying superior methods of production? For example, during the Industrial Revolution (1750–1830), England held a position of technological leadership, which it later lost (Mokyr 1990, chapters 5, 10). What factors determine the timing and path of technological and economic revolutions? (Mowery and Nelson 1999, chapter 9). Second, there is the puzzling variation among nations in their ability to borrow, adapt, and apply production methods that innovating nations already have developed. What conditions and forces prevent some countries from employing modern methods of production? This study is not concerned with the nature of growth leadership, the sources of new technologies, or the strategies of second-tier nations (R. R. Nelson 1996).

Instead, I tackle the second puzzle, the inability to either create or imitate new technologies.

This chapter briefly analyzes the evolution of modern growth theory in economics and looks for explanations of economic stagnation in low-income countries. According to the division of labor in the field of economics, growth theory has the task of studying long-term economic growth and is therefore a logical starting point for this inquiry into the problems of growth laggards. We will see that growth theory is concerned with equilibrium properties of successful growing economies and does not explicitly examine the role of social institutions in growth.[6] Yet its latest version, the so-called new or endogenous growth theory, implicitly explains poor growth performance by appealing to unspecified social barriers that prevent countries from drawing on the stock of world knowledge to upgrade their production methods. In this study I distinguish between two categories of applied knowledge that are relevant for economic growth, production technologies and social technologies, and argue that inability or unwillingness to apply appropriate social technologies is the main cause of relative economic backwardness. The problem of successfully introducing new social technologies is the organizing theme of this volume.

Chapter 2 outlines the basic argument about why social technologies rather than production technologies constitute the crucial barrier to growth. The chapter also introduces key tools and concepts that I use to analyze these issues. My approach is a modified version of the new institutional economics. The traditional tools of economics are not appropriate for studying important aspects of social technologies. I believe that unblinking faithfulness to standard economics would bias the selection of variables and possibly make us turn a blind eye to important social phenomena (Stiglitz 1999). Ideally, the study of institutions and social technologies requires a robust theory of social systems, which economics and social science in general lack.[7] The result is my eclectic approach.

Learning from Growth Theory

The Three Waves

Since it first appeared around the middle of the twentieth century, modern growth theory has evolved through three phases, all focusing on the relationship between physical inputs and outputs rather than on the social environment of producers. As a general rule, growth theory identifies two ways of raising a country's average output per worker. First, if a country's economy is inside the production possibilities frontier, which is determined by the best available production technologies, the theory suggests that the country is combining its inputs in inefficient proportions. In this instance, the country is able to raise average output per worker and move toward the production frontier by adjusting its factor (input) ratios, which usually means raising the ratio of physical and human capital to basic or unskilled labor services. Second, when a country is on its production possibilities frontier, only new technology that moves out the frontier can further raise output per capita. In growth theory, new technology is the ultimate engine of growth.[8]

In its first two phases, the theory simply assumed that new technology followed a time trend and did not attempt to explain technological change. The third phase, endogenous growth theory, does not explain growth in terms of *exogenous* technological change and fails to analyze in any detail what social circumstances favor the production and application of knowledge.[9] Endogenous growth theory, however, has abandoned the traditional assumption that all countries have ready access to state-of-the-art production technology, which implied that variation in national economic performance is always caused by different factor ratios.[10]

In sum, growth theory tells us that countries are relatively poor because they have failed to accumulate inputs, particularly capital in its many forms, except that the recent endogenous growth theory recognizes that poor countries somehow are not able to use world knowledge to upgrade their production capacities. We now look at these findings in more detail.

The Harrod-Domar Model Creates Path Dependence

Modern growth theory originates in the theoretical world of J. Maynard Keynes (1936), the father of modern macroeconomics.[11] The Great Depression of 1929 and the parallel ascendance of Keynesian macroeconomics changed the worldview of most economists and eclipsed the idea of a self-correcting market system. Equilibrium at low levels of employment now appeared to be an empirical and theoretical possibility, and thoughtful people wondered whether growing economies, even more than stationary ones, were prone to unemployment or overheating. Evsey Domar (1946) set out to answer this question, and his work (and earlier work by Roy Harrod [1939]) put mainstream growth theory on a path that it has followed through the changing landscapes of the last half century.[12]

The Harrod-Domar model emerged in response to concern about a possible imbalance between a country's growing production capacity and the increase in total demand required to keep up with increasing capacity. The reason for the uneasiness was that unemployment increases when the capacity to produce grows faster than the demand for output. As the original focus of the analysis was not on the sources of economic growth, Harrod-Domar models simply assume that some rate of technological change is given—and that it is of the labor-saving variety.[13] The theory also makes the critical assumption that labor and capital must be used in fixed proportions because the inputs cannot be substituted for each other.

It follows from the stringent assumptions of the model that a Harrod-Domar economy contains no internal equilibrating mechanism that guarantees balanced growth. Balanced growth depends on the relationships among four variables: the saving rate, s; the capital-output ratio, v; labor saving technical change, a; and population growth, n. All these variables are determined outside the model; they are exogenous. Formally, balanced growth requires $\frac{s}{v} = n + a$, but the two sides are equal only by mere chance.[14]

The problem of balancing aggregate supply and aggregate demand in a growing economy certainly is an important issue, but it is not the heart of the matter when we try to understand Third World poverty. Yet economists lost no time applying the Harrod-Domar model outside its intended (and in retrospect questionable) sphere of competence to provide theoretical foundations for the view that capital accumulation is the key to economic development. The premise that capital and labor are used in fixed proportions appeared to make sense for developing countries undergoing structural change, especially when combined with W. A. Lewis's (1954, 1955) famous dual-economy model of economic development with unlimited supply of labor. By merging the two images, economists made lack of saving the primary cause of poverty and supply of saving the key policy variable.

The story goes like this. Developing countries typically have a dual economy made of a modern manufacturing sector, which has a relatively high and (practically) fixed capital-output ratio as well as a traditional labor-intensive agricultural sector where the marginal product of labor is (close to) zero, indicating hidden unemployment. In such situations, economic development involves structural transformation, especially transfer of labor from the traditional sector into the modern (usually manufacturing) sector. Although the social rate of return in the manufacturing sector is high, in part because of the low marginal opportunity cost of labor, very little new investment and output expansion occurs in the modern sector. The reason is that developing countries lack investment funds (domestic saving or foreign funds), and labor cannot be substituted for capital in the modern sector. Yet if they somehow could manage to increase their investment quota, developing countries with surplus labor could for a while achieve very high rates of growth simply by expanding the modern sector and shrinking the traditional sector. Later we will have more to say about the image of insufficient investment funds as the main barrier to growth.

The Capital-Output Ratio Becomes an Endogenous Variable

The second stage in the evolution of growth theory, neoclassical growth theory, originated in the work of Solow (1956) and Swan (1956) and responded to the Harrod-Domar vision of a growing market economy as being inherently unstable and prone to overheating or unemployment. Technically, the obvious way to avoid the gloom of Harrod-Domar growth theory is to model as endogenous at least one of the four underlying variables and hope that the equation $\frac{s}{v} = n + a$ will then have a solution most of the time (Solow 1994, 46).[15] Neoclassical growth theory made v, the capital-output ratio, endogenous, but let the saving ratio, population growth, and technological change retain their status as parameters. An endogenous v implies that labor and capital are substitutes in production and that unemployment ceases to be a problem. When the labor force of a country grows faster than its capital stock, labor substitutes for capital and the flexible capital-output ratio simply shrinks. Having made v endogenous, economists waited some thirty years, or until the 1980s, before they again tried to fundamentally remodel growth theory, as the following section discusses.

Neoclassical growth theory formally models the economy of a country as a single production function.[16] A simple production function makes national product, Y, depend on the level of production technology, A, and two inputs, capital, K, and labor, L, which we can write as $Y = (A; K, L)$. Improved production technology—technological change—is introduced as an increase in A. When a country arrives at the optimal capital-labor ratio, technological change is the only source of increase in per capita output, but the theory makes no attempt to explain why A changes—A is an exogenous variable.[17] Furthermore, the theory boldly assumes that all countries have access to modern technology; they all have identical production functions.

The lack of concern for both the origins and diffusion of production technologies may seem curious, but again, it is best explained by the initial motivation of the economists who developed neoclassical growth theory. The original purpose and use of the theory was to analyze long-term growth paths for mature industrial economies, and neoclassical growth theory offers some striking findings. The theory predicts that the long-run (steady-state) growth rate of a country is independent of its saving rate, that all countries will achieve the same steady-state growth rate, and that all economies eventually will converge on an identical output per head.

The original intentions were soon forgotten, and economists, in their eagerness to generalize, improperly applied neoclassical growth theory to the study of poor countries in the Third World, reinforcing the findings of the Harrod-Domar approach about the causes of underdevelopment.[18] If all countries employ the same production function and have the same value for A in $Y = f(A; K, L)$, differences in output per person, $\frac{Y}{L}$, must result from differences in the capital-labor ratio, $\frac{K}{L}$, assuming constant returns to scale in the production function.[19] Developing countries are poor because on average their workers are supported by relatively few capital assets.

The first two waves of growth theory seemed to indicate to economists and policymakers that the problem with the poor is that they lack capital. By assuming a fixed (average or incremental) capital-output ratio, the Harrod-Domar model made it easy to calculate, even on the back of an envelope, how much new investment is required to meet short-term goals for increasing the national product. Empirical estimates of the average ratio of capital to output and also the incremental capital-output ratio are easily available for most countries. If the incremental capital-output ratio equals 4 (a common value), then new investment must be four times greater than planned increase in the output level. After the necessary level of investment is determined, the next step is to estimate whether domestic saving and spontaneous foreign investment add up to the required increase in the country's capital stock. When these calculations reveal a gap and additional funding is required, many experts have concluded that filling the "financing gap" with foreign aid will enable developing countries to meet their targets for growth (Easterly 1999). International organizations such as the World Bank have relied on the financing gap model as a primary tool for linking growth targets and foreign aid: "Over 90% of country desk economists at the World Bank, for example, use some variant of the financing gap model today to make growth and financing gap projections" (Easterly 1999, 424).

In sum, until the 1990s many development experts who had received traditional training in economics held rather mechanical views of the development process and framed the problems of poor countries in terms of capital accumulation and macroeconomic relationships, paying little attention to individual incentives or social institutions. The financing gap model assumes implicitly (a) that aid translates automatically into investment projects and (b) that in the short run there is a fixed linear relationship between growth and investment. Easterly (1999) finds neither satisfactory theoretical nor empirical support for the financing gap approach. Comparing actual growth rates in countries that receive aid with growth rates predicted by the financing gap model, Easterly (1999, 434–36) shows that the model fails entirely to predict growth performance of these countries; in fact, there is a slight negative relationship between actual and predicted outcomes.[20] The case of Zambia is a striking example of the irrelevance of a crude capital accumulation approach to economic development. Although Zambia has received substantial development aid, its per capita income has remained stagnant since the country's independence in 1964, hovering around $600 measured in 1985 prices. The country's growth dilemma obviously involves factors other than financing. Financing gap calculations that take account of all aid received by Zambia indicate that by 1994, the country should already have reached per capita income of about $20,000, measured in 1985 prices.[21]

The durable influence of the financing gap model illustrates one of the main themes of this volume: Nobody—not social scientists, not administrators, and not the general public—can grasp the full complexity of social systems. Instead, we all rely on simplified images, both for general understanding and to plot relationships between means and ends. Unambiguous tests of social theories are relatively rare compared with tests in many of the natural sciences, and people often habitually rely on familiar models. Also, actors may stick with particular models for strategic reasons (perhaps to avoid social sanctions), and in some instances social models are even a significant source of emotional gratification.

A Note on Growth Accounting

In the 1930s and 1940s, images of the national economy as a huge factory that turns inputs into output and the launching of national income statistics invited a new activity, called growth accounting: attempts to measure the contributions of various types of inputs toward economic growth. In the 1950s and 1960s, growth theory, with mathematical formulation and statistical testing of national production functions, further enhanced the prestige and popularity of growth accounting among economists.[22] The basic model $Y = (A; K, L)$, where the national product depends only on the level of technology, A, and inputs of capital, K, and labor, L, was modified to introduce, among other things, more fine-grained definitions and measurements of inputs. Missing from all these adjustments was an explicit measure of A. In growth accounting, the contribution of changes in A (technology) to growth in per capita income is not measured directly but is assumed to equal the unexplained residual remaining after all contributions of measurable inputs have been accounted for. The growth accounting literature refers to this indirect measure as the growth in total factor productivity.[23]

The early growth accounting studies, including Solow's (1957) investigation, indicated that capital, defined narrowly to include only physical capital, made a very small contribution to growth in the periods examined; the unexplained residual accounted for nearly all recent growth. Solow's (1956) neoclassical growth model, however, is not an entirely clear guide to what one should expect growth accounting studies to reveal. In an economy that is moving along its steady-state growth path, output per person, labor-saving technological change, and the capital-labor ratio all grow at the same rate. Alternatively, when an economy is edging toward the optimal capital-labor ratio, its growth path shifts up as capital accumulates, and during such adjustments both capital and output can grow at a faster rate than technology or total factor productivity (Easterly 1999).

In any case, the economics profession saw the very large growth-accounting residual as suggesting problems with the measurement and reflecting a need for better research methods. The residual became known as the "measure of our ignorance."[24] The ensuing rush to reduce the residual led to a comprehensive definition of capital, which now included human capital, and to findings showing that investment in education, skills, and training is an important source of growth. International organizations such as the World Bank and the Organization for Economic Cooperation and Development responded swiftly to these findings by requiring developing countries to present education and manpower plans to qualify for aid. The story was essentially the same: the poor are poor because they lack capital, now including human capital.

The Third Wave: Technological Change Becomes an Endogenous Variable

By the late 1960s, significant new contributions to neoclassical growth theory had become scarce, probably because there was not much left to say in terms of this particular paradigm. For macroeconomic growth theorists, the great remaining challenge was to explain one of the theory's exogenous parameters, technical change, but other scholars wondered whether macroeconomic models at the highest level of aggregation were appropriate tools for exploring conditions that stimulate innovations (R. R. Nelson 1996). Various historical developments in the late 1970s and early 1980s helped create demand for a new growth theory, developments that included a puzzling slowdown in productivity growth in the industrial world, growth miracles in Asia, economic failures in Africa, and signs of economic collapse in the Soviet Union and socialist Eastern Europe. The new or endogenous growth theory surged in the mid-1980s (Romer 1986; Lucas 1988), supported by new mathematical techniques and, on the empirical front, by a recent availability of massive country data that includes not only economic variables but also social and political ones (Maddison 1982; Summers and Heston 1988, 1991). The formal models of new growth theory are rigorously built from traditional economic variables, but an emerging literature of cross-country growth regressions is less restrained, often adding political, social, and geographic variables to the regressions without even informal systematic theoretical justification.

Endogenous or new growth theory is a research program far more diverse than neoclassical growth theory and is unified by a commitment to explaining long-term equilibrium growth in a formal economic model that does not rely on exogenous technological change.[25] Economists initially used three approaches to wrestle growth theory from the three-layered straitjacket of constant returns to scale, exogenous technological change, and long-term growth rates that are independent of saving and investment rates.[26] Consider first neoclassical growth theory's well-known finding that (developed) countries cannot pursue long-term growth by raising the ratio of capital to labor because sharply diminishing returns to physical capital eventually set in as the relative scarcity of labor increases. To counter the effects of increasing relative scarcity of labor, new growth theory has developed models that allow countries, even those with a stationary labor force, actually to increase the supply of labor services through investment in human capital. With this addition, the models show that long-run growth no longer is independent of the saving and investment ratios, as neoclassical growth theory concludes, and national growth rates and income levels need not converge (Romer 1994).

Second, other new growth models have introduced economies of scale and made growth self-propelling. Compared with small markets, large markets are capable of accommodating more extensive specialization and supporting production units of a larger optimum size. The theoretical apparatus of the basic neoclassical model, however, assumes perfect competition, which requires constant returns to scale, and perfect competition is a core assumption of neoclassical growth theory. New growth theory found a way both to retain perfect competition and to introduce increasing returns to scale by assuming that private and competitive investment in physical and human capital gives rise to positive spillover (external) effects. In other words, when they invest in human and physical capital, economic actors, operating in competitive markets, raise not only their own productivity but also that of other actors. New knowledge arising from these investments, including the knowledge that workers acquire when they learn to use new equipment, spills freely over to other actors in the same market, raising A (total factor productivity) in the aggregate production function. The introduction of positive spillovers, however, makes competitive markets inefficient. Private investment is at suboptimal levels because investors do not receive the full benefits flowing from their projects (Romer 1994).

What do these two strands of new growth theory tell us about the problems of growth laggards? First, we encounter once again the old story that countries are poor and grow slowly because they have low investment ratios, now involving both physical and human capital, which may result from a low saving ratio, from the government's failure to subsidize private investments (including investment in education), or from a lack of foreign investment and foreign aid. Second, the spillover thesis indicates that per capita output is positively related to the size of the market. Spillover benefits that flow to each economic unit increase as the total volume of investment activity becomes larger, and the volume of investment usually increases with the size of the market. In other words, assuming closed economies, the production function shifts upward more rapidly in large countries than in small countries. Small countries, however, can avoid unfavorable small-scale effects by opening their economies to international trade.

In its third liberating mode, endogenous growth theory partly severs its relationship with competitive markets by introducing profit-oriented actors that operate in markets with monopolistic competition and produce new technologies (Romer 1994). Unlike their treatment in neoclassical growth theory, new technologies are no longer free goods but are costly outputs of business firms that produce innovations by using scarce resources and compensating input owners. The idea that private firms produce innovations obviously has an empirical counterpart in the research divisions that many large firms operate. According to economic theory, private firms lack the incentive to create new technologies unless they somehow have proprietary control of the knowledge they create. A firm operating in competitive market does not invest in a cost-saving innovation that automatically becomes available to its competitors and reduces their costs. Why should a private firm pay for an innovation that lowers the cost curves of all the firms in its industry and fails to improve the innovator's relative position?

New growth theory solves this dilemma by assuming that firms in the market for innovations have some degree of monopoly power. The original models often assume that the innovative activity involves investments that increase the quality or variety of intermediate goods. The social profitability of these investments increases with the size of the market because the demand for quality and variety is relatively great in a large market, which again introduces economies of scale into the aggregate production function, giving growth advantage to large countries and to countries open to international trade. The lesson here is that, other things being equal, poverty is associated with small and isolated economies.

The new interest in cross-country growth regressions emerged concurrently with endogenous growth theory, although many such studies bear only a token relationship to new growth theory. The cross-country regressions often introduce a large number of economic, political, and social variables but frequently do so only on the basis of intuition, hunches, and availability of data. Other studies draw explicitly on various branches of social science, including the new institutional economics.[27]

Summary: Growth Theory and Growth Laggards

In his 1994 survey "The Origins of Endogenous Growth," Paul Romer calls for a growth theory that goes beyond "the standard neoclassical prescription—more saving and more schooling" (20). Romer wants a growth theory that examines such detailed issues as the implications for growth of the link between firms and universities and that seeks answers to such questions as "In a developing country like the Philippines, what are the best institutional arrangements for gaining access to the knowledge that already exists in the rest of the world?" (21). In spite of such hopes, a macroeconomic growth theory that has something novel and important to say about governance structures and institutional environments has not emerged, suggesting that the analytic level and modeling methodology of modern growth theory may not be well suited for exploring the sources of growth. New growth theorists seem to prefer to work with proximate or immediate growth variables and rather than to concern themselves with producers' basic organizational variables or institutional environments. Firms are simply characterized by the type of market in which they operate, and the 1980s introduction of noncompetitive markets in growth models was seen as a major theoretical breakthrough in the study of growth. When new growth theorists try to explain why a particular country does not adopt superior technologies from abroad, the explanations usually focus on variables that are friendly to the theorists' style of modeling, such as the price of capital, temporary shortage of skilled workers, and learning-by-doing processes (Rebelo 1998). In other words, when studying the deeper sources of growth, mainstream growth theorists seem to be handicapped by their reigning methodological standards (R. R. Nelson 1998).

In their most ambitious moments, endogenous growth theorists assert that their theory offers or soon will offer explanations of technological progress and the diffusion of knowledge. Romer (1994, 12) emphasizes the undeniable fact that "technological advance comes from what people do" and, therefore, that we should be able to explain and predict such behavior. While he recognizes that individual success in research and development often appears to be a random event, Romer (1994, 13) argues that the "the aggregate rate of discovery is still determined by what people do." Robert Solow (1994, 47) recently has sought to explain the logic behind his original decision, when building neoclassical growth theory, to assume instant diffusion of knowledge and treat technological progress as an unexplained (exogenous) variable.[28] In defending his approach, Solow expresses doubts about the ability of formal aggregate growth models, grounded in standard economic theory, to predict technological change, although technical progress "might be entirely understandable in some reasonable but after-the-fact way, only not as a systematic part of the model itself" (48). Solow does not deny Romer's point that people purposefully seek technological progress, for example by allocating resources to research and development or by introducing patent laws, but he questions "whether one has anything useful to say about the process, in a form that can be made part of an aggregative growth model" (48). Similarly, Richard Nelson (1998) argues strongly that new growth theory is concerned only with the immediate causes of growth, a phrase coined by Abramovitz (1952). Nelson's main concern is that endogenous growth theorists' self-imposed (neoclassical) modeling standards will give rise to new theories that fail to incorporate and therefore tend to obscure important insights of more informal microlevel theories and empirical work concerning the origins and transmission of technological knowledge, the impact of business organization and systems of property rights on the incentive to innovate, the role of universities in technological progress, and national innovation systems.

CHAPTER 2

Barriers to Growth
Institutions and Social Technologies

Theories and Their Spheres of Competence

New growth theorists and other scholars sometimes claim that they have taken the first step toward a general theory of economic systems, yet a satisfactory general theory has not emerged. Lacking a unified theory of economic systems—one that explains how diverse economic systems operate, how they are nested in a wider social system, and how their internal dynamics create paths through time—social science relies on specialized theories. Each of these specialized theories has a sphere of competence, a comparative advantage in analyzing a particular set of issues at a particular analytic level. The intellectual history of growth theory (outlined in chapter 1), as well as the history of other fields, shows that scholars are tempted to apply their favored theories not only inside but also outside their spheres of competence. Spheres of competence admittedly are discovered through trial and error when testing theories in new domains, but in practice scholars sometimes are blinded by their pet theories or act in a self-serving imperial manner.

Social scientists sometimes make outlandish claims for their fields—for example, by arguing (a) that their theories and methods have universal application; (b) that the sphere of competence for their theories contains all questions worth asking (economics offers a case in point); and, as last resort, (c) that their particular techniques for modeling problems is the only legitimate scholarly approach. Issues that resist this way of modeling should be left alone until scholars are able to formulate them in the one and only appropriate manner.[1] At the end of the 1980s, when the Soviet-type economies of Eurasia collapsed, one or more of these three viewpoints encouraged mainstream economists to rush in with advice on the transitions from socialism to markets. Without a theory of economic transitions and ignoring political and social dynamics, these experts confidently provided advice on how to build a market system, drawing on theories originally intended for analyzing market exchange in environments of solid exclusive property rights and stable expectations (Stiglitz 1999).

In this study of social institutions and economic performance, I pursue a multidisciplinary approach associated with the new institutional economics and limit myself to arguments that build on individual decisions and their consequences (methodological individualism). In addition to relying on economics, I borrow theories, insights, and empirical results from other fields such as political science, sociology, anthropology, history, law, and cognitive science.

Strict rational-choice methodology, which standard economics uses, works best when choice situations are stable, structured, and repeated—for example, when people shop for their daily household necessities (Clark 1998). However, decisions about fundamental changes or reforms of economic and political mechanisms and systems rest on more uncertain foundations than do household decisions or routine business decisions. When dealing with social systems or the physical world, actors usually have incomplete understanding of the relevant causal relations and may not even know all the elements in their choice sets.[2] My approach to such ambiguity or uncertainty is to assume that actors cope by relying on simple and incomplete (mental) models of their physical and social environments but then act rationally in terms of their mental constructs.[3] Social models are used to analyze and evaluate social structures.

Social Technologies as Barriers to Growth

As we saw in chapter 1, during its evolution since the Second World War, growth theory consistently has brought a single unifying theme to the fore: Intensive economic growth of the past 200–250 years is best explained in terms of the discovery and application of new knowledge. Furthermore, prominent early theorists ranging from Karl Marx to Joseph Schumpeter, each in their own way, saw new knowledge as the engine of growth, and so do most modern economic historians (Mokyr 1990). As for the emergence of revolutionary new production technologies, the historical evidence shows that a small number of countries have led the way, with the leadership position periodically passing from one country to another (Mokyr 1990).[4]

Economic theory usually classifies new knowledge as a public good. By definition, pure public goods are immediately and freely available to everyone, but these (alleged) properties of knowledge impinge on the basic puzzle with which we grapple in this study: What factors prevent poor countries from accessing already available world knowledge and upgrading their production technologies? Consider country j that is relatively poor. In country j, the potential maximum output per person, y_j^*, is a function of the current state of world knowledge, W^*. We can write $y_j^* = (W^*)$. If the actual output in country j is only y_j, and $y_j^* > y_j$, it appears that we have a case where $y_j = f(W_j)$, where $W^* > W_j$. In other words, j uses only a subset of available world knowledge. When $y_j^* > y_j$, we obviously need to know more about the factors that determine a country's willingness and ability to absorb, adapt, and apply relevant production technologies from the global stock of knowledge. We need to know how W_j is determined.[5]

My answer is that y_j, per capita output in country j, depends on the country's ability to implement two complementary types of technologies: social technologies and production technologies. Later in the chapter I define key concepts used in this study, but I will simply say now that social technologies describe methods or mechanisms whereby social institutions create patterns of behavior. Production technologies describe methods for transforming inputs into outputs, but production processes are effective only within appropriate institutional frameworks. Production technologies travel relatively well between countries (as pure public goods do), but the task of transplanting social institutions is more difficult (see chapter 11). Growth theory in economics has been concerned almost entirely with production technologies, except for occasional references to social technologies, institutions, and organizations—for example, by introducing monopolistic competition.

In this study I argue that:

1. Social technologies and physical technologies complement each other: to function effectively, production technologies need the support of appropriate social institutions (or one of several compatible institutional frameworks).
2. Successful transfer or introduction of new social technologies is a more complex phenomenon than the transfer of new production technologies because preexisting institutional arrangements often undermine the effort. Successful institutional reforms depend on active support from a large portion of relevant actors, which may not be forthcoming. Compliance often requires prior resolution of deep political conflicts as well as synchronization of individual social models.

3. Problems with applying new social technologies are the critical barrier to growth in poor countries.[6] Although secrecy, patents, and other restrictions can temporarily slow the diffusion of production technologies, the technical problem of transferring methods of production between countries is a relatively simple matter involving domestic and perhaps foreign engineers, technicians, and scientists; foreign consultants; multinational firms; and investment in human capital.

Key Concepts Revisited

My analysis of how social institutions contribute to poverty traps draws on the new institutional economics and, with some modifications, uses its frameworks, concepts, and theoretical insights (Williamson 1985; Libecap 1989; Eggertsson 1990; North 1990; Furubotn and Richter 1997). The following is a synopsis of the key concepts in this study:

Social models are a general term for various types of mental constructs that actors use to cope with uncertainty and complexity in their social environment. Social models describe causal relationships, usually incompletely, and provide justification for social values. Actors also rely on (incomplete) models to cope with their physical environment.

Social technologies are social models that describe how social institutions create social outcomes.

Policy models are the operational models that guide decision makers, whether in the private or public sphere. Policy models define for the actor his or her choice set, rank the elements in the choice set, and describe relationships between means and ends (instruments and targets). Policy models are social models, range from being crude schemas to elaborate plans, and include the concept of social routines.[7]

Social institutions are humanly made constraints and their enforcement mechanisms (North 1990) that generate incentives, behavior, and outcomes in social groups. Institutions have both observable and unobservable aspects. Outcomes, rules, and formal enforcement mechanisms are relatively visible elements of an institution, but individual policy models that guide behavior are less visible.[8] Institutional rules include laws and regulations as well as social norms. Enforcement is both decentralized (self-restraint, third-party enforcement, or dyadic enforcement) and with formal organizations (police, courts, private boards).

Property rights are social institutions that regulate the use of scarce resources by assigning and enforcing rights and duties (Barzel 1997). Legal theory uses a narrower definition of property rights than does the new institutional economics.

Organizations are social mechanisms for pooling resources and directing production in the widest sense of the term. The institutional framework in which organizations operate influences their form or structure, but organizations (such as legislative bodies) also "produce" institutional change (North 1990).[9]

Institutional policy is the art of implementing social technologies to create new institutions or remedy existing ones. Laws, regulations, and formal enforcement mechanisms are the usual instruments of institutional policy, although attempts are also made to influence social values and beliefs about social technologies. Institutional policy, except for marginal adjustments, is a knowledge-intensive activity compared with policy aimed at operating established social systems.[10]

Transaction costs are the costs of control in a social system. Transaction costs arise when individuals try to acquire new ownership rights, defend their assets against transgressions and theft, and protect their resources against opportunistic behavior in exchange relationships.

Contracts are tools used in exchange for lowering transaction costs. Institutional frameworks and organizational forms also affect transaction costs. When analyzing organization and exchange in all domains, not only in the economic one, the new institutional economics emphasizes the role of transaction costs, institutions, and contracts.[11]

The concept of transaction costs has created certain confusion in the literature, especially when we fail to distinguish clearly between realized (and, in principle, measurable) transaction costs and expected or potential transaction costs. It is enough that transaction costs be anticipated for them to have profound impact economic organization and outcomes (Allen 1991; Klaes 2000). For example, in long-term contractual relations between buyers and sellers of inputs, expected transaction costs (fears of opportunistic behavior by the other side) often create powerful incentives to vertically integrate firms or sometimes abandon promising projects (Williamson 1985). At the national level, growth-promoting institutional reforms often are not undertaken because it is too costly (the transaction costs are too high) to make credible agreements (contracts) for sharing expected costs and benefits from the reforms (North 1990).

Imagine a farming community that uses social institutions (and underlying social technology) Y which are so ineffectual that the typical farmer spends a third of her working hours guarding the property and another third of her labor time protecting herself against unscrupulous buyers and sellers—for example, by checking their identity and trying to enforce contractual clauses. In other words, two-thirds of the farmer's labor supply is assigned to protection and only one-third is allocated to regular production. Furthermore, the farmer's choice of production technology, types of output, and markets is likely to be strongly influenced by the relative cost of defending her assets against theft and cheating. If transaction costs become high enough, market transactions may shrink and virtually disappear, which is likely to reduce realized or actual transaction costs. Farmers may decide to avoid cash crops altogether and engage only in subsistence farming to feed their families. With no output contracts to monitor or valuable products to defend, the farmers' actual transaction costs may sink to a very low level. The poor are now very poor, but expected high transaction costs rule out all plans to reverse the trend and produce valuable commodities for the market.

Next consider social institutions (and technology) Z that is much more effective than Y because it provides the average farmer with strong protection of her assets and contracts, freeing labor and creating incentives to select lines of production that have high consumer values (net of standard production costs) rather than choosing products and processes that are easy to protect. Now the farmers decide perhaps to use their land for orchards rather than for grazing cattle because under social technology Y for protecting their property rights, grazing was attractive only because of relatively low monitoring (transaction costs). This example tells us that a comparison of actual transaction costs under property rights regimes (institutions) Y and Z does not reveal much about barriers to progress and may even mislead us. Total transaction costs of operating relatively productive social technology Z may even be higher than the costs of operating unproductive system Y.[12] Social technology Z might involve costly (but effective) enforcement by specialized actors, whereas under Y enforcement costs are at a low level because there are relatively few valuable assets and transactions to protect. As the following section argues, comparative institutional analysis is conceptually the appropriate way to evaluate the two systems.

Comparative Institutional Analysis

For evaluating the relative economic effectiveness of social technologies Y and Z, more appropriate than attempting to measure realized transaction costs is using comparative institutional analysis and contrasting total benefits and total costs (i.e., net value) of aggregate economic activity under the two institutional regimes. Theoretically, there are two equivalent ways of making such comparisons. Holding output constant at some level, we can compare all costs (transformation costs and transaction costs) under Y and Z to discover which arrangement is cheaper, or, holding total costs (transformation plus transaction costs) constant at some level, we can compare outputs under Y and Z.

If a community learns of a new institutional arrangement or a system of property rights, Z, that is more wealth enhancing than its current system, Y, but does not switch to Z, what could possibly create such inertia in a society of intendedly rational, goal-oriented individuals? In answering such puzzles, the new institutional economics usually emphasizes various types of transaction costs that bar reforms. Relevant actors see as being very high the anticipated transaction costs of negotiating, coercing, or otherwise arranging a transition from system Y to Z. When high transaction costs make it impossible *ex ante* for the potential winners to credibly commit to compensating the losers, those who expect to lose from institutional reforms will fight the proposed changes.[13] Institutional reforms are further complicated by pervasive uncertainty about the identity of potential winners and losers that the reform measures will create.

It has recently become standard fare in the literature to analyze how commitment problems and uncertainty about winners and losers undermine institutional reforms. While emphasizing these issues, this study also identifies imperfect social models and pervasive uncertainty about social technologies as additional barriers to reforms.

Imperfect Knowledge and Institutional Reform

Chapter 5 discusses how political economy explains the unwillingness or inability of rational political leaders to create institutional environments that favor economic growth. These varied explanations usually have one thing in common: they do not explain failed transitions or reforms in terms of incomplete policy models and ignorance of social structures. Instead, they emphasize constraints and narrow (rather than encompassing) interests of political leaders and political coalitions. Sometimes, however, growth-oriented governments fail in their attempts at reform—their measures do not reach the desired goals, even when there is no organized political resistance. I will now discuss three overlapping explanations of such failures: microlevel incompatibility, macrolevel incompatibility, and ideological drift.

Microlevel Incompatibility

Public or private reformers who desire to upgrade institutions that govern activities at the micro level (for example, in public or private organizations) without changing the basic structure of society usually attempt to do so by changing relevant public laws, regulations, and enforcement mechanisms; by introducing new private laws (rules and bylaws of private organizations); and sometimes by trying to influence the players' social models and social norms. These attempts can fail when the new institutions clash with old and still prevalent institutions unless the reformers know how to solve the conflict and are able to do so.[14] Necessary tools for removing dysfunctional institutional elements (including social norms) are sometimes unavailable, or when they are available, the reformers, with their incomplete models, sometimes may not know how deep to dig until the new institutions take root.

Consider the simple example of policymakers in a Third World city who want to lower the high costs of frequent traffic accidents by imitating the social technology that regulates vehicular and pedestrian traffic in the Swiss city of Geneva. How radical are the required measures? Is it enough to simply throw out existing traffic regulations and enact into law the traffic rules of Geneva, or are additional measures necessary? Exactly what is required?

Let us assume that the reformers find out that the imported traffic rules do not function properly in their city unless the general public—drivers and pedestrians—adjust their personal policy models and strategies. In particular, the new traffic rules will not become an effective institution unless both public enforcement officials and the general public comply and, by and large, uphold the new system. For the policymakers, it is therefore of central concern to establish, preferably *ex post,* whether the new written rules will gradually bring about voluntary compliance and spontaneous enforcement. Yet little is known about the interactions between new formal rules and preexisting social norms. If spontaneous enforcement does not emerge, policymakers find themselves in a quandary because they have little direct control of social norms or other factors that might bring compliance.

The effectiveness of new rules and enforcement mechanisms depends on how individuals perceive their new circumstances after the new measures have been introduced. Actors respond to rules aimed at creating new institutions by forming (1) perceptions about the transition path from the old to the new regime; (2) perceptions about the properties of the new system when it is in equilibrium—for example, whether it will involve hard or soft constraints; and (3) perceptions about responses by fellow actors to issues (1) and (2) and how best to adjust to these responses. Individuals draw on their social models to evaluate the properties, including legitimacy, of new institutions, and an effective shift to a new social system requires readjustment and coordination of individual models through trial and error and other forms of learning. Ideally, reformers would want to know how individuals adjust and coordinate their social models and how those processes affect the outcomes.

Macrolevel Incompatibility

There is no obvious line demarcating microlevel and macrolevel institutional reforms, but the latter generally involve fundamental changes in a country's economic and/or political systems. Modern social science has relative advantage in explaining the operations of stable macrosystems (such as the operational properties of a market-based economy). Less is known about the relationship between individual structural components of a social system, how they substitute or complement each other, and how they coevolve.[15] The literature has looked at the way in which economies coevolve with the general social system in which they are nested, but firm conclusions are lacking. We do not fully understand, for example, how in the long run a market economy impacts a nondemocratic polity or vice versa; how synthetic capitalistic market institutions (such as the ones that the Chinese and before them the Yugoslavs have tried) will evolve or decay; or whether, in terms of economic effectiveness, the long-term dynamics of a market system in a democracy are self-correcting or self-destructive. With incomplete knowledge of the dynamic macroproperties of social systems, mistakes and unexpected outcomes are a common feature of institutional policy.

Ideological Drift

Microlevel and macrolevel incompatibilities could be avoided if policymakers fully understood such problems prior to introducing institutional reforms. In fact, our knowledge of social technologies is limited and uncertain, and social models often change over time because of both advances in knowledge and fashions and fads. In chapter 3, I discuss the phenomenon of correlated shifts of individual social models, even at times when (in retrospect) the changes are not motivated by important new discoveries in social science. Readiness to dramatically revise social models emerges especially in times of crises. When pivotal actors come to believe that the current system is critically flawed, their intense uncertainty often gives rise to correlated drifts of individual social models—for example, along the centralization-decentralization axis. Models of the physical world (including beliefs about production technologies) and are less prone to drifts of this nature; at any given time, experts and other relevant actors usually agree more closely on physical models than on social models.

During much of the twentieth century, experts, policymakers, and the public debated whether decentralized markets or central management produces better economic outcomes. Early in the period, the median social model shifted toward centralization; then, in the last decades, the pendulum swung back toward decentralization. And twentieth century social science has done little to remove pervasive uncertainty about social systems: the twenty-first century began with sharp disagreements about the economic effects of substantial tax cuts, about the long-term effects of particular social programs on work incentives, and about the appropriate sequence and speed of institutional reforms in transitions from central management or traditional economies to markets. No solid theory exists that explains why only some of the reforming countries in Eastern Europe respond well to their medicine.

Limited knowledge about complex social systems invites emotional involvement with social models, which contaminates attempts to empirically test hypotheses concerning social technologies. Dysfunctional social technologies often gain popularity while the riding appears to be good, whereas random shocks can create panic and make communities do away with relatively effective social arrangements.

Conclusion: Social versus Production Technologies

My claim that problems with implementing new social technologies dwarf those of installing new production technologies is somewhat exaggerated because the two technologies are closely interwoven. The introduction of new production technologies often devastates traditional industries such as agriculture, and opposition to new forms of property rights in land may also reflect opposition to mechanized agriculture. It may therefore appear a bit capricious to assign to the domain of social technologies all social and political factors involved in the transition from one mode of production to another, but my reason for this classification is simple. I want to put to one side the conventional physical and resource constraints of the transition process, which has been the traditional topic of economic analysis, and examine other factors that economic analysis usually takes for granted. By emphasizing this dichotomy, I direct a focus on political, social, and even cognitive factors without denying the importance of the traditional concerns of economics.

The distinction between social and physical technologies is a way of separating immediate explanations of economic growth (accumulation of capital and technological change) from deeper or underlying causes—namely, inability or unwillingness to install appropriate social technologies. Having said this, two qualifications must be made. A full-fledged theory of economic systems obviously must eventually focus jointly on social and production technologies. Second, by distinguishing between the two technologies, we must not obscure the fact that new production technologies often give rise to new social technologies, and vice versa. The rise of the modern corporation is a complex story of interacting innovations involving both social and physical technologies (limited liability; bills of exchange; telephones; railways). Looking toward the future, new physical technologies (electronics) may make it practicable to monitor schools of fish in the ocean and even individual fish. New monitoring technology could then conceivably create new forms of ownership in live fish in the ocean that resembles current property rights in cattle.

In conclusion, while granting that social and physical technologies are closely related, this study examines the hypothesis, largely ignored in the modern growth literature, that inappropriate social institutions and inability or unwillingness to adopt new social technologies are the critical barriers to growth in low-income countries.[16] According to this argument, the financial and technical problems of implementing foreign production technologies is a lesser barrier than the social, political, and cognitive problem of providing appropriate institutional support for new production technologies. Physical problems and resource constraints, real as they are, come second to institutional dilemmas.[17]

CHAPTER 3

Competing Social Models

Introduction: How Much Do the Rulers Know?

Rational-choice analysis rarely appeals to uncertainty about social models and social technologies to explain institutional change. Instead, rational choice emphasizes redistribution. Actors may lack data (but often know the probability density functions) for particular variables, but the analysis typically assumes that they understand the basic logic of their social environments.[1] Olson's (2000, 101–54) recent work on the structure of the classic Soviet system under Stalin falls neatly in this category. Olson claims that Stalin's system was a response to new industrial technology that had created opportunities for an unprecedented level of exploitation. The novelty of the system lay in a new social technology for modifying the supply disincentives of exploited citizens and channeling more economic resources to the dictator and his winning coalition (see chapter 5) than had previously been possible. To overcome the usual disincentives of private investors who fear appropriation, the Stalinist state took over the ownership of physical assets and directly managed the entire economy, including investment decisions. To modify disincentives in the labor market, wages and salaries for skilled and unskilled workers were set so low that people had to work overtime to meet their basic needs. Because low skill differentials of daytime wages discouraged people from acquiring human capital, the state made it up to educated workers and stimulated them to work long hours by maintaining huge skill differentials for overtime work. In addition, highly skilled workers were given relatively easy access to durable and other scarce consumer goods, which also rewarded human capital. Privileged groups could shop in special stores stocked with luxury goods and otherwise unavailable commodities.

According to Olson (2000), Stalin and his cronies had no illusions about their system, and they understood its long-term dynamics. Although structural features of early twentieth century production technologies (especially in heavy industries) facilitated Soviet leaders' task of running their economies (more or less) as one large factory, opportunism in agency relationships created a cumulating array of unsolvable problems. Yet Stalin's horizon of a normal human lifetime made these problems irrelevant to him personally because he expected that the difficulties would not come to a head during that time.[2]

Olson's model is an insightful and clever retrospective analysis, but it also obliterates the biggest political and economic debate of the twentieth century: the worldwide intellectual confrontation between those who favored state ownership and central management and the supporters of decentralized markets. In Olson's analysis, the Soviet system is simply a modern version of Weingast's divide-and-rule exploitative equilibrium in a feudal society (see chapter 5).[3] What has changed is that new monitoring methods and new production technologies have made theft more efficient: the exploited are made to work harder and give up a larger surplus than previously had been possible.

It is difficult to reconcile the Olson story with widespread support for the Soviet system both at home and abroad. Many Western economists (not the least Hayek and von Mises) gave the system highly negative ratings, but at the time many other intellectuals of high standing, including major figures in the economics profession, saw Soviet economic and social institutions as a magnificent breakthrough. The supporters believed that the Soviet system was vastly superior to the market economy for generating economic growth, not to mention (economic) justice.[4] In fact, Olson's interpretation of the Soviet system would be uninteresting (which it is not) if he were describing only how the case is commonly viewed.

Mainstream economists and many other rational-choice social scientists are reluctant to associate poor economic performance with uncertainty about social technologies. Bueno de Mesquita and Root (2000, 1) concede that until late in the twentieth century, poor economic performance sometimes was caused by uncertainty about the appropriate economic model; by the end of the century, however, they claim that

> Substantial variation in economic performance can no longer be attributed to ignorance about what makes an economy grow; observers must look elsewhere than at competing economic theories to explain national economic failure. Today, the key to economic success or failure—indeed, to a broad array of policy successes or failures—lies within the political institutions of sovereign

states. Political arrangements create incentives for political leaders to foster growth or steal their nation's prospects for prosperity.

Only the future can tell whether the free-market model has permanently claimed the world stage for itself as the ideal economic system for creating wealth or whether serious contenders will reemerge. Modern history indicates that intellectual competition among social models is unlikely to produce an ultimate winner that everyone accepts—for example, by recognizing markets and democracy as the victors with universal prosperity as the payoff. Instead, recent history records cyclical swings in the support for democracy and free markets that seem to be linked to changing material circumstances, power politics, and the rise and fall of ideas. The political science literature identifies three waves of democratic transitions: from 1828 to 1926; from 1943 to 1964; and from 1974 to 1990. In between these upsurges, we find reversals or antidemocratic waves (Diamond and Plattner 1996). In roughly the same periods, long waves of promarket and antimarket institutional arrangements have passed through the world economy, although political and economic waves are not entirely synchronized. Moreover, Siegmund (1996) detects empirical evidence worldwide in the twentieth century for short-term nationalization-privatization cycles of enterprises.

Social institutions rise and fall because of (1) changes in the political balance, (2) new material circumstances, or (3) the changing fortunes of social models. These factors can be interrelated in a complex manner, involving both redistribution and reorganization of production. Scholars wedded to the standard economic approach (of rational choice and selfish motivation) usually take pride in demonstrating that social models are a neutral factor in economic and political developments. Others scholars prefer to let ideas have the dominant role. But a compromise solution, which I prefer, has actors make rational choices concerning their economic and political interests in the context of imperfect social models.

This chapter focuses on sharp changes in the organization of production and discusses the propensity of governments in various parts of the world to reverse rather suddenly their institutional policies in this area, which can lead to cycling and sometimes synchronous change across regions. Instead of the usual attention to low-income countries, the focus here is primarily on first- and second-tier economies that utilize state-of-the-art production technologies. I conclude that sharp reversals in the organization of production are likely to reflect both conflicting or uncertain social models and remedial (productivity-enhancing) adjustments of institutions to new production technologies or new material circumstances. A look at the historical evidence suggests that massive industrial reorganization often is tied to revisions of social models, although new production technologies also play an important role.

Why Do Social Institutions Cycle?

If we look to standard neoclassical economics for an explanation of why countries make major changes in the organization of production, sometimes in a cycling manner, the theory points to pure remedial adjustments as the cause. There is no other obvious explanation, given the usual assumptions—namely, that the economy utilizes the best available production technologies, reaches its production-possibilities frontier, and automatically adjusts social technologies to efficiently accommodate new production technologies. When social models are neutral, sharp change in industrial organization must reflect discontinuous changes in production technologies.

There is, however, a general impression that production technologies tend to change gradually and piecemeal—natura non facit saltum. In purely neoclassical terms, outright sudden policy reversals (for example, from centralization to decentralization of economic management) are especially unlikely if we consider only technological change; rather, we expect to see gradual adjustments in economic institutions. The main exception occurs when innovations come in bundles, especially when nations invest massively in research and development to support major wars or prestige projects such as space programs and high-speed transport. The fruits of such projects usually hit the general economy with a considerable lag, sometimes creating discontinuous structural changes, although mostly in select industries. For example, a large number of innovations, clustering in the years of the Second World War, were commercialized fifteen to twenty years later. These innovations lowered entry barriers in industries (microwave technology), increased capacity (wide-bodied aircraft), changed economies of scope (electronic transfer of funds, automatic teller machines), and altered perceptions about market failure and the need for government regulation in particular industries (Vietor 1990, 17). Vietor (1994, 18–20), for example, discusses how, in the late 1960s, new technology began to undermine the natural monopoly in telecommunications in the United States.

As I discuss in chapter 5, political constraints and distributional motives often affect the organization of production and pull economies off their production frontiers, making them decline relative to leading economies. Although such forces interfere with productive efficiency to varying degrees in all countries, the discussion here is limited to high-income countries that are relatively free of these impediments: in other words, their politicians are inclined to separate production and distribution, maximize the size of the pie, and then divide it according to their political preferences. Here one would not expect to see abrupt changes in the organization of production unless such changes served to redistribute wealth but did not seriously impact productivity or unless uncertainty existed about social technologies.

New social models often come to the fore with new political leaders, and political change is usually discontinuous, although the forces underlying political change usually move slowly. Economic contraction or expansion in an industry, a region, or a country; population growth; expansion of the urban working class; an increase in the relative importance of service workers; and comparable factors usually generate smooth time series, but consequent political changes generally have sharp turning points. Expansion of the franchise and other changes in electoral systems, revisions of internal procedures of legislatures, coups, and rebellions can produce rapid changes in the political balance as well as related swings of the public policy pendulum. The British iron and steel industry, which went through two rounds of nationalization and denationalization in the period after the Second World War, is a notable example of policy cycling (Singleton 1995). It is unlikely that these reversals reflect only struggles over redistribution and not conflicting ideas about efficient organization of production.[5]

New social models of industrial organization do not emerge solely through change of governments; for various reasons, often involving persuasion and learning, sitting governments sometimes make radical changes in their policies. New ideas also emerge from complex diffuse social processes in which actors initially hide their ideas for fear of social and other sanctions (Kuran 1995). After a sufficient number of individuals somehow signal their true beliefs, social change can occur rapidly, as it did in Iran in 1978–79 and in Eastern Europe in 1989. New social models, however, are likely to involve both efficiency and distributional issues, and the task of empirically isolating the two is a formidable task. Yet I argue that changing social models have had a crucial role for the efficiency of economic organization, and changes often occur abruptly.

When our knowledge of social mechanisms is scarce, policymaking can become a walk in the dark. The intellectual history of the gold standard, which in the late nineteenth and early twentieth centuries linked the monetary systems of several major countries with fixed exchange rates, illustrates this metaphor. Specialists both at the time and later (United Kingdom, Parliament 1918; McCloskey and Zecher 1976; Ford 1989) offer conflicting explanations of why the system worked well from 1870 to 1913 "in the sense of eliminating balance of payments imbalances without exchange rate changes in a rapidly changing world economy" (Ford 1989, 197). The disastrous reintroduction of the gold standard in the interwar period is a telling example of how incomplete models affect economic outcomes (Moggridge 1989). It is virtually impossible to argue that those responsible for reviving the system did so to serve the short-term interests of a particular support group, knowing all along that the experiment would fail miserably.

Individuals with comparable experience and interests usually have faith in similar social models and social institutions: their models cluster. If we assume that social models are incomplete, different, and volatile and that the diverse models favored by different groups sometimes make correlated shifts along an important policy axis (or axes), the shifts can result in discontinuous institutional change, irrespective of which political group is in power. If clusters of social models both within and across countries simultaneously shift in the same general direction, global discontinuous changes in institutional policy may result.

Bueno de Mesquita and Root (2000), writing at the end of the twentieth century, contend that nonmarket solutions to the economic problem have forever lost their luster, but in the years immediately prior to the Second World War, the market model was at low ebb, and many people believed that the future belonged to central management. In the prewar era, even the British Conservative Party had a statist faction that called for the introduction of various forms of central management. In his 1938 manifesto, *The Middle Way,* Harold Macmillan, a member of the party and later its prime minister, lists various services and industries that he sees as being ripe for nationalization.

Macmillan was concerned about the high levels of malnutrition in British cities. He thought that private wholesalers and shops were incapable of providing good food at a price which working-class mothers could afford. Under Macmillan's plan, bread and margarine would have been delivered to the housewife's door by an organization resembling the Post Office. High technology National Bakeries would be built in order to secure economies of scale, although the production and distribution of scones and fancy cakes would remain in private hands. (Singleton 1995, 19)

In the social science literature, Hirschman (1982) offers perhaps the best-known explanation of medium-term private-public cycles. Hirschman draws on social psychology to explain how these cycles are caused by coordinated shifts in personal preferences. Hirschman's explanation is based on the notion that exposure to consumer goods, especially certain types of durables, creates more comfort than pleasure and that comfort saturates and disappoints consumers, who then turn to other activities, especially to public life, to meet their needs for pleasures. Similarly, frustrations of public life eventually discourage actors and send them back to private action and consumerism. According to Hirschman, this reversal is coordinated across nations that enter the phase of mass consumption at about the same time.

Hirschman's insight is based on a single observation that certainly weakens the work. Hirschman began his study in 1978, fascinated by the puzzle why the "Spirit of 1968" had turned into apathy ten years later. His work does not explicitly analyze whether these private-public cycles, driven by saturation, maintain constant amplitude, explode, or peter out, but there is a presumption of constancy. However, if society does not receive repeated impulses of a magnitude comparable to or greater than the initial entry into mass consumption, it is conceivable that people eventually learn to balance private and public action, which would dampen the cycles. Although there is a grain of truth in the Hirschman thesis, I do not consider his shifting consumer preferences as the fundamental force driving the private-public cycles of the twentieth century (and probably neither did he).

When policymakers come to believe that their institutions malfunction and are willing to revise their models and policies, various factors can delay remedial actions. The next section discusses three reasons for such lags.

The Declining Years of Failed Social Models

The introduction of incomplete and evolving social models into the causal chain of economic analysis is not a decisive break with the methods of modern economics (see chapter 8). In its initial models, rational-expectations macroeconomics assumes that economic actors have

complete (accurate) models of the economy, enabling them to anticipate and often avoid costly public policy measures. Although these
extreme assumptions were useful initially because they simplified
mathematical formulations and bonded with standard general equilibrium analysis in microeconomics, the rational-expectations hypothesis
"does not imply that all agents have the same information, or that all
agents know the 'true' economic model; it simply means that agents
use available information in the best way and collect further information only if the expected benefit exceeds the cost" (L. E. O. Svensson
1996, 3).

Counterproductive policy models need not have harmful effects if
policymakers promptly recognize undesirable results and make appropriate adjustments in their models. Yet governments—even in the
advanced industrial countries—often delay corrective measures, and
imperfect institutions seem to become semipermanent. There are at
least three reasons for such delays. First, policymakers, typically lacking knowledge of measures' medium- and long-term impacts, often
find to their surprise that regulatory regimes that function relatively
well at the outset sometimes deteriorate. The erosion results from
cumulative adjustments of expectations and strategies by actors living
under the regimes, and decades may sometimes elapse before such
institutions become seriously dysfunctional in a manner obvious to
all.[6] Studies of the regulatory regime that governed the airline industry
in the United States from 1938 to 1978 provide evidence for a negative
cumulative process. As the government compelled the airlines to
refrain from price competition, they chose to compete on various non-
price margins, and perverse competition gradually spread from one
margin to another. Toward the end of the period, attempts by the U.S.
Civil Aeronautics Board to control valuable margins of service provided by the industry involved "writing regulations that defined the
size of a coach class seat and the amount of meat that could be lawfully
served on a sandwich" (Noll and Owen 1983, 156). The regulatory path
created an upward trend in operating costs and rent seeking among
employees and suppliers, until broad political support for deregulation
finally arose.

A second, related explanation, which does not necessarily depend
on institutional decline, is the difficulty in a complex world of establishing unambiguously whether institutional failures or random shocks
and transient forces are the cause of undesirable and unexpected outcomes. Setbacks can be either a onetime blip and a reparable problem
or a sign that the relevant institutions ought to be discarded and

replaced with new ones. Inability to correctly distinguish the two situations is particularly likely to occur when the institutions were originally chosen without much deliberation—without experimentation, evaluation, and international comparisons.[7] Knowledge about possible alternative institutions and how they would function is likely initially to be scant. After a community installs specific institutions, it seeks additional knowledge primarily about aspects of the existing arrangements rather than about alternatives, at least while the going is still good.

When imperfections are finally recognized, political impotence is the third reason why governments continue to live with social institutions that fail to meet their original goals. Policymakers may discover that they are politically unable to reform the relevant social structures; they are locked into the status quo (Killick 1995). Those who benefit from imperfect institutions are often well organized and control the policy process, and fears of sanctions may sometimes even compel people to withhold information about institutional failures.

Economic Institutions: The Modern History of Long Waves

The history of government control of the economy in Europe and the United States during the modern age is consistent with the idea that correlated shifts in institutional policy are driven by the confluence of technological change, power politics, and shifting beliefs in social models that are often preceded by unexpected social developments. Although there is no evidence to indicate that the complex mixture of power politics, technology, and imperfect social models creates anything resembling mechanical cycles, looking back at two centuries of European and North American economic history, many scholars discern a long wave of decentralization and another of centralization, with each wave not fully synchronized across countries and lasting approximately a century.[8] In the last two decades of the twentieth century, the world seems to enter a new phase of decentralization with the revival of economic liberalism and the collapse of most Soviet-type economies.

The various contributions in volume 8 of the *Cambridge Economic History of Europe* (Mathias and Pollard 1989), which deals with the development of economic and social policies in the industrial economies, tend to support the idea of the two long waves of government control and decontrol. Schremmer (1989, 362) provides crude quantitative evidence in a diagram showing changes in the share of central government expenditure in gross national product. Time series for Britain and France, which extend back to the 1780s, are U-shaped and bottom out somewhere around the middle of the nineteenth century, after decreasing by about half from the previous high of mercantilism and mutual warfare. The French, however, hit the low point earlier than the British, and in the 1910s both series return to eighteenth-century levels. In Prussia and in the German Reich, the ratio of central government spending to gross national product shows a sharp increase that begins in the last quarter of the nineteenth century.

The work of Adam Smith, Jean-Baptiste Say, James Mill, and David Ricardo as well as the American Declaration of Independence in 1776 and the French Revolution of 1789 mark the emergence of dominant clusters of laissez-faire or liberal models (Bairoch 1989, 4–5). Yet the long liberal wave contained much variety and more state intervention (especially at the local level) than many people assume. Britain moved toward free trade late in the eighteenth century, the trend was interrupted by the French wars, but it culminated in the repeal of the Corn Laws in 1846, which marked the beginning of a free-trade era in Britain that lasted until 1914 (Bairoch 1989, 13). The other countries of Western Europe and the United States leaned more toward protectionism than Britain, the world's industrial leader. The phase of European free trade was short, lasting from 1846 to 1861 (Bairoch 1989, 36–50). Prior to the Second World War, the United States followed a policy of protectionism except for a phase of liberalism or moderate protectionism that lasted from 1846 to 1861 (Bairoch 1989, 140). Yet the historical evidence makes clear that the emerging industrial nations untied the knots of mercantilism, put fewer restraints on private property, released market forces, and encouraged competition—if not internationally, then domestically or within free-trade zones, such as the German *Zollverein*.[9] The state's direct role in production, distribution, and exchange was minimal compared with earlier and later periods, and when the state was active, the activity generally was concentrated at the local rather than national level, which is particularly relevant for America (Letwin 1989).

A strong move toward greater state control in the industrial countries began late in the nineteenth and early in the twentieth century. The turn reflected not only a shift in political power from the middle to the working class, which the state gradually enfranchised, but also fundamental revision of social models as these nations grappled with new methods of production and unfamiliar economic realities.[10] Industrialization had brought new problems and new opportunities. Among new problems were rapid decline and dislocation in agriculture, industrial accidents, serious spillover effects such as pollution, and dissolution of traditional rural social security networks. There also was concern about the role of women and children in industrial society, the low educational level of the labor force relative to the new production techniques, lack of infrastructure services for industry, and insufficient service utilities and housing for fast-growing urban areas.

The Industrial Age, with its new production technology, mechanization, and scale economies, saw vast increases in wealth, which at this time of bewildering change gave credence to claims by political entrepreneurs and utopia peddlers that the end of scarcity was near. Improvement in communications and transportation, the concentration of economic activity in urban areas, and a huge increase in the scale of production suggested opportunities for central planning. It now seemed feasible that some form of central direction by the state could accelerate industrialization and, at the same time, bring the unruly process under control. Ronald Coase (1992 [1991]) reports being perplexed in 1931 by the apparent conflict between a denial of the possibility of effective central planning and the current success of large corporations. In particular, Coase found it puzzling that in the industrial countries, the corporation had in part taken over the coordination function of the price mechanism.

> The Russian Revolution had taken place only fourteen years earlier. We knew then very little about how planning would actually be carried out in a communist system. Lenin had said that the economic system in Russia would be run as one big factory. However, many economists in the West maintained that this was an impossibility. And yet there were factories in the West and some of them were extremely large. (716)

The structure of emerging industrial society, an unprecedented phenomenon, was poorly understood, and, as the nineteenth century wore on, public opinion leaders increasingly diverged in their views of appropriate social technologies for the new society. Early in the twentieth century, social models favored by leaders in Europe and America spanned a spectrum from a decentralized market economy with few restrictions on private actors through a regulated market system with centralized industrial policy to full state control of production and central planning. As we know, statist solutions emphasizing varying degrees of central control won the day. America introduced extensive regulations of many of its industries, especially infrastructure service industries, whereas Europe nationalized many of these industries (Vietor 1990). National governments in America and Western Europe assumed responsibility for the health and well-being of their citizens, with Europe taking a larger step toward a welfare state. And in 1928, following an intense industrialization debate, the leaders of the Soviet Union embarked on a massive centrally managed program of forced industrialization (Davies 1989).

During the 1970s and 1980s, a trend away from state control became apparent. Hopes for the effectiveness of central planning dwindled, as did belief in state-sponsored industrial policy. Even France disemboweled its once admired system of indicative planning beginning in 1976 with the seventh plan (Hall 1986, 185). The United States entered a phase of deregulation of various infrastructure service industries, and in 1979 Britain under the Thatcher government began a move toward liberalism. By the 1980s, few people believed that state ownership of enterprises was an effective way to achieve economic efficiency, financial accountability, necessary restructuring, and pleasant work environments. History seemed to support the raw statement by a 1949 Tory pamphleteer:

> The Socialists were never more wrong than when they believed that nationalization would send their miners sprinting to the pithead and keep them slogging all day long as merrily as the Seven Dwarfs. (Singleton 1995, 25)

As public ownership and various regulations of private industry increasingly lost their support because they became perceived as flawed social technologies, the popularity of decentralized solutions and market-oriented systems increased. The collapse of the Soviet Union in 1991 appeared to seal these developments.[11]

The reversal of government control of the economy in the last quarter of the twentieth century, which in some ways is comparable to the move toward liberalization that began some 200 years ago, raises the following questions:

1. Does the drift beginning in the 1970s–80s signify a fundamental reversal of the previous century-long trend toward public control? Is the world economy headed toward a new century (or many centuries) of liberalism, riding a downward curve of reduced public control?

2. What forces brought about this new direction in social organization? In particular, does revision of individual social models play an important causal role in recent reversals of institutional policies, or does the explanation entirely rest with shifts in political power, new technologies, and requirements of new production methods?

My response to these puzzles is no more reliable than are my own incomplete social models. I have a hunch, however, that in modern democracies, with their large winning coalitions and rising levels of education, the political incentive to promote economic growth is very strong. Modern democratic societies are unlikely to reject recent liberal economic trends as long as citizens and their leaders believe that reversal of free-market policies would certainly bring serious economic difficulties and sharp decline in growth rates. A major reversal of institutional policy, if it occurs, is likely to be preceded by a crisis perceived (rightly or wrongly) as catastrophic, creating fundamental uncertainty about social models.[12] Such an event would be an opening for alternatives to the liberal market regime—for alternative social models waiting in the wings for their cue. At the end of the spectrum opposite the liberal market regime are models that predict calamitous consequences for life on Earth if the world economy continues to grow at its current rate and generally see environmental damage as being irreversible. In this view, positive economic growth, as it is usually defined, is a negative destructive process. The associated policy models often suggest a complete reversal of current policies involving an end to economic growth as we know it, strict limits on free international trade, direct redistribution from rich to poor countries, and return to the simple lifestyles of old. Hence, it may be too soon to relegate the concept of cycling social models and institutional regimes to the dustbin of history.

CHAPTER 4

Stable Poverty and Unstable Growth

This study refers to social institutions as "imperfect" when they are thought to cause relative economic backwardness of economic units, large or small. This chapter considers two aspects of imperfect institutions, stability and fragility—the stability of dysfunctional institutions and the fragility of growth-promoting institutions. First, I discuss how traditional societies have created nonmarket institutions to lower the cost of dangerous risks from nature and other sources. These institutions, which often play a vital role in survival at early stages of social development, usually become deeply embedded in the communal culture. However, when opportunities arise because foreign technologies become available, because new markets open, or for other reasons, traditional institutions often block change: they create a poverty trap. The latter part of the chapter considers the opposite problem, institutional fragility. Many societies that have succeeded in introducing property rights supportive of growth are unable to weather exogenous shocks; their systems are fragile and liable to collapse. International statistics reveal that punctuated growth is quite common, and in this context I turn to an empirical study by Dani Rodrik (1998) for explanation of the phenomenon.

The discussion of stable poverty and unstable growth does not consider the motives of those who set institutional policy, the topic taken up in chapter 5, which turns to political science to explain why rational leaders tolerate imperfect institutions.

Coping with Shocks from Nature and from Trade

When asked to explain why some countries are poor while others are rich, a natural response for many people is to mention adverse external circumstances. Countries are poor because of hostile or changing climate (historical Iceland, sub-Saharan Africa); because of exploitation by colonial powers (India); because leading countries harm developing countries by manipulating the terms of international trade (Latin

America); because the countries lack abundant natural resources (Japan while it was still relatively poor); because of an unfavorable geographic location (landlocked and equatorial countries); or because of disease and foreign invasions. In social science, the importance of such external factors in economic development wanes and rises with the times. Some recent studies, for example, indicate that abundant natural resources actually harm rather than help the long-term growth prospects of a country (Sachs and Warner 1999; Gylfason 2001). Of course, external shocks have often had devastating consequences, particularly for poor countries that use primitive technologies, thereby limiting such countries' ability to avert catastrophes. Moreover, in the case of unavoidable external events, it is relevant to ask whether a country, rich or poor, employs sound governance and effective institutional policy (given its level of development) to cope with adverse impulses or whether inadequate policies actually aggravate external shocks.[1]

Several recent studies interpret social institutions in traditional societies as a rational response to the physical environment given the low level of technology in these communities. Because specialization has not advanced far in traditional societies, social institutions often simultaneously serve several functions. Institutions for maintaining order, protecting property rights, and supporting and regulating exchange sometimes also provide insurance against risks from nature. The section on emerging economies in this chapter provides an introduction to studies of this kind by looking at methods used in poor farm and agrarian communities to insure against risks. As an illustration, I explain how traditional society in historical Iceland organized to cope with harmful events. The historical Icelandic system, which in modern times has parallels in the Third World, allows us to consider how traditional institutions often serve their purposes relatively well yet later, when new opportunities arise, become barriers to growth. These institutions create perverse path dependence. Hoff (2000, 7–8) draws the following lessons from modern information and transaction-costs economics:

> A very general insight of recent theoretical work is that while institutions may have, as their intention, the improvement in economic outcomes, there is no assurance that that will be the case. Institutions may be part of an equilibrium, and yet be dysfunctional. For example, Arnott and Stiglitz (1991) consider the consequences of the social institutions that arise as a result of the incomplete insurance provided by markets because of moral haz-

ard problems. They show that informal social insurance may crowd out market insurance and lower social welfare. Developing countries may be caught in a vicious circle in which low levels of market development result in high levels of information imperfections, and these information imperfections themselves give rise to institutions—for example informal, personalized networks of exchange relationships (Kranton 1996)—that impede the development of markets.

Premodern Iceland relied on a decentralized system of social security that coped tolerably well with most types of shocks, given the country's poverty and primitive production technologies, except when the shocks were severe and widespread. Yet I argue that harmful disincentives were embedded in these institutional arrangements. I briefly outline the dynamic inefficiency of the system at the end of this chapter and continue the case in chapter 6, which discusses inefficient social norms and economic development. I claim that Good Samaritan norms supportive of the welfare system barred systematic livestock management and strategic storage of hay. The faulty management policies of the farm community had dire consequences because shortage of fodder during cold spells frequently decimated the livestock. Chapter 7 then discusses in detail how the country's welfare institutions were a contributing factor in a game with external and internal components that blocked the development of a specialized fishing industry in Iceland.

Risks, Institutions, and Disincentives in Traditional Societies

Responding to General and Specific Risks

Random environmental factors such as climatic disturbance or disease can cause large variation in the outputs of poor agrarian communities that operate with low levels of technology.[2] As lives may be at stake, traditional societies have a strong incentive to seek ways to reduce consumption variability over time, but high costs of transacting in these communities usually prevent or limit the use of insurance, credit, and other intertemporal markets. Recent studies show that traditional societies stabilize their consumption and lower the cost of risks by relying on various nonmarket institutional arrangements and adjustments in production.[3] Typically, this work has ignored the political problem of coordinating social responses in a risky environment, but it is often implicitly assumed that the arrangements reflect spontaneous or local decisions that are motivated by threats to the community's existence.

The literature on risk management distinguishes between covariate or general risks and uncorrelated or specific risks. If the risks faced by individual economic units have high positive covariance (misfortune strikes most of the units simultaneously), they are general risks, and much of the gains from pooling and sharing risks are removed. Weather-related risks, for example, have a positive correlation when all economic units in a community belong to the same climatic zone, and risks of disease are correlated when proximity exposes human or animal populations simultaneously to infection from contagious diseases. Consider a community of farmers on an island, all operating in the same climatic zone and facing a high positive yield variance for their crop. Although pooling their yield risks in the current activity would not help (even if transaction costs were low), the farmers might be able to reduce their risks by diversifying into new lines of production—for example, by reallocating some of their inputs to coastal fisheries. If the correlation between outcomes in the old and new activity is less than 1, each farmer has reduced his or her overall risk but probably has done so at the expense of foregoing output due to lack of specialization.[4]

Specific risks are individual mishaps such as accidents, nonepidemic diseases, localized fires, or drowning of people and animals. The members of a social group can reduce the cost of specific risks by pooling and sharing the risks. Informal insurance systems may cover extended families, the labor force of a farm, the members of a village, a township, or a whole nation. Informal insurance schemes in traditional societies tend to cover relatively small groups because primitive measurement techniques and weak formal enforcement mechanisms usually confine social networks of reciprocal obligations to small groups. However, the covariance of risks often falls when the size and geographic span of the insured group increases, and the choice of insurance groups involves a trade-off between insurance costs and transaction costs.

Although the literature on nonmarket insurance arrangements in traditional societies usually assumes that given the circumstances, these institutions are efficient, inefficient institutions are not unknown. Because knowledge is incomplete, societies may introduce imperfect institutions and then get locked into an unfavorable social equilibrium that precludes reforms. Additionally, institutions that are efficient at one point often become inappropriate when circumstances change—

for example, with the introduction of new markets or new technologies—and may block necessary restructuring of the economy. The decentralized system of social security that prevailed in historical Iceland is a good example of the ambivalent nature of traditional social institutions.

Local Institutions for Coping with Risks in Historical Iceland

The traditional system of social security in historical Iceland was based on relatively sophisticated local institutions for sharing and lowering the cost of risks (Eggertsson 1998b). Icelandic farmers cultivated grass to provide fodder for livestock in a climate that was extraordinarily marginal for farming. In the premodern period, the major source of general risks in the farm community were random cold spells, although volcanic eruptions and epidemics were also important sources. To deal with general risks, farmers stored food. They also diversified production by entering the country's rich coastal fisheries, but only in small open boats, on part-time basis, and during the off-season in farming.[5] The polity supported the arrangement by enforcing a ban on specialization in the fisheries.

For coping with specific risks, which can be pooled and which include illness, accidents, fires, floods, avalanches, and local weather conditions, the community relied on local institutions. The origins of the social safety net are found in the laws of the commonwealth (930–1262), which are collected in the Grágás and probably were first put in writing in the eleventh and twelfth centuries.[6] As is customary in traditional societies, the Icelanders were responsible for the welfare of their relatives, and *kin* was defined broadly, but when family support failed, local governance units, some 160 communes, or *hreppar,* became the centerpiece of the social safety net. The law required adjacent farms to form a *hreppur,* but these communes were fairly autonomous self-governing bodies. The law provided each *hreppur* with tax revenue (a share in the tithe, which was introduced in 1096), and specified in detail the rights and duties of communes and their members in dealing with risks. The old law of Iceland shows sophisticated awareness of moral hazard, for example in its stipulations of how to compensate for fire damages on farmsteads.

In the labor market, general use of linked or tied long-term employment contracts was an important insurance mechanism whereby labor power was exchanged in return for a payment that linked basic remuneration with credit and social security (Bardhan 1983, 1989).

Hunger Insurance: Incentives and Outcomes

Because they were responsible for the welfare of all individuals in their commune, Icelandic farmers became preoccupied with potential abuses of the system. The farmers feared not only that the system would make people lazy and irresponsible but also that it would create incentives for experimenting with new activities and leave the cost of failed experiments—for example in the fisheries—with the farmers. The farm establishment is on record as opposing technological advances in the country's fisheries (see chapter 7), in part to prevent upward pressures on the pay of farm servants. The farmers also used informal methods to enforce population control, preventing most people from marrying before they could afford to rent or buy a farm. In 1703, some 44 percent of all Icelandic women fifty years and older had never been married (Gunnarsson 1983, 16).[7]

This decentralized system of hunger insurance, which generally worked well for specific risks, could not cope with the most severe general risks (Eggertsson 1998b). The eighteenth century was Iceland's worst. One in nine Icelanders perished in the famine of 1756–57, some 24 percent of the population perished in the famine of 1784–85, and even more people died in a smallpox epidemic of 1707–9. Vasey (1991, 344) reports that the excess death rate in 1784–85 was double the size of most estimates of mortality from the Irish Potato Famine and was comparable to the worst local famines in early modern Europe.

The Icelandic system, with its disastrous outcomes, is not without redeeming qualities. The country's welfare system appears to have done rather well, given the country's primitive production technology and the risky subarctic climate. Within these constraints, the social welfare system was relatively egalitarian and not blatantly dysfunctional.[8] In his study of the famine of 1784–85, which is associated with one of the most massive volcanic eruptions in human history and belongs to the category of general risks, Vasey (1991, 340–43) reports that servants, adopted children, and people on assistance generally did not have lower survival rates than farmers and their immediate families.

From a dynamic perspective, however, Iceland's ancient social policies and institutions contributed to an underdevelopment trap. The country avoided all economic experiments and preserved Viking-age farm technology and organization well into the nineteenth century. In chapter 6, which discusses social norms, I argue that norms of reciprocity that supported the country's informal welfare system contributed to a dysfunctional equilibrium in farming by creating incentives for farmers not to maintain stores of fodder (hay) beyond the requirements of a normal year. The social technology used by the farm community to manage livestock made it unprepared for cold spells and other random shocks, with drastic consequences. As mentioned already and discussed later in greater detail, the country's welfare system was also one of two critical factors preventing rationalization and technological improvement in the country's fishing industry, which at the time was the country's only feasible way out of a vicious cycle of poverty and its best insurance against starvation.

Emerging Economies—Fragile Growth and Trade Shocks

The Record: Punctuated Growth

Observing contemporary economic growth over periods of thirty or forty years, economists have noted for countries worldwide that growth in the early part of a period is a poor predictor of growth in the latter part. In other words, the growth performance of a country varies considerably from one subperiod to another, even when there are no major changes in its domestic institutional environment or policy regime.[9] Easterly et al. (1993), who drew attention to this phenomenon, suggest that punctuated growth is caused by exogenous shocks such as wars or external trade impulses that at times interrupt economic progress.

Economic theory is concerned with technical economic issue of how to respond to trade shocks, whereas political institutions, political calculations, and political bargaining shape the actual responses. Depending on their severity, efficient adjustments to external trade shocks sometimes require only fiscal and monetary measures; in other cases, however, major structural changes are also needed, including the development of new industries and the shrinking of established and often politically powerful industries. When adverse trade impulses such as a sharp fall in the value of a major export commodity reduce real national income, governmental attempts to allocate the burden often initiate costly struggles among social groups. When developments in external markets undermine established industries, its owners, managers, workers, and even suppliers frequently seek protection and subsidies from the state. When macroeconomic adjustments are required, some groups favor import controls over devaluation of the currency, while other groups may prefer devaluation accompanied by wage controls (Rodrik 1998, 2). When reduction in aggregate spending is called for, organized groups often call for higher taxes on others than on themselves or advocate cutting government spending in areas where they are not affected. The worst scenario for growth is created by governments that respond to these various pressures by allocating the cost of external shocks through inflation and by protecting and subsidizing declining industries without providing incentives for new industries to develop. Ineffective policy responses can magnify the economic cost of trade shocks and make adverse effects linger long after the original external conditions have reversed themselves and become favorable again.

Easterly et al. (1993) conclude from their empirical evidence that, for the medium term, exogenous shocks are the chief cause of punctuated growth. Rodrik (1998, 5–9) provides evidence indicating that different responses to trade shocks explain why growth in East Asia (excluding China) diverged in the mid-1970s from growth rates in Latin America, the Middle East, and to some extent Africa. From 1960 to 1973, the growth performance in all these regions except Africa was roughly comparable. The Middle East led with 4.7 percent growth in gross domestic product per capita, but even many countries in Africa did well. In Africa, eight sub-Saharan countries had growth rates of gross domestic product per capita that exceeded 3 percent. The data show that during 1973–94, productivity growth collapsed in all these regions except East Asia, where growth continued at about the same rate as it had during 1960–73. Rodrik (1998) contends that during the 1970s, terms-of-trade shocks triggered different responses in East Asia than in the other three regions. His detailed comparison of policy responses in South Korea, Turkey, and Brazil reveals that Korea, the country that during the 1970s was hit harder by changes in world prices than the other two countries, made efficient adjustments in its macroeconomic policy, whereas Brazil and Turkey failed to adjust. And only Korea kept growing at a rate comparable to the pre-1970s rate.

The Rodrik Model of Punctuated Growth

This section introduces a theoretical model that Rodrik (1998, 9–13) uses to explain punctuated growth in terms of social conflict and describes how the model was tested empirically. The chapter's last section discusses Rodrik's explanation and how it fits with our view of imperfect institutions. I dwell on this study because it suggests that punctuated growth is a critical problem for emerging nations and, furthermore, that the problem is linked to imperfect institutions. Rodrik's study, however, does not isolate the basic political factors that prevent countries from responding successfully to exogenous shocks.

Rodrik (1998, 9–13) offers two basic explanations of why countries fail to adjust their economic systems to shocks originating in their international trade relations. The countries (a) are constrained by latent social conflict and (b) lack effective institutions for conflict management. Using a simple formal model, he predicts that external shocks have the largest impact on growth in countries that both are plagued by serious social strife and lack effective institutions of conflict management. Successful countries either are relatively free from social strife or experience social strife that causes little harm because strong institutions of conflict management neutralize the conflict. Rodrik's model is typical of the interest-group approach in public-choice theory. The expectations, the incentives, and the behavior of organized pressure groups drive the story, but the state is in the background, providing a playing field for these groups. A simple equation roughly captures the essence of the model:

$$\Delta \text{ growth} = -\text{external shocks} \times \frac{\text{latent social conflict}}{\text{institutions of conflict management}}$$

Given the various assumptions of the model, the value of two variables determines whether the political system will magnify the negative impact of an external trade shock. One, ø, measures the effectiveness of national institutions of conflict management, and the other, π, measures the expectations by each group that the other group will fight—their expectations about latent social conflict. Low ø (weak institutions) causes the dominant strategy for both of the model's two groups, A and B, to be fighting; high ø makes cooperation a dominant strategy—in both cases regardless of the value of π. When ø takes on an intermediate value, the value of π, the indicator of latent social conflict, drives the outcome. Cooperation is dominant for low values of π, and fighting is dominant for high values of π.

The recent availability of data sets containing comparable social, political, and economic variables for a large number of countries has made it possible to test empirically various conjectures about the general impact on economic growth of both economic and noneconomic variables. These econometric tests involve high levels of aggregation, relatively crude proxies for social and political variables, potentially large measurement errors, and doubtful statistical assumptions.

Underlying the approach is the premise that we can derive general principles about the long-term development of economies by comparing countries at different levels of development.[10] Although we may doubt the ability of international cross-section regressions to give reliable answers, they are fruitful tools of discovery and insights and for generating new hypotheses. Findings from cross-section regressions can be retested by other means such as time-series analysis for individual countries, statistical studies of individual industries in several countries, or in deep case studies that rely on various methods of inquiry.

In Rodrik's empirical test of his social conflict theory, the dependent variable is the growth differential between 1960–75 and 1975–89 for each country. His proxies for latent social conflict are (a) income inequality (measured by Gini coefficients) and (b) an index of the ethnolinguistic diversity in a country. The quality of institutions of conflict management is measured by the International Country Risk Guide index (ICRG), which for each country covered gives numerical values to factors such as rule of law, bureaucratic quality, corruption, expropriation risk, and government repudiation of contracts. The ICRG index, therefore, measures the quality of social outcomes—the security of economic property rights. The other main proxy for measuring the quality of institutions of conflict management is the Freedom House index of democracy, which is composed of indicators of civil liberties and political rights. Again, the index is outcome oriented, but its emphasis on political outcomes provides a deeper explanation of growth than does the ICRG index. The nature of political outcomes presumably influences expectations about secure property rights, which in turn influences economic behavior and the allocation of resources.[11]

The regression analysis appears to strongly support Rodrik's thesis about the link between social conflict and economic performance. In various versions of the regression model, key coefficients have the predicted sign and are nearly always statistically significant. Many of the regressions explain (as indicated by adjusted R^2), about two-thirds of the country variation in growth performance. However, dummy variables for regions, such as Latin America and East Asia, remain significant after the social conflict and institutional variables have entered the regressions, suggesting that growth performance is influenced by region-specific factors.

When they enter the regressions, the social conflict and institutional variables usually render statistically insignificant the variable measuring the size of the trade turbulence that a country faced in the 1970s.

The apparent lesson here is that external trade impulses have insignificant impact on economic growth when latent social conflict is under control. The study also produces empirical evidence showing that trade shocks do not affect growth primarily by reducing a country's rate of investment but do so by affecting the productivity of investments.

Finally, Rodrik creates an (outcome-oriented) index of macroeconomic mismanagement that combines the increases between 1960–75 and 1975–89 in the rate of inflation and in the premium for foreign currency on the black market. The index of bad policy has a very strong negative correlation with economic growth, suggesting that social conflict and poor institutional arrangements influence medium-term growth by affecting the quality of macroeconomic policy (and poor macroeconomic policy presumably reduces the productivity of investments).

The findings of the Rodrik study are striking and direct our attention to an important feature of economic decline that the new institutional economics often neglects: the interaction between the quality of the institutional environment and the effectiveness of macroeconomic policy. The study shares with other comparable work the assumption that policymakers possess correct economic policy models for designing measures to neutralize external shocks (Rodrik 1998, 2). In other words, it is assumed that the policymakers know exactly what policy measures must be taken to effectively limit the impact of trade disturbances on the economy but avoid such measures when poor economic policy is good politics. Yet in the 1970s (and later), many politicians appeared to believe sincerely that "bad" policies such as import controls and subsidies were the right way to go.[12]

If we accept the findings of the Rodrik study, we still have some way to go to understand why some countries suffer punctuated growth and others do not. First, ethnic diversity and income equality are often targets of government policy rather than fixed parameters. Second, the study does not tell us what circumstances enable some countries to combine high levels of ethnic diversity and income inequality with secure political and economic rights. Third, Rodrik's main finding is perhaps that governments that support secure property rights also have the incentive to follow sound (growth-friendly) macroeconomic policies. The finding is not surprising because the value of property rights is closely related to macroeconomic stability. Missing from the analysis, however, is an examination of the burning question of why some governments tolerate insecure property rights and pursue imperfect macroeconomic policies. The absence of such topics in the study is not surprising: a single essay cannot explore punctuated growth at all analytic levels—for example, by examining the motives and constraints of political leaders. Chapter 5 turns to political science, exploring the question of why bad economics is sometimes good politics.

CHAPTER 5

The Political Logic of Bad Economics

Introduction: The Political Rationality of Inefficient Economic Systems

Social scientists seldom explore simultaneously all dimensions of a large research question. Instead, researchers bring available tools to manageable aspects of the problem. One aspect of imperfect institutions that is well suited for standard rational-choice analysis is the question of why rational rulers support policies that are known to bring economic decline. This chapter discusses theories about rational rulers who see bad economics as good politics. These theories do not appeal to incomplete knowledge (imperfect social models) to account for destructive economic policies but interpret the policies as rational political strategies. The literature pessimistically concludes that utility-maximizing leaders will sooner or later embark on destructive economic policies unless they are appropriately constrained. I sample this literature and begin by discussing two conditions that give rulers reason to sacrifice economic growth: their time horizon and the size of their support group. Unless they are constrained, rulers who discount the future have an incentive to appropriate without delay available resources and ignore long-term growth. Similarly, rulers who rely on small support groups thrive politically by transferring resources to their small bands of supporters, even amid economic decline.

Rulers who need to please a large group of supporters have less left from the national surplus for their personal use and grandiose plans than those who rely on small groups. Therefore, unless doing so threatens their political lives, rulers have reason to prefer a small coalition to a large one, which they can achieve by setting powerful social groups at each other's throats and thereby divide and rule. If we accept this negative view of the basic propensities of rulers, it is evident that the only way to secure long-term growth is for society to constrain its leaders. The difficult task of constraining rulers calls for coordination and cooperation among various groups and avoidance of prisoner's-dilemma situations.[1]

The chapter's final section considers the following question: Can we explain the logic of limited government purely in terms of interactions between selfish rational actors, without appealing either to ideas (social models) or constraints imposed on their historical paths? Recent studies of the emergence of limited government in England and elsewhere indicate that the particular way in which actors model their social environment has been a critical element for the emergence of democratic institutions.

The Horizon Effect and Bad Economics

The rational-choice story about political preferences for bad economics often begins with an analysis of the strategies of an autocratic ruler in a simple setting containing only two types of actors: a ruler and subjects. Olson's (2000) analysis of roving and stationary bandits, which is motivated by the historical example of China's warlords in the 1920s, is a colorful example of such studies. Olson was struck by the puzzle of why people were particularly eager to live under a certain Feng Yu-hsiang, an unscrupulous bandit. The apparent answer is that he suppressed thievery by others than his own gang in the district that he controlled.[2] In this lawless period, Chinese warlords usually behaved as roving bandits or thieving armies on the march through a foreign territory, stealing all valuables that they could carry. Feng Yu-hsiang apparently built enough military power to claim possession of a substantial geographic area and keep other bandits out. He chose, therefore, to become a stationary bandit, a Mafia-type ruler who does not immediately plunder his region but invests in protecting and expanding the economy, the tax base.

Roving and stationary bandits are comparable to fishers before and after a fishery becomes exclusive property: with open access, the fishers plunder the fishery; under exclusive ownership, their strategy is optimal harvesting. Olson (2000) uses a simple neoclassical model to elaborate why the self-interest of a stable autocrat leads her both to supply public goods and to restrain taxation. A rational ruler who wants to maximize tax revenues must reckon both the negative supply effects of high taxes (because high taxes reduce effort) and the positive impact on tax revenues from growth-enhancing public goods.[3] A maximizing ruler continues to invest in public goods as long as new public services yield more tax revenue (through economic growth) than they cost.

Similarly, the ruler increases tax rates as long as higher rates yield greater tax revenues and stops when disincentive effects of taxes outweigh higher rates. This means that a stable autocrat may be inclined to promote growth but that such favorable outcomes are inherently unstable.[4] With time, various factors usually make autocrats lower their horizons and behave like open-access fishers. These factors include aging and problems with succession, new military technology, and external or internal threats.

Olson also uses his model to analyze the difference in behavior between an autocrat and a democratically elected leader when both leaders take the long view. The model suggests that the leader of a selfish majority in a democracy invests more resources in growth-oriented public services than a growth-friendly autocrat because the autocrat is interested only in the impact of growth on tax revenues.[5] A democratic majority is interested in both the impact of public services on tax revenues (which it controls) and on its personal incomes. A democratic majority, therefore, receives more benefits from each dollar invested in public goods than does an autocrat and therefore is ready to invest more.[6] However, Olson's theoretical insight that democracies will lead the growth race may fail when, for personal reasons, autocrats give highest priority to growth. Yet autocratic growth paths are unstable. At any time, leaders are liable to switch priorities to suit their immediate needs.

The critical problem with autocratic rulers who control an economy is that they ignore the external effects of their actions. To continue the fisheries metaphor, under open access, both autocrats and fishers are isolated from the full returns and full costs of their investments, which means that they do not allow for external effects (fail to maximize joint wealth). Economic theory tells us that external effects emerge when exclusive property rights are incomplete or missing, particularly the rights of exclusion, use, and transfer. External effects can be modified, the theory also tells us, by introducing new property rights and redefining existing ones or by regulating the actors. Practical considerations (high transaction costs) sometimes rule out the definition and enforcement of exclusive property rights. In ocean fisheries, for example, exclusive ownership of individual fish before they are caught has not been practical with existing technologies.[7] Similarly, defining and enforcing exclusive ownership rights over an economy and its tax base are not straightforward tasks. We already have argued that exclusive individual ownership of economies is unlikely to bring sustained growth. A market for economies or countries could theoretically raise the level of efficiency under autocracy, but that solution is not relevant or desirable in the modern world.[8]

The ultimate ownership rights to a country and its economy can also rest with the nation, implying communal ownership where a representative government acts as an agent of the citizens. In a world of full knowledge and zero transaction costs, joint decisions by the citizen-owners would account for all costs and benefits and maximize the joint wealth of the nation. In practice, the problems of internal governance and agency rule out such ideal outcomes. Consider first the problem of internal governance. When resources belong to thousands or millions of rational and selfish co-owners, selfish actors will free ride and ignore group interests unless effective regulations or other institutions modify their behavior. Similar reasoning applies to a multitude of fishers who co-own their fishing grounds. Agency problems arise because the citizens are too many to directly manage the state. They must appoint and empower agents to run the police, the courts, the armed forces, and other public organizations. The evidence makes clear (see, for example, the public-choice literature) that even in mature democracies the citizen-owners are not fully in control; the agents usually have considerable leeway. Yet limited government is a reality, and although less than ideal, democracy often works well—property rights are secure and representatives of the people promote the general welfare. Modern social science understands rather well the strengths and weaknesses of democratic governance; less is known about the art of effectively transforming the institutions of nondemocratic states into democratic ones.

The following section discusses yet another theory that explains public policy and poor economic outcomes in terms of the personal incentives of government leaders. The focus is now explicitly on the logic of political survival and on how the survival logic varies from one regime type to another, which is treated as an exogenous variable. The chapter's final section looks at studies that explain the rise of limited government in terms of strategic choices.

Winning Coalitions, Selectorates, and Inefficient Policies

All rulers rely on support groups for their political survival. The political life of a leader or a government depends on the loyalty of what Bueno de Mesquita (2000) refers to as the winning coalition. The necessity of placating its winning coalition broadly determines the basic political and economic strategies that a government chooses. According to Bueno de Mesquita's (2002) selectorate theory, a government buys support from its winning coalition in exchange for public and private goods.[9] In this context, "public goods" refers to social services, economic infrastructure, secure property rights, and sound macroeconomic policies, whereas "private goods" are grants to specific individuals of money, commodities, and various privileges, such as the right to monopolize industries or be exempt from specific laws. In this definition, public goods are growth friendly, but private goods represent debilitating cronyism. It follows that a theory of how regimes buy support through mixes of private and public goods can also account for the political logic of bad economics and the political sources of economic growth.

The political economy literature has long recognized that the harmful effects of pressure groups are related to their size (Olson 1965). A small group usually expresses narrow interests, but a relatively large group is more likely to have encompassing interests (Olson 1982). Groups with narrow interests often request government favors or programs that benefit these groups but hurt the national economy. The traditional theory of rent seeking is concerned primarily with the demand side, leaving the supplier of favors, the government, in the background as a passive player. With the selectorate theory, Bueno de Mesquita et al.(2000, 2003) take the additional step of analyzing the supply side, giving the government an active role in determining how supporters are rewarded.

The selectorate model rests on three pillars. The theory assumes that the primary goal of leaders is political survival, that all governments face budget constraints (there are limits to taxation and borrowing), and that leaders minimize the cost of buying support. It follows that different strategies are appropriate for buying support from small winning coalitions than from large ones, which leads to the theory's basic proposition: All else being equal, the supply of (growth-friendly) public goods by the government is an increasing function of the size of the winning coalition, whereas the supply of private goods is an inverse function of coalition size.

The reason is simple. A ruler who relies on a small number of cronies minimizes costs if he buys their support mainly with private goods (money, commodities, and various individual privileges).[10] When a government depends on a very large winning coalition, particularly a democratic majority, budget constraints and cost minimization exclude primary reliance on private goods. The optimal manner of securing the loyalty of a large winning coalition is to supply public goods, including effective property rights and sound macroeconomic policies. In these cases, the government offers general economic prosperity rather than benefits designed for particular individuals.

Turning to our exploration of the politics of imperfect institutions, this parsimonious model suggests that all else being equal, economic stagnation is inversely related to the size of a regime's winning coalition (holding population constant). As small winning coalitions are a typical feature of various nondemocratic polities such as monarchies, dictatorships, and juntas, the theory suggest that the economies of such regimes tend to perform poorly. Bueno de Mesquita (2000) and Bueno de Mesquita et al. (2003) have empirically tested these propositions in a study using data for a large number of countries. These studies furnish evidence of significant positive relationships between indicators of economic performance (including growth rates) and the size of a polity's winning coalition.

The selectorate theory, like all social models, relies on various simplifications. For example, a thin red line does not separate the winning coalition of a regime from other social groups. The political survival of even brutal dictators, such as Stalin or Kim Il Sung, depends in part on widespread social acceptance in addition to support from their key cronies. Dictators require a substantial mass of popular support to enforce their programs because sole reliance on naked force is costly and impractical. Compliance is admittedly often a manifestation of outright fear, but other forces are also at play, including those embedded in the reputational reward mechanism.[11] Individuals in large numbers support these regimes, including brutal dictatorships, to fulfill the psychological and material need to be accepted. At stake are both social acceptance and access to job promotions and other scarce resources. Yet criticism along these lines is not fatal for selectorate model, which emphasizes predictive power rather than realism.[12] What matters is whether it is feasible to unambiguously rank countries according to the size of their winning coalitions and whether empirical studies support the hypotheses derived from the model.

If statistical tests reveal a great variation in economic performance among regimes that rely on winning coalitions of about the same size (holding population constant), the finding would challenge the theory. To reduce such variation for regimes that have small winning coalitions, a new variable, the selectorate, is added to the model. The selectorate is the set of individuals from which the leaders of a nation and their supporters (winning coalition) are drawn. The relevance of the selectorate derives from the assumption that political leaders minimize the cost of paying for support: they pay the members of winning coalitions only the bare minimum necessary to keep them from defecting. For regimes where the winning coalition is small (primarily various nondemocratic regimes), the price that a government pays for support depends directly on the following ratio:

$$\text{Index of the price for loyalty} = \frac{\text{size of winning coalition}}{\text{size of selectorate}}$$

The size of this ratio influences the future political chances of individuals who plan to defect from a current winning coalition. The probability that a defector will belong to next winning coalition depends directly on the size of the winning coalition relative to the size of the selectorate. To facilitate empirical tests, selectorate theory makes the simplifying assumption that nature randomly assigns members of the selectorate to the winning coalition when a new government emerges. For example, when a political system has a winning coalition that contains 100 individuals and the selectorate contains 100,000 individuals, a defector sees the probability as 1:1000 that she will belong to the winning coalition of the next government. A very low probability of joining the next government coalition is an incentive not to defect from the current one. The model assumes that the members of a winning coalition rationally calculate the costs and benefits of defecting and defect when a prospective government offers them a better deal than the current one. All other things being equal, when the ratio of the winning coalition to the selectorate increases, offers from opposition leaders become more tempting, and a sitting government must raise its price to supporters to prevent them from defecting, provided it is willing and able to do so.

I conclude by citing a few of the insights offered by the selectorate theory (Bueno de Mesquita et al. 2003). Consider what happens in a nondemocratic regime when the size of a small winning coalition increases and with it the winning-coalition/selectorate ratio. First, the minimum price that current rulers must pay for political support will rise. Because of budget constraints, they now have fewer resources to expend on their personal consumption and pet projects. A second consequence of an expanding winning coalition is that the payments for support increasingly consist of public goods rather than private goods because of cost considerations. Third, as the winning-coalition/selectorate ratio increases, the cost of defecting decreases (the probability of belonging to the next winning coalition increases). Specific offers from opposition leaders now become more attractive, other things being equal, causing defection rates to increase and leader turnover to become easier.

In nondemocratic countries, small selectorates are common in traditional or class-based societies—for example, where only members of the nobility can enter the political domain—but larger selectorates are often found in autocracies where social stratification is not pronounced. Some right-wing dictatorships encourage mock elections and have a broad-based selectorate, and the former Soviet Union was a regime characterized by a lethal combination of a small winning coalition and a large selectorate. Here three unfortunate conditions coincide: A relatively large selectorate stabilizes the regime because defection is risky; the small winning coalition is rewarded with growth-blocking private goods; and high costs of defecting and low price for loyalty permit the rulers to use a large share of the surplus for personal projects.[13]

The Race to Be First and Destructive Winning Coalitions

The selectorate model offers a convincing explanation of an underlying propensity of democratic governments to promote long-term economic growth. Yet various democracies, at least in the short and medium term, seem to follow economic policies that border on the irrational. Rodrik (1996) discusses some of these tendencies. Years can go by before democratic governments reverse policies that generate negative growth and serious overall economic losses. Democratic governments even reintroduce economic policies that in an earlier period brought economic disaster. What precisely is the underlying logic?

Rational-choice political economists of a new generation have explored with the help of relatively sophisticated formal models why many democratic countries, for example in Latin America, pick destructive economic policies (Sturzenegger and Tommasi 1998). The new theories usually assume that the actors fully understand underlying economic structures but lack knowledge of the distribution of important variable(s). As an illustration, let us assume that everyone knows with certainty that proposed institutional reforms would bring large net economic benefits in the aggregate, if implemented. With some probability there would also be costs randomly distributed among the various categories of actors. Finally, it is known that losers will not be compensated. A skillful theorist can now construct a model showing that rational pivotal actors, uncertain about their share in the costs, will not support the reforms until the economic crisis has reached some critical level.

The new literature models various phenomena that the old literature on interest groups left unexplored or explained informally, including the dynamics of the rent-seeking process. Why, for example, do factions within rent-seeking coalitions frequently create political crises by calling for economic reforms well before their rents are depleted and before a state of full-scale economic crisis is reached? If these calls for reforms are heeded, the reform measures appear to make the instigators worse off by hastening the removal their privileges.

Tornell (1998) illustrates the new style by offering a rational-choice explanation of both vigorous rent seeking and subsequent early calls for reform. He observes that uncertain property rights cause excesses and even destructive behavior by holders of various government privileges. The possession of quotas, monopoly rights, and special favors is often linked to the life of the current government, these rights frequently are not transferable, and they are vulnerable to various groups' attempts to capture these rights. In the extreme, the situation resembles open access, where actors race to be first to deplete a resource with uncertain ownership.

According to Tornell (1998), the beneficiaries of uncertain economic privileges may call for reforms before their destructive race hits bottom because they seek to control the agenda of expected government reforms when it becomes apparent that reforms cannot be avoided. By taking the reform initiative, a group hopes to minimize its cost of future reforms and pass disproportionate burdens onto other groups. The Tornell model shows how competition to avoid the burdens of economic reforms influences timing, which is set at a relatively early date because the factions are unable to solve their collective-action problem and present a united front.

Constraining the Government: Social Structures and Social Models

So far, our examination of wasteful economic policies has been restricted to rational-choice explanations. The explanations share the following characteristics: (1) poor economic outcomes result from strategic decisions by rational actors who have full knowledge of the underlying social structures (social models are neutral); (2) destructive economic policies and outcomes are rooted in high transaction costs, which prevent side payments and credible commitments necessary for maximizing joint wealth; and (3) social structures that constrain rulers are exogenous.

Theories of this nature are not well suited for explaining why certain countries get stuck in poverty traps while other countries evolve political structures supportive of long-term economic growth or why some countries have political structures capable of weathering severe exogenous shocks that devastate other countries.[14] To handle these difficult issues, we need a theory that has the growth-friendliness of political and social institutions as the dependent variable. Fragmentary evidence indicates that historical forces embedded in path-dependent social institutions, organizations, and social models shape the opportunity set of polities and often restrict opportunities for reform.

Because the evolution of political institutions has a historical dimension, several American scholars have mined English history in search for the roots of limited government. In a well-known study, North and Weingast (1989) analyze the evolution of institutions governing public choice in seventeenth-century England, and Weingast (1997) has revisited the case. North and Weingast emphasize individual choice but do so against the background of organizations and institutions and in the context of specific social models.

Weingast (1997) attempts to capture the essential features of political developments in seventeenth-century England by using a simple game-theoretic model that analyzes the relationship between a ruler and two social groups. The study models the ruler's ability to set the groups against each other. Weingast assumes that the two groups can repel transgressions by the ruler only when they coordinate their response and act jointly; acting alone, neither group is capable of resisting the ruler. Consequently, the ruler has an incentive to make neutrality attractive to the group that is not under attack by sharing with it some of the resources confiscated from the targeted group.

In the Weingast model, the ruler acts first and decides to transgress against (for example) group X. In a one-shot game, Y's best response is to acquiesce and not challenge the ruler. If Y comes to the aid of X, Y will bear costs of war, even when X defends itself and together X and Y overpower the ruler. Y gains nothing by helping to defeat the ruler (except perhaps feeling good about it) because Weingast makes the strong assumption that X and Y cannot appropriate the ruler's wealth. If Y does not come to the aid of X, X loses a large part of its resources, but Y suffers no losses. There is no urgent need for the ruler to share with Y some of the assets taken from X to keep Y neutral. By the same token, a rational X stays neutral when the ruler transgresses against Y.

Although the divide-and-rule strategy dominates nonrepeated games, when we introduce repeated play the situation becomes more complex. In repeated games, as the folk theorem tells us, a whole range of equilibrium outcomes is possible. Now all parties choose their strategies with future games in mind, recognizing that repeated play enables the players both to signal and punish each other. The divide-and-rule outcome, where one group is attacked and the other acquiesces, is still a potential Nash equilibrium outcome, which the ruler can reinforce by sharing the wealth of a targeted group with the neutral group. But nonaggression is also a potential Nash equilibrium if the ruler expects the two groups to support each other against her transgressions. In terms of the model, nonaggression enables economic growth; in the long run, it is the best joint outcome for X and Y. Moreover, in repeated play, a group that acquiesces in one round (stays neutral while the other group is attacked) may itself become the target of state aggression in a future round, creating an incentive for zero tolerance of serious state transgressions.

Various scholars, not always using game theory, claim that in England and the Netherlands a transition from divide-and-rule equilibrium to limited monarchy and nonaggression equilibrium was a necessary condition for early emergence of sustained economic growth. These studies, however, usually, rely on exogenous events or new social models to explain breakdowns of divide-and-rule equilibria and the transition to limited government.[15] A recent paper, for example, emphasizes the role of Atlantic trade in releasing modern economic growth in Europe (Acemoglu, Johnson, and Robinson 2002).[16] Although Atlantic trade extended to the Americas, Africa, and Asia and included colonial extraction and slave trade, the empirical evidence indicates that, relative to the gross domestic product of the European countries, income and profits directly generated by the trade were not large enough to explain the upsurge in economic growth. Yet Acemoglu, Johnson, and Robinson argue that the Atlantic trade was central to the rise of Western Europe because of the indirect impact on economic institutions.

The argument is as follows. From around 1500, Atlantic trade created profit opportunities for new commercial groups in Europe but did so only in countries that met two conditions: access to Atlantic ports and freedom for new merchants to enter and prosper from the trade.

The latter condition excluded countries governed by divide-and-rule monarchs who monopolized the trade, usually sharing the spoils with their close supporters. Britain and the Netherlands, however, met both conditions. Substantial direct profits from Atlantic trade empowered a new mercantile class in England and the Netherlands to demand capitalistic institutions for facilitating private enterprise and market transactions. In both countries, relatively weak monarchs were unable to suppress these demands. Induced by its self-interest, a powerful new merchant class demanded new institutions that promoted economic growth, not only in the trading centers but also in other regions and sectors that were not directly involved in Atlantic trade. The diffusion effect initiated modern economic growth in Europe. In this view, modern growth is rooted in a historical accident: the interaction between Atlantic trade and initial political and economic conditions in England and the Netherlands. The rise of the Western world depends on diverse historical forces in the two countries that prior to 1500 had created a new balance of power and new ideologies.

The case of Spain and Portugal further illustrates the exogenous or chance element in economic development, which is implicit in the work of scholars such as North, Weingast, and Acemoglu. Both countries were deeply involved in Atlantic trade—indeed, Portuguese advances in ship design helped launch the Age of Discovery. Spain and Portugal received considerable direct gains from Atlantic trade but not indirect gains in the same measure as England and the Netherlands because the initial conditions were unfavorable. Around 1500, for various historical reasons, the balance of power had not yet turned against the monarchs of Spain and Portugal. Powerful monarchs were willing and able to block the emergence of a new merchant class. Instead, the crown and its key supporters monopolized the trade. Those in power had no need for modern capitalistic institutions, which did not emerge, and high taxes paralyzed private enterprise. Although the trade increased the wealth of Spain and Portugal, their economic might declined relative to the leading powers of Europe.

The Lessons

Recent studies provide several interesting insights into the political logic of imperfect economic institutions. First, when rulers have uncertain political control over their subjects or when their time horizons are limited, they have an incentive to plunder the wealth of their nations instead of creating institutions supportive of growth. Second, authoritarian governments are prone to dividing and ruling, usually creating small winning coalitions; therefore, authoritarians tend to reward their immediate supporters with private goods (including various privileges) and usually undersupply growth-promoting public goods (secure property rights and essential infrastructure). Although growth-oriented autocrats are well known in history, rapid economic growth under autocratic governments is usually a temporary phenomenon. Moreover, when autocrats try to create a strong economy, they are not typically concerned with the needs of an average household but with their personal projects, including military ones. Limited government, especially democracy, creates opportunities for sustained long-term growth, but democracy by itself is not a sufficient condition for growth, as the public-choice literature has explored.

Since limited government is an important step toward sustained growth, a theory of institutional reform ideally should instruct reformers about how to constrain autocratic rulers. Modern game-theoretic approaches, such as Weingast's (1997), assume that limited government is a self-enforcing institutional arrangement, created by the readiness of pivotal groups spontaneously to punish political leaders who violate communal standards for "legitimate behavior" and infringe on basic rights. These studies, however, are of little use for policymakers because they treat social conditions that enable cooperative equilibrium as exogenous variables. The conditions appear in an unexplained manner at some point in the historical evolution of social systems, creating opportunities for a cooperative equilibrium in the political domain and secure property rights in the economic one.

In political science, the literature, both rational choice and other approaches, roughly follows three separate paths in explaining the origins of limited government (Weingast 1997). A venerable line of research claims that democratic values come first and limited government follows: Limited government becomes self-supporting only when pertinent actors somehow have internalized democratic values. The precondition is that the actors share social models of legitimate governance and develop strong preferences for opposing illegitimate political acts, irrespective of whose rights are breached. Common policy models and shared political values remove the otherwise stubborn problem of coordinating the responses of different groups and their individual members in the face of divide-and rule-strategies by a ruler. Values-first theories, however, are not of much direct use to reformers. The theories usually are stated in general terms and offer little practical guidance about how to spread democratic values.

The second class of explanations identifies historical circumstances where an overall balance is struck between the power of the ruler and the power of significant social groups. In this view, limited government comes first and democratic values follow. The evolution of multipolar centers of power limits the ruler. Values initially play no role in this balancing act, but as time passes, experience with limited government makes people adopt democratic values. Values do not lead the process; they come later.[17]

Weingast also suggests a third scenario: limited government and democratic values arise simultaneously. Social groups facing a rapacious leader manage to agree on terms of engagement and coordinate a response. The resulting political equilibrium involves both institutions of limited government and democratic values.

In few words, the logic behind the third alternative is roughly as follows. Leaders of major social groups sometimes coordinate their responses to recurring aggression by autocratic leaders. In game-theoretic terms, the leaders set up common trigger strategies (or make pacts) for harmonizing their defenses. To establish a growth-friendly political equilibrium, the groups must agree *ex ante* on what conduct (transgressions) by the ruler will automatically trigger their joint response. If the various groups honor the trigger strategy, new growth-friendly political equilibrium has emerged because a rational ruler will not violate the trigger rules and risk defeat. The new balance involves both limited government and democratic values—the trigger rules. Weingast emphasizes that the various groups need not share exactly the same social models of legitimate state behavior. A self-enforcing pact can emerge even if the various groups do not share exactly the same values about constitutional affairs. Joint trigger rules imply, however, similar policy models for responding to aggression by the ruler, which implies that their constitutional models must substantially overlap. To this we add that Weingast does not deal explicitly with the problem of coordinating responses within each social group.

How does Weingast's theory compare with the two other explanations of limited government? His coordination equilibrium is an amalgam of the two previous models, thereby actually raising the bar. As a prior condition, Weingast's limited-government solution requires both a new balance of power—the emergence of two or more powerful groups that are capable of restraining autocrats without themselves resuming absolute power—and minimal overlapping of social models required for enabling a joint trigger strategy. Like the other two approaches, the Weingast theory offers little assistance to policymakers. The task of creating convergence of appropriate social models and decentralized hubs of political power is beyond the usual realm of policymaking. Indeed, as Weingast emphasizes, trigger strategies and limited government have often grown out of pacts between powerful groups attempting to restore order in the aftermath of cataclysmic events, such as civil wars. Similarly, North, Summerhill, and Weingast (2000), in their discussion of empirical cases, emphasize the role of turbulent historical developments in creating conditions for limited government.

We draw a mixed lesson from our excursion into the political logic of bad economics. The first lesson is that there are few immediate opportunities for basic reform in countries firmly ruled by autocratic leaders and small winning coalitions. In these countries, social and political upheaval apparently is a necessary (but not sufficient) condition for reform. Yet one should be careful in generalizing. Special circumstances can give rise to growth-oriented autocrats who take the long view and on their terms create stable conditions for economic activity. Moreover, in many democracies, political support for growth-oriented policies is fragile and is prone to collapsing when external impulses jolt the economy. The second, main conclusion concerns the role of social models in reforms. Except for theories that visualize a chain reaction beginning with decentralization of political power and leading to democratic political institutions and finally democratic values, social models seem to play a critical causal role in the transition to limited government.

Weingast compares his solution to a coordination game mixed with elements of prisoner's dilemma, but he cannot escape the social-models issue. In pure coordination games, people value coordination in itself. They are indifferent *ex ante* to the form coordination takes.[18] The various approaches in constitutional games aimed at deriving limited government often have very different wealth consequences for key players, who are likely to have strong preferences for particular sets of rules. Constitutional games also involve beliefs concerning sources of legitimate power and a good measure of uncertainty about cause and effect. The players often honestly disagree about the likely effectiveness of alternative constitutional rules. Our excursion into the political logic of imperfect economic institutions leads us to the conclusion that history and social models play a crucial role in defining limits and opportunities for reform.

CHAPTER 6

Inefficient Social Norms

Introduction: Norms Matter

A research program that identifies institutions as a crucial determinant of economic performance must deal with social norms, which are included in nearly all definitions of social institutions. Indeed, the literature has paid increasing attention to this complex phenomenon. North (1990) explores the links among ideas, institutions, and economic performance; Greif (1994, forthcoming) analyzes how informal social structures of individualist and collectivist societies affect economic performance; Weingast (1997) claims that shared beliefs, values, and focal points, often incorporated in pacts, have helped establish limited-government equilibrium and stable markets (see chapter 5); Bates, Figueiredo, and Weingast (1998) analyze how rulers threatened by economic reforms exploit latent beliefs to redirect the nation's policy focus toward social strife and away from reforms; Putnam, Leonardi and Nanetti (1993) use variation in the historical social capital of Italian regions to explain their uneven development; Barro (1997) adds cultural variables to his growth-accounting regressions; and Eric Posner (2002) studies the relationships among norms, law, and economic behavior.[1]

The assumption that information is scarce and transactions are costly has brought social norms and other cultural variables to the surface. Information scarcity makes it costly for traders to verify (measure) the quality of complex commodities, discover their partners' motives and standards of honesty, and enforce contracts (Eggertsson 1990; Barzel 1997). Costly measurement and monitoring discourages exchange, and fears of opportunistic behavior by the other side can make traders forgo lucrative options (Williamson 1985). Explicit recognition of transaction costs brings to our attention not only problems of measurement, enforcement, and control through legal mechanisms but also the role of reputation, trust, and norms in both political and economic exchange.

Mainstream economists have long avoided social norms, although their opposition has recently softened. These economists are concerned that ad hoc appeals to social norms for explaining theoretical anomalies would lower scientific standards in economics. A young field, the economics of religion, has shown that these fears are not always warranted. Studies in this area often introduce religious norms as preferences in individual demand functions and test hypotheses about conventional price and income effects in religious behavior.

In academic economics, opposition to norms is an instance of a "norm against norms," and the following section of this chapter irreverently uses the case to explain the enforcement of norms and their impact on behavior and social outcomes. Although many scholars recognize both efficient and inefficient norms, others lean toward functionalism and assume that norms tend to be efficient. For their part, functionalists try to discover the many ways in which norms contribute to efficiency. The third section of the chapter discusses this tendency. The fourth section argues that social norms need not be any more efficient than laws and regulations. The fifth section introduces an empirical case, claiming that an ancient norm of sharing in historical Iceland contributed to a high-risk strategy in farming. Icelandic farmers consistently failed to use stores of fodder effectively as insurance against random cold spells and other acts of nature. My intention with this case is to support the claim that norms are often embedded in a wider social system and cannot be considered in isolation. I claim that a dynamic analysis of beliefs and values is required to understand the Icelandic hay-storage puzzle. The sixth section discusses policy strategies for undermining and erasing undesired norms with reference to the Icelandic case. The strategies all aim to give the so-called cooperation-defection differential a negative value (E. A. Posner 1996b). The concluding section discusses attempts to develop dynamic analyses of social norms and in particular dynamic analysis of beliefs and values.

The Norm against Norms in Economics

Many graduate students of economics have learned that their peers and superiors will punish them for using social norms to explain behavior that is not easily explainable as standard maximization by a selfish agent. The students also assimilate the received research methodology (a social model), which makes them appreciate the harmful consequences of trivializing economic methodology. In short, the neoclassical culture of academic economists has (at least until recently) enforced a norm against norms. In "What Happened to Economic Development?" Ruttan (1991, 276, quoting Huntington 1987, 22) states,

It would be hard to find a leading scholar in the field of developmental economics who would commit herself or himself in print to the proposition that "in terms of explaining different patterns of political and economic development . . . a central variable is culture . . ."

At the outset of the twenty-first century, Ruttan's statement may sound dated or pessimistic. The resurgence of game theory, which derives norms as outcomes in noncooperative and evolutionary games, and recent interest in new institutional economics and transition economics has made many economists reconsider their opposition to norms as an important explanatory variable (Coase 1937, 1960; R. R. Nelson and Winter 1982; Axelrod 1984; Williamson 1985; Eggertsson 1990; North 1990; Binmore 1994; Drobak and Nye 1997; Furubotn and Richter 1997). Yet there is a natural tendency in economics to analyze norms in a manner that is consistent with standard prize theory, as illustrated by many studies in the economics of religion (Hardin 1997; Iannaccone 1998).

The economics of religion tackles religious beliefs with market metaphors, models churches as firms or clubs, and uses variation in the opportunity cost of time to explain aspects of religious behavior such as differences in religious observance by age and sex; the timing of religious switches; and the frequency of same-religion marriages. Religious norms are treated in the same manner as preferences for tea and coffee, and the studies examine how religious behavior is affected by changes in income or in the relative price of religious observance.

The fixed-preferences approach to religious behavior has turned up interesting results, showing that religious behavior responds as predicted to income and relative prices. Yet the methodology has obvious limits. A leading scholar in the field readily admits that a static approach (fixed beliefs and preferences) is not well suited for explaining the origins of religious beliefs or surges in religious activity. According to Iannaccone (1998, 1467), narrow economic analysis has problems accounting for "the resurgence of evangelical Christianity in the United States, the rise of Islamic fundamentalism in the Middle East, the explosive growth of Protestantism in Latin America, the religious ferment in Eastern Europe and the former Soviet Union, [and] the role of religion in political conflict world wide."

We can add that recent theoretical developments, particularly the assumptions of imperfect information and transaction costs, create difficulties of their own. Consider Azzi and Ehrenberg's (1975) pioneering attempt to model religious behavior as demand for afterlife consumption.[2] Transaction-costs economics suggests that contracting for afterlife consumption is likely to involve severe measurement and enforcement costs. Rational consumers must verify or form rational expectations about the quality of a high-price service before they purchase it. Afterlife consumption is not a search good with qualities that consumers can verify prior to purchase. It is an experience good with infinite *ex ante* measurement costs (P. Nelson 1970). With experience goods, the proof is in the pudding. Unless information about the quality of afterlife consumption passes from current consumers to potential buyers on Earth, rational actors will not trust the product. In fact, by the logic of transaction-costs economics, the market for afterlife consumption should disappear or not even emerge.[3]

Modern institutional analysis defines norms as decentralized social mechanisms that regulate behavior and affect social outcomes. The traditional norm against norms in academic economics well illustrates the phenomenon. The norm is propagated and diffused in informal interactions among professors and graduate students in economics departments in the United States and other countries; there are no formal laws or regulations that restrict scholarly work on social norms. As is the case with all active norms, enough actors stand ready to sanction those who violate the norm against norms to make enforcement effective. The enforcers are ready to punish even personally unknown scholars and to do so at the enforcers' expense. The punishment varies. Violators may receive gentle rebukes, lose their reputations as serious scientists, have their papers rejected by mainstream journals, or be denied tenure.

The threat of sanctions influences how scholars choose their research strategies, preventing at least some of them from "polluting" the research environment by applying "cheap" solutions to difficult problems. Efficient social norms improve the allocation of resources— for example, by correcting spillover effects arising in imperfect or incomplete markets. The efficiency of norms depends on the properties of the (sometimes forgotten) social models that support them. The economics profession derives its norm against norms from shared social models of how best to design social inquiry, and the efficiency of the norm against norms depends on the relevance of these models. Inefficient norms survive for various reasons such as inertia and incomplete knowledge or lock-ins resulting from preference or knowledge falsification (Kuran 1995).

An Efficiency Bias?

In a classic paper, Demsetz (1967) has made the most influential contribution of any economist to the study of norms. Demsetz suggests that social norms (and other institutions or property rights) emerge in a community (in some unspecified manner) if they are expected to increase its aggregate net wealth. Those who favor the Demsetz explanation often support their case by referring to corrective forces such as nature or market competition that filter out inefficient social arrangements (Demsetz 1980).[4]

Demsetz (1967) discusses the utility of new norms in terms of internalization of external effects. Economic theory talks about external or spillover effects when actors make decisions about the allocation of resources in a social setting without considering all the costs and benefits of their actions. When making their production plans, profit-maximizing entrepreneurs who are free to pollute air and water in their community will ignore whatever pollution costs (external effects) they impose on others. The same is true of sloppy scholars who contaminate research in economics. To eliminate external effects and make actors adjust their planned activities accordingly, the actors must become responsible for all costs of their decisions and receive all benefits. At least in theory, laws, regulations, and norms can be used to eliminate external effects.[5]

The fundamental message of the functional approach is that social problems create their own solutions—for example, through the introduction of new norms. To illustrate the functional approach, we revisit the economics of religion and look at an interesting study by Hull and Bold (1994). The authors explain why some communities rely on religious beliefs and norms to keep the social order and how these beliefs and norms readily adjust to the tasks at hand. Hull and Bold argue that least-cost methods for maintaining social order vary with the developmental stage of a community. Heavy reliance on religious norms for social control is cost-effective for communities that have left a primitive stage, where order is best established through personal interactions in small isolated groups (clans), but have not reached a higher stage, where complex bureaucracies are the least-cost solution.

The study then ponders why some communities base their enforcement of socially useful behavior on promises of afterlife in heaven as well as threats of torture in hell, while other communities emphasize only rewards in heaven and make no reference to hell. The answer involves simple microeconomics. In relatively stable communities, vague promises of heaven provide necessary incentives for keeping order. In more restless societies, both the carrot and the stick become necessary because reliance on only one of the instruments soon runs into diminishing returns. Maximum effectiveness requires gilding the promises of heaven and magnifying the tortures of hell until a balance is struck where the last block of investment in each method gives the same (marginal) rate of return. The solution assumes that additional threats and promises have positive but eventually decreasing impact on behavior. It is further assumed that people assign finite (rather than infinite) values to prospects of eternal afterlife of pain or pleasure.

The Hull and Bold study contains several features that are typical of functionalism. The study does not explain how norms emerge: we are simply told that society finds or selects appropriate norms for each societal stage. Moreover, it is implicitly assumed that (most) people are ready to adopt whatever beliefs about heaven and hell are needed for maintaining order in their community. Hull and Bold (1994, 451) do not propose a theory of learning, but they cite an author who claims, "No purely religious urge can run counter to economics and ecology for a long time." Yet whatever the shortcomings, the functional approach can generate testable hypotheses. To test their theory, Hull and Bold use a data set with information about religious beliefs and other social institutions in a large number of traditional communities at various developmental stages. The statistical tests find support for their main propositions about the relationship stages of social development and the nature of religious beliefs.

Unlike functional approaches, game-theoretic studies of norms do not assume efficiency. In repeated games, where actors are able to signal their types and punish defectors, selfish players with selfish motives can reach either efficient or inefficient outcomes (Nash equilibria). The problem with repeated games is indeterminacy. Game theorists sometimes embed their games in historical environments that provide particular circumstances—some feature of the culture or historical background of the players—that give the game a focal point, leading it to a particular equilibrium, either efficient or inefficient. The term *analytic narratives* has been used to describe this marriage of game theory and history (Bates et al. 1998). Game theorists sometimes refer to regularities in behavior associated with Nash equilibria as social norms (Binmore 1994; Greif 1994). Finally, the evolutionary branch of game theory is also suitable for studying norms and how norm efficiency depends on what assumptions the models make about filtering or selection mechanisms.

After we leave behind both game theory and straightforward extensions of neoclassical methods and reasoning, we run into an embarrassment of riches, a bewildering variety of models and theories that do not necessarily see norms as being functional or efficient.[6] I do not attempt to evaluate these different contributions but simply distinguish between static and dynamic analysis. I refer to theories as being static when they assume stable preferences and stationary social models. Dynamic institutional analysis has on its agenda analyzing and explaining origins and changes in knowledge, beliefs, perception, preferences, and identities.[7] Ideally, we would like to see a theory of norms (and institutions in general) that is capable of explaining both the evolution of common knowledge and parametric or strategic decisions by actors, but we are not quite there yet (Katzenstein, Keohane, and Krasner 1998, 678–79).[8]

A likely future development in institutional analysis is its division into static and dynamic theory. Indeed, Aoki (2001) attempts such division.[9] Dynamic analysis would seek "to understand how preferences are formed and knowledge is generated, prior to the exercises of instrumental rationality," which is the proper domain of static analysis (Katzenstein, Keohane, and Krasner 1998, 681). The final section of the chapter returns to these issues and discusses attempts to build bridges between static and dynamic analysis. The next two sections discuss in static terms the concept of inefficient norms.

Inefficient Norms

Sampling the new literature on norms or informal institutions, readers may come away with the impression that actors, at least in competitive environments and homogeneous groups in stable surroundings, usually find ways to develop norms for efficiently organizing their affairs (E. Ostrom 1990; Cooter 1996). If efficiency is desired, the correct policy response by the state is to provide local and regional communities with a secure general framework of property rights but to allow relevant social groups to develop their own rules. The central government perhaps can later usefully solidify informal local institutions by acting them into law.

Not everyone agrees that norms tend to be efficient, even in compact local groups. Stiglitz (1994) and various coauthors have argued that information problems (moral hazard, adverse selection) can undermine private groups' ability to efficiently organize their affairs. Information problems can even push activities such as formal insurance services off the market (or never allow them to enter). When particular services are not available on the market because of high transaction costs, social groups such as extended families or tribes sometimes provide comparable services informally and in limited versions, relying on norms and social sanctions to deal with opportunistic behavior. Stiglitz (1994) (somewhat implausibly) argues that as a general rule. the state should either directly manage these troubled activities or regulate them through industry-specific rules. Yet nothing can be said a priori about the state's willingness and ability to improve the provision of such goods and services or its capacity to deal with information problems, including its agency problems.

Eric Posner (1996a) also has doubts about the general efficiency of norms. He vigorously argues that social norms often produce less efficient outcomes than statutes and customary law because in many circumstances norms are inferior tools for solving the social dilemmas of cooperation and coordination. Using game-theory analogies, Posner shows that social groups that rely on norms rather than laws depend on appropriate but haphazard focal points to find an efficient social equilibrium. The social outcomes resulting from decentralized strategies chosen by individual actors depend on various cultural factors. These points of coordination are historical accidents, whereas law need not depend on the accidental availability of appropriate focal points, he argues. Posner also maintains that dispersed social groups, although well informed about local conditions, are often poorly prepared to evaluate and properly respond to changes in external circumstances such as technological developments. Local groups may fail to adjust their social norms when new conditions arise, but judges and national legislators have better access to specialists and to aggregate sources of information. For complex cases that call for investigation by specialists, social sanctions are a less efficient method of enforcement than is reliance on the police and the courts. Finally, a close-knit social group is likely to ignore various costs and benefits (external or spillover effects) that its activities create for other groups, whereas courts and legislatures usually take a more inclusive view.[10] As a counterweight, we should add that in many countries, the legislature, the administration, the courts, and the police are corrupt, which diminishes their effectiveness relative to social norms.

No matter which side we take in this debate, it is clear that economic outcomes depend on the prevailing mix of norms, statutes, regulations, and judge-made laws, and it is not obvious that social forces will always calibrate the mix of institutions to ensure maximum welfare. Even when a social subgroup creates norms that effectively solve its internal problems, these norms are efficient only within the group's institutional environment. An efficient decentralized adjustment of norms to an inefficient overall institutional environment is likely to lead to a globally inefficient outcome.

Katz (1996, 1754) reminds us that Coase (1937, 1960) casts institutional policy as a search for second-best solutions in a world with transaction costs where policymakers must choose whether to rely on markets, business firms, or government agencies.[11] Katz (1996, 1774–75) augments Coase's list of possible solutions by suggesting that reliance on private groups and their norms is the fourth way for allocating resources:

> Such groups are structurally different from markets, business firms, and government agencies; they face different constraints and use different procedures for making rules. Thus they will have different transaction costs and will be better suited to solving certain sorts of allocation problems and worse suited to solving others.

Evaluations of the effectiveness of social technologies should not focus on individual rules or norms and their enforcement but on bundles that usually contain various combinations of formal and informal institutions. Norms in themselves actually can combine to form a complex system. According to Ellickson (1994), norms often mimic an entire legal system where specific norms govern substantive entitlements and others regulate remedies and procedures. Then there are controller-selecting norms that specify for each type of activity the appropriate methods for achieving social order. In some circumstances, controller-selecting norms even forbid a grievant from using the legal system (Ellickson 1994, 98).

The transition from inefficient to growth-promoting norms is not well understood in the literature. Game-theoretic analysis often relies on particular historical circumstances to explain past events, validating Eric Posner's complaint about haphazard focal points. Scholars are hard-pressed not only to predict the likely direction of institutional change—for example, when attempts are made to transplant modern law to target country—but also to evaluate the properties of prevailing norms. The case study that follows explores these issues.

A Bad Good Samaritan Norm?

As mentioned previously, many scholars are optimistic about the ability of small homogeneous groups to create efficient norms and other rules to govern their affairs. In these circumstances, low transaction costs often facilitate the evolution of efficient property rights (Coase 1960; Eggertsson 1990, chapter 4). When basic property rights are secure, Williamson's governance structures (1985), Barzel's (1997) organization of markets, the informal institutions of Ellickson's (1991) ranchers and farmers, and Elinor Ostrom's (1990) common-pool regimes tend to be wealth enhancing unless a distant central government for its own reasons distorts the local institutional environment.

Premodern Iceland's small farm community of roughly 50,000 individuals was potentially an ideal setting in which efficient norms could emerge. Premodern Iceland was almost entirely a rural community of farmers and their servants, who raised livestock, mostly sheep. Some 160 local communes, each consisting of between 100 and 500 individuals, provided social security in a decentralized manner, relying on a mixture of social norms and formal rules. To a high degree, public order and enforcement of rules depended on decentralized enforcement of norms (see chapter 4). In the last centuries of the premodern period, Iceland was a Danish dependency or colony. Denmark did not maintain military presence in Iceland but relied on a handful of (usually Icelandic) regional administrators, and Iceland had neither an army nor a police force.

Climatic conditions made Icelandic farming marginal, and hostile nature made the cost of inefficient institutions very high. According to the country's decentralized welfare system of mutual help, individuals or families who had suffered some misfortune could appeal to their communal leaders for help (Eggertsson 1998b). The members of the commune would share food and housing with the needy, and the level of support was determined by the wealth of each contributing household. The welfare system, which was a primitive farm society's substitute for an insurance market or a welfare state, generally appears to have functioned well in cushioning individual misfortunes (specific risks), but the system could not cope with general risks that affected whole regions (see chapter 4). The historical evidence shows that the farmers feared opportunism by the welfare recipients and were preoccupied with the threat of moral hazard and adverse selection. They thought that guarantees of support were likely to create incentives not to work or even motivate people to undertake risky ventures and count on help from their commune if their projects failed.[12]

Chapter 4 introduced a branch of the transaction-costs literature that examines how traditional countries cope with their climatic conditions. The Icelandic system of grassroots social security in many ways resembled the methods of risk management in traditional agricultural and farm communities of present-day developing countries. The literature uses functional arguments to explain the structure of these informal insurance institutions, relating the arrangements to types of risks involved and measurement and enforcement efforts required for controlling cheating, but complex interactions with the wider social system make it difficult to evaluate the efficiency of a particular social norm or institutional arrangement. Still there are reasons to believe that a Good Samaritan norm of sharing that required farmers to share surplus fodder (hay) with their neighbors had harmful effects.

The Icelandic system had all along created disincentives for storing hay. The first substantive instance of taxation in the country, the tithe introduced in 1096, treated hay reserves as taxable wealth if the supplies were more than one year old. A law from 1281 gave farmers no choice: On request from neighbors, a farmer was required to hand over surplus hay at a fixed price that was independent of economic conditions. Those who resisted sharing their hay supplies virtually lost all rights.[13] The evidence does not tell us whether the 1281 law simply codified a prevailing norm of sharing or whether the law created such a norm, but there is no reason to believe that the legislation was out of touch with contemporary values and practices. Evidence from the centuries following the law's enactment shows clearly that the farm community vigorously enforced a hay-sharing norm.

In historical Iceland, temperature fluctuations were a major source of general risk. Sporadic cooling of the climate sometimes merged winter and summer, caused meager fall hay crops, and shortened the available period for outdoor grazing. Pooling risks was not a practical solution in this case, but the farmers could self-insure by storing hay and adjusting their livestock, thus preparing for exceptional weather conditions. Incentives for long-term storage of fodder, however, conflicted with the general norm of sharing that undermined farmers' property rights over their stocks of hay. According to local custom, farmers who were well supplied with fodder could be forced to share their hay in late winter and early spring, even before it was clear whether they had enough fodder if the summer arrived exceptionally late. Uncertain rights took away the incentive from cautious farmers to create buffers to prevent fodder crises and mass starvation of farm animals when two or more lean years coincided. The evidence clearly shows that the farmers did not take such precautions. During cold spells, even as late as the early twentieth century, a large portion of the country's livestock starved to death.[14]

Already in the seventeenth century, reformers argued strenuously in writing that failure to store fodder was a major cause of crises in the farm community.[15] I have found no records of legal judgments based on the hay-sharing law of 1281, but there is much evidence that the Good Samaritan norm of sharing hay was strictly enforced. In 1806, when a royal decree formally abolished the hay-sharing law, the farmers did not modify their behavior and take up storage and long-term livestock management. In the nineteenth century, as in previous centuries, farmers who needed fodder turned to their neighbors. In exchanges with hay, contemporary accounts show that late or no payment was considered a relatively mild offense and was not a cause for serious loss of reputation, but breach of contract or theft involving sheep and horses was a major offense (Eggertsson 1998b, 22).

The attempt to erode the hay-sharing norm and introduce long-term storage of fodder was led by Icelandic experts and intellectuals who had received education abroad, especially in Denmark, and by agents of the government—in 1770–71, for example, by a high-level royal commission. Copenhagen had appointed the commission to find solutions to the country's economic ills following a near collapse of the economy. Some of the commission's many recommendations aimed at improving livestock management by requiring public supervision of livestock size on every farm, punishment of farmers whose flocks exceeded prescribed numbers, and central stores of hays managed by community leaders.[16] In 1874, when Denmark gave Iceland the right to govern its internal affairs, several bills dealing with the provision of fodder and prudent management of livestock almost immediately were introduced in the Alþing and passed into law (Eggertsson 1998b, 19). These laws had no effect at all. The evidence shows that the public did not obey these laws and that local authorities did not enforce them.

Bjarnason (1913, 201–4) reports that during the nineteenth century, a couple of communes attempted coordinated livestock planning relying on volunteer inspectors. He has information that one of these communes survived the notorious winter of 1881–83 with all its livestock intact, whereas in the country as a whole a large portion of the animals starved to death. The two communes soon abandoned their experiment because skilled inspectors no longer were available for free, and livestock planning did not catch on in neighboring districts.[17] The farm community's lack of interest in livestock planning is puzzling and raises questions about the durability of the hay-sharing norm as well as the ability of the authorities to undermine it. We now turn to these issues.

I can think of four explanations for why the Icelandic farm community did not adopt a long-term strategy to trim its livestock and store hay in preparation for hard times.[18]

1. The farmers were rational agents except that their subjective policy models were incomplete. The models underestimated the large payoff from livestock management and long-term storage of hay. They selected a wrong decision rule because of limits to their knowledge of appropriate institutions for organizing farming in Iceland.

2. Their policy models recognized the benefits of long-term livestock management and the farmers were fully rational, but they were trapped in an inefficient equilibrium. The outcome is a standard case of failed collective action and is comparable to the prisoner's dilemma.

3. In spite of recurrent massive losses, the farmers' livestock strategy was actually efficient. They were rational agents following a wealth-maximizing strategy. In Iceland's unstable environment, the best policy was to live for the moment and not engage in long-term planning. The farmers maximized their wealth by raising large flocks of sheep in good years and taking their chances in lean years. This high-risk strategy involved losing most or all of their animals in hard years, but the farmers would simply start over again or, at the worst, give up farming and become farm laborers. The risk was worth taking.

4. The standard rational-choice model does not accurately describe the farmers' behavior. Iceland's informal institutions for insuring against specific risks were embodied in a cluster of norms that included the norm of sharing animal fodder. The

norms formed an integral cognitive system from which the norm of sharing fodder could not be removed; its removal would cause unsustainable cognitive dissonance.[19] Most farmers avoided seriously contemplating the benefits of long-term storage. Seen in isolation, weak exclusive property rights in hay were costly, but strong rights and long-term storage would have undermined the country's system of social security.

I am inclined to reject the first hypothesis. I find it hard to believe that rational farmers for some 1,000 years misperceived the basic nature of their environment, misinterpreted the feedback they received, and in their livestock strategies drew on fundamentally faulty policy models. The evidence admittedly shows that the farmers did not adjust creatively to their environment or adopt new technologies. Only toward the end of the premodern era did the farmers learn to dig up peat and use it as fuel, and very elementary but highly productive improvements in scythes waited until the nineteenth century (Þorsteinsson and Jónsson 1991, 214, 290). Yet it is hard to believe that rational actors (as usually portrayed in social science) were unaware of the costs and benefits of high-risk and low-risk management strategies. Lack of knowledge cannot explain their behavior.

I find the second hypothesis wholly unconvincing. A switch to a new management strategy in farming would have involved substantial coordination and commitment problems if the farmers had to act individually. In fact, the authorities stood ready to coordinate a transfer to a low-risk strategy, but the farm community firmly refused to cooperate (as the following section discusses in some detail).

The third hypothesis is likely to appeal to many mainstream economists and scholars oriented toward functionalism: the farmers, being rational, correctly concluded that periodic massive loss of livestock was an unavoidable costly side effect of the best available strategy. The high-risk strategy made good economic sense because the gains in good years outweighed the losses in bad years. Unfortunately, I am not aware of historical data that would allow me to empirically test this hypothesis. Again, I rest my case on circumstantial evidence. In a recent study of these issues (Eggertsson 1998b), I find clear evidence that leading experts and higher authorities in Iceland and Denmark saw long-term livestock management and storage as superior to the high-risk arrangement. For example, in the late nineteenth and early twentieth centuries, the most visible and passionate proponent of the storage strategy was Torfi Bjarnason, an agronomist educated in Scotland, a farmer, and in 1880 the founder of Iceland's first agricultural school. There is little doubt that in a technical sense, the farm community had the capacity to stabilize its livestock by storing and adjusting the flocks to long-term fodder supplies (Eggertsson 1998b, 21).

Having rejected the first three hypotheses, I come to the fourth and final thesis, postulating lumpiness in the Good Samaritan norms of sharing that were central to Iceland's system of social insurance. Of the four explanations, I find the final one more plausible than the other three, but I offer only an informal psychological explanation, avoidance of cognitive dissonance. The question of lumpy norms belongs to a dynamic theory of institutions that explains the formation of social models, beliefs, and preferences. The literature contains many models of behavioral dynamics, but it is fair to say that no consensus has emerged on any particular approach. The chapter's last two sections survey some of the issues concerning the stability and change in social beliefs and social norms.

Policies for Eroding Undesirable Norms: The Cooperation-Defection Differential

The government of a country can employ various means to undermine norms that conflict with the goals of public policy, but success is often uncertain. Eric Posner (1996b, 137–44) uses a theoretical framework, which he refers to as the cooperation-defection differential of potential norm violators, to classify the most important of these antinorm measures. Posner's study is representative of recent scholarly work that links rational individual choice with macro outcomes without producing (in my opinion) a full-fledged dynamic theory of beliefs and values. Posner's differential compares the net gains of observing a norm to the net gains of violating it. When the net gains of violating the norm become greater than the net gains from observing it, a rational actor stops observing the norm. In a rational calculus, the net gains to an individual actor from observing a norm depend on two factors: The sum of benefits that the actor attributes to the norm minus his or her total costs of enforcing it. Net gains from defection or violation of a norm include the value of the best available alternative after allowing for the punishment costs that a violator should expect. When a positive cooperation-defection differential begins to shrink, actors initially can attempt to restore the differential by withdrawing their participation in costly enforcement while still observing the substantive norm. When the differential becomes negative, rational actors no longer observe the norm, and the social routines that the norm supports are no longer sustainable.

The elements of the cooperation-defection differential suggest what measures governments can use to uproot inefficient or undesirable norms (E. A. Posner 1996a, 1728–36). In Posner's terms, the aim of antinorm policy is to turn a positive differential into a negative differential, which can be done by (a) trying to lower people's perceptions of the direct benefits from supporting the norm; (b) raising the costs to norm followers of enforcing the norm in their group; (c) lowering the punishment for those who violate the norm; or (d) providing attractive new social arrangements that compete with the arrangements supported by the norm.[20]

In their attempts to undermine the hay-sharing norm, the authorities in premodern Iceland explored virtually all avenues suggested by the Posner framework.[21] To lower punishment costs for norm violators who refused to share their stocks of hay with the neighbors, the authorities formally made individual farmers legally responsible for satisfactorily feeding their animals. If a farmer's lack of hay in midwinter is legally seen as a proof of negligence or even criminal behavior (unless the shortage is caused by fire, flooding, or other such accidents), the social stigma of farmers who refuse to help negligent neighbors may be diminished. Similarly, if the farmers are directly supervised and compelled to maintain sufficient emergency stores of fodder, the norm of sharing hay would become obsolete. Attempts at compulsion included a 1746 royal decree issued in Copenhagen that instructed local authorities to monitor the hay reserves of all farmers in their districts and to ensure that supplies were adequate. Comparable official recommendations, rules, and laws that require official monitoring of reserves and forbid farmers to starve their animals are common during a period stretching from at least 1702 until the end of the nineteenth century. The most notorious of these edicts was the Starvation Act of 1884, which imposed fines on farmers if they were found to have starved their animals and to have ignored recommendations by communal authorities concerning appropriate hay reserves. An 1889 revision of the Starvation Act provided in extreme cases for the imprisonment of offenders. Historians agree that farmers and local law enforcement officials alike entirely ignored all these attempts for two or more centuries, which is the central puzzle of this story (Eggertsson 1998b, 19–20).

The authorities and reformers also tried to affect the cooperation-defection differential by using cognitive approaches—campaigns of persuasion—to lure farmers to upgrade their social models and recognize the costs of their high-risk strategy as well as the benefits of the hay-storage alternative. These attempts also did not succeed; farmers were not willing to give up their game against nature.

Introducing new social arrangements that the players find more profitable than the old norm-supported arrangement is perhaps the surest method that a government can use to erode a positive cooperation-defection differential of a norm. The new arrangements, which sometimes rely on government subsidies, can make the old norms irrelevant. In Iceland, the eventual solution to the livestock-management problem, which in the first part of the twentieth century both stabilized the country's livestock and undermined the hay-sharing norm, falls in this category. The new system was one of a central (rather than individual or local) storage, and the initiative came from the national legislature, the central government, and a new national association of farmers. The program received substantial financial support from the central government and relied on new technologies and new industrial organization. The country's system of communications—on land, at sea, and in the air—had improved, a modern fishing industry provided fish meal as fodder, and imported supplies were now available on short notice. Finally, in the emerging urban environment of the twentieth century, formal government social services and commercial insurance replaced the traditional commune system of sharing as a method for coping with risks (Þ. Jóhannesson 1948, 107–14; Björnsson 1979, 277–78).

Building a Dynamic Theory of Norms

In this section, I discuss recent attempts to model dynamic aspects of social norms: the origins of the rules themselves and associated social models or beliefs; the evolution of enforcement strategies; and the dissemination of informal rules and behavior patterns. A dynamic theory ideally would integrate all three aspects, but, as we shall see, the first topic is less well developed than the other two, and robust empirical studies and formal tests of hypotheses are relatively rare.

Game theorists often define norms as regular (Nash equilibrium) patterns of behavior that emerge in interactive relationships. Iterated uncooperative games are characterized by multiple equilibria, leaving the theory open-ended, whereas evolutionary game theory comes to the rescue and provides tools for formally analyzing the selection of strategies. Bendor and Swistak (2001), drawing on their own work and that of others, provide a lucid account of how evolutionary game theory is useful for studying the dynamics of social norms. Consider a social group with members that interact in pairs, with the pairs randomly chosen for each round of the game. The individuals, who seek to maximize their expected payoffs, pause periodically to reevaluate and possibly change their current strategies after observing the game as played by all the players. Bendor and Swistak use iterated prisoner's-dilemma games to illustrate the approach, although their analysis is applicable to other types of games. The players, in their regularly recurring revisions, evaluate the payoffs yielded by strategies such as always defect, tit-for-tat (TFT), or TF2T, which implies cooperating in periods 1 and 2 and then defecting if and only if your opponent defected in the previous two periods. The reevaluations make the players discard low-yield strategies or, in the language of evolutionary game theory, "the more fit a strategy is in the current generation, the faster it increases" (1506). A strategy played by all the members of a group is evolutionarily stable if it can resist the invasion of "mutants"—new behaviors that invade the group. The native strategy is weakly stable if it prevents the spread of mutants and is strongly stable if the invaders decrease in frequency. Bendor and Swistak conclude that social norms are necessary for stabilizing behavior in a large class of evolutionary games. The authors also find that evolutionary forces do not necessarily ensure Pareto optimal outcomes, although native strategies tend to be more robust (have greater survival chances) the more efficient they are.[22]

Studies applying evolutionary game theory to social norms tend to be highly abstract and weak on empirics. Recent empirical studies of social norms that use noncooperative game theory often rely on exogenous cultural and historical elements to explain, on a case-by-case basis, why a particular social equilibrium came to be selected. Such studies have provided interesting insights, but the analysis is essentially of static nature (Bates et al. 1998).[23]

The diffusion of social norms through society can be swift and sometimes unexpected. The sudden diffusion of ethnic animosity in the former Yugoslavia startled many insiders and outsiders. Kuran (1995, 1998), whose approach is not (formally) game-theoretic, employs a model with turning points and reputational cascades to explain both persistent low levels of ethnic activity and explosive increases in such behavior. The model also offers general insights into the dynamics of norms.

Kuran (1998) obtains his results by adding two new categories of variables to the standard individual utility function: reputational utility, which emanates from social (ethnicity related) responses both in one's own ethnic group and in out-groups, and expressive utility, which is a discontinuous variable that registers how much people value their current lifestyles. The model assumes that people vary in their willingness to change their lifestyles and allocate resources to ethnic activities solely for reputational reasons.

Two factors can upset the prevailing social equilibrium of ethnic activities and ethnic norms: new expectations and new inherent taste for ethnicity. Both factors are external to the Kuran model. An upsurge in expectations about rising (or falling) ethnic activity overall in the community makes individuals allocate more (less) of their personal resources to ethnic activity to avoid social sanctions, but individual responses vary because of different needs for social acceptance and self-expression. Moreover, the configuration of these factors produces a distribution of thresholds.[24] In the model, expressive utility has two important implications: *ex ante,* the thresholds are not directly observable (they are a feature of individual utility functions), and individual threshold differences can create multiple equilibria of both the stable and unstable varieties.

Finally the model contains a diffusion function that charts the relationship between expected and realized societal levels of ethnic activity. It is assumed that expectations adjust downward when overshooting realized levels and upward when underestimating the levels. Building on these foundations, Kuran (1998) shows how a small change in expectations about the overall level of ethnic activities may lead, via reputation effects, to huge changes in the realized levels. Large effects are likely when the prevailing equilibrium is unstable or when changes in expectations exceed the sphere of gravity of a prevailing stable equilibrium. In either case, the size of the change depends on the distance to the nearest equilibrium point.[25]

The second factor that can alter the level of ethnic activity in society is a change in the inherent utility that people derive from ethnic activities, as distinct from social pressures to engage in such activities. Most theories of ethnification emphasize only the direct utility effect, leaving out the possible role of reputational cascades. In the Kuran model, a direct utility effect shifts up the diffusion curve, leading to a new equilibrium. The move to a new equilibrium will always involve an intrinsic effect and in some cases will also involve a magnifying reputational effect.

In sum, relying on the concepts of unobservable tipping points and reputational cascades, Kuran derives results that are interesting and intuitively sensible but also disappointing from the viewpoint of social science. In this view, ethnification is an unpredictable phenomenon, as is the stability of low (or high) societal levels of ethnic activity. Also, the reputational effect and the intrinsic effect of an ethnification process are probably empirically almost indistinguishable. The core problem blocking progress appears to be our lack of empirically usable theory of how people restructure their social models.

Models of the physical and social world are driven by human imagination and creativity, which appear to be inherently unpredictable phenomena. Students of norms differ in their views of how well we understand the mental models part of norm dynamics. Eric Posner (1996a, 1709–10) believes that we lack a satisfactory psychological theory to explain why people sometimes feel emotional and psychological compulsion to follow norms. Other scholars claim that psychologists and cognitive scientists have developed rich and useful theories of mental models and internalization of norms (Denzau and North 1995; Cooter 1996, 1661–62; Clark 1998). In a recent volume on values and organization in economics that contains nineteen essays by leading scholars, the editors pessimistically conclude, "The subject of norms, values, and preference formation is increasingly attracting the attention of economists. . . . Yet this field of inquiry, now in its initial stages, still lacks a unified analytical framework and . . . a common set of conclusions. In particular, there is little empirical evidence to support or refute various theoretical claims made in this volume" (Ben-Ner and Putterman 1998, xxiii–xxiv).

To illustrate the role of social models, let us return briefly to Iceland, this time in the early modern period, which saw a gradual erosion of the norms of sharing in farming and of norms prohibiting specialization outside agriculture. Nonetheless, traditional values, models, and norms lingered and delayed the country's modernization. When Iceland gradually gained independence from Denmark in the late nineteenth and early twentieth centuries, Iceland's political parties adopted and fought over three contrasting social models: the capitalist-entrepreneurial model, the socialist (including Marxist) model, and the traditionalist model. The traditionalist model saw the Industrial Revolution as a perverse historical episode that might bring a temporary increase in wealth. Yet in the long run, industrialization with factory work and urban living would in this view undermine the social fabric and lead to moral and economic decline.[26] The traditionalists called for an agricultural rather than industrial revolution, rural rather than urban living, regulated international trade, and strict control of foreign investments. They only accepted small-scale manufacturing, located in rural areas and integrated with farming.[27]

Recent studies of the political history of Iceland in the last quarter of the nineteenth century and the first half of the twentieth century show that traditionalists influenced political parties across the left-right spectrum. Ásgeirsson (1988) suggests that the fundamental divide in Icelandic politics was not the usual capitalist-socialist split but capitalists-socialists versus traditionalists. The political parties were divided along traditionalist-nontraditionalist lines, and traditionalists in the various parties joined hands, sometimes by reaching across party lines to cooperate in coalition governments, fighting to delay urbanization and industrialization.[28] The traditionalists retarded economic development and modernization in Iceland for several decades, particularly by blocking investment in hydroelectric power plants, aluminum smelters, and railways and by delaying urbanization.[29]

If we refuse to believe that social arrangements such as laissez-faire markets, African socialism, and Soviet central management reflect only the material interests and relative power of key players and nothing more, an important question arises: How do national elites acquire or select particular social models of economic development along with the related values and norms? Chai (1998, 282) takes a step toward answering this difficult question when he attempts to explain the "striking relationship between an experience with Western colonialism and a tendency toward state economic intervention" in countries that recently have broken away from colonial rule. Just like the Icelanders, leaders of other newly independent countries faced a range of foreign models of social and economic development. Tests of contending social models are seldom unambiguous, and ambiguity permits different interpretations. Fundamental choices of policy depend not only on political processes and the power of organized interests but also on the appeal of alternative social models. Chai argues that in the former Western colonies, well-understood psychological processes, which he discusses, led to internalization of "opposition ideologies" and motivated the rulers' initial choice of social models. The opposition ideologies were attempts at homegrown policies that differed from those of the former masters. According to Chai's empirical evidence, developing countries that had not experienced colonial rule did not go through a similar phase of opposition ideologies and policies in the postwar period. Iceland, which became a sovereign nation in 1944, fits well with Chai's findings, although the country is not included in his study. After the Second World War, Iceland lagged fifteen years or more behind other West European countries in dismantling state control of the economy and introducing market arrangements.

The Kuran (1998) model analyzes how norm entrepreneurs can initiate reputational cascades by stirring up expectations of increasing ethnic activity. Another way to model these interactions is to assume that individuals use Bayes's rule to update their prior beliefs.[30] Political leaders are in a special position to manipulate events and news about events and to create particular responses both in their own group and in outside groups. Social groups share symbols, models, and collective memories of historical events, such as ethnic strife, that people use for filtering data and interpreting current events. These cognitive structures provide opportunities for manipulative leaders to rekindle latent suspicions. Bates, Figueiredo, and Weingast (1998) examine two cases in these terms: the overthrow of the United Independence Party in Zambia in 1991 and the outbreak of ethnic tension and violence in the former Yugoslavia. In the latter case, Bates, Figueiredo, and Weingast's model formalizes how President Milosevic sought to save his political skin by raising expectations about ethnic activities in the former Yugoslavia and shifting preferences away from ongoing postcommunist reforms, which threatened his authority, to ethnification and civil strife.

Bates, Figueiredo, and Weingast's study contains interesting insights, but, as the authors recognize, their model lacks a dynamic element. In the Yugoslav case, the players observe only actual events—and corresponding pieces of information relevant for updating their beliefs and expectations—that are associated with the equilibrium path. Yet equilibrium behavior also depends on expected values of outcomes that never happen. Behavior along the equilibrium path can be analyzed using Bayes's rule; behavior off the equilibrium path cannot (Bates, Figueiredo, and Weingast 1998, 627). In other words, Bayes's rule has rational actors adjust their beliefs only after observing (what they consider to be) actual events or actions, but "perceptions, debates, persuasions, influence, and rhetoric: these processes rather than rational decision making and experience, govern the calculations that inform the choice of strategies off the equilibrium path" (628).

PART II

Empirical Interlude:
Poverty Trap — A Case Study

CHAPTER 7

Why Iceland Starved

Of Yseland to wryte is lytile nede Save of Stokfische . . .
—*The Libelle of Englyshe Polycye,* 1436

Introduction: The Mystery of a Missing Industry

This chapter reflects on the dismal equilibrium that held the Icelandic economy at low or even declining levels of income and technology from the late Middle Ages until the nineteenth century. With the Icelandic case, I hope to bring to life some of the main themes of the book's theoretical section concerning imperfect institutions and poverty traps. I have chosen this particular case because of its simplicity and educational value. In my thinking, historical Iceland has role similar to that of formal mathematical models, which, when they are successful, bring transparency to complex issues and highlight important relationships that more opulent images would obscure.

The golden age of the Icelanders, when they traveled widely, discovered North America, and created original literature (the sagas) that is still in print in major world languages, petered out in the thirteenth century, which saw civil war, increasing isolation from Europe, and loss of independence. From the sixteenth century on, living conditions deteriorated, culminating in a series of eighteenth-century famines that caused Danish rulers to contemplate moving the Icelanders to Denmark. In the twentieth century, the world has seen disastrous social outcomes that flow from the human propensity to make great experiments, which often generate monumental failures because of the perpetrators' unrealistic assumptions about knowledge, information, and incentives (V. Ostrom 1993, 1997). As Hayek (1945, 1960) never tired of emphasizing, in these social experiments, the central authority frequently overestimates its ability to restructure, monitor, and enforce. In the Icelandic case, centuries of economic failure reflected the inability or unwillingness to experiment at all—a social paralysis in which both domestic and external institutions thwarted economic progress and trapped the community in poverty.

The economic history of Iceland is a story of a stationary population of some 50,000 individuals who, undeterred by the country's marginal conditions, gave priority to farming and attended only part time to one of the world's most valuable fisheries, which surrounds the country. It is a story of the distant monarchs of the Danish-Norwegian kingdom who lacked incentives and capacity to expand their tax base, partly because of limited control of resources and agents on the distant North Atlantic island. When the nineteenth century dawned, industrial technology and industrial organization in Iceland had not advanced substantially since the Viking age, and the rise of an independent fishing industry had to wait for the last decades of the century (Magnússon 1985).

In my analysis of the case I focus on economic, political, and social institutions that shape individual behavior and channel collective action. For example, I examine institutions for regulating choice in the labor market, local governance systems such as the Icelandic communes (*hreppar*), and the administrative structure the Crown used to rule Iceland. My argument, consistent with the theme of this book, is that social institutions were the fundamental factor holding back economic development in Iceland; in a supportive institutional environment, the country would have mastered and benefited from superior (known) production technologies. Incomplete social models guiding the country's elite, the landowning class, played an important role in maintaining the poverty trap. The elite obviously did not employ modern economics and use a general equilibrium model to analyze how the removal of restrictions would affect their wealth. Instead, they used what we would now characterize as an "informal partial equilibrium model" to predict that permitting independent fisheries would ruin farming. I argue, however, that defectors, lured by the promise of profits in the fisheries, would have destroyed the coalition of landowners had the Danish Crown not participated in enforcing the status quo for its own reasons, which I discuss in some detail.[1]

I begin by discounting two ideas that are inappropriate for explaining why Iceland did not develop an effective fishing industry: (a) isolated Icelanders were unaware of both state-of-the-art fisheries technology and potential export markets abroad and (b) the culture in Iceland was adverse to commercial activities. First, consider the notion that the Icelanders' lack of knowledge about fisheries technology and exportation was the ultimate cause of centuries of stagnation. Is it possible that the Icelanders did not develop an effective fishing industry because they knew only small rowboats and fishing lines with single hooks and had no conception of exports and export markets? The evidence does not support this view. Inshore fishing was a part-time activity of farmers from the time of the country's settlement around 900 A.D.; substantial exports of fish began in the thirteenth century, gradually replacing woolen products as the country's major export; and from around 1400, when English fishermen first appeared, Icelanders were exposed to state-of-the-art fishing technology through their contacts with foreign fishing fleets.[2]

Second, consider the hypothesis that the Icelanders failed to develop an independent fishing industry because their values were in a fundamental conflict with commercial exchange—that the chief objective of the actors in the country's primitive household economy was to satisfy basic needs rather than to accumulate wealth through exchange. History again fails to support this alternative (B. Lárusson 1967; J. Jóhannesson 1974; Byock 1988; W. I. Miller 1990). In point of fact, the desire to accumulate was unbridled in premodern Iceland, as is evident in the sagas that deal with the Viking period and from the extremely unequal distribution of private wealth. The Icelanders were never shy about commercial exchange: land was priced and exchanged; agricultural and marine products were exported, and luxury and other commodities were imported; and in the commonwealth period not only were seats in the national assembly, the Alþing, traded, but the law allowed actors in court cases to sell to third parties the right both to prosecute cases and to enforce verdicts.[3] Even if the Icelanders aspired to ensure only survival, institutional change was required because the premodern economy often could not meet basic needs, which led to frequent Malthusian cycles of epidemics and famine (Gunnarsson 1983; Gunnlaugsson 1988).[4] Finally, the argument that prevailing value systems hostile to change by themselves blocked economic development cannot account for the economic takeoff in the late nineteenth century, when labor and capital overcame formal institutional barriers and flowed into urban areas, into the fishing industry, and even out of the country. During the transition in the nineteenth and early twentieth centuries, powerful elements of the traditional community waged ideological and political wars against urbanization, the new wage-earning class, the fishing industry, and industrial development; however, these forces retarded but did not reverse the trend (see chapter 6).

While mindful of the ideological opposition, I emphasize the lure of defection from the landowner coalition and identify the strategies of the Danish Crown as the critical factor perpetuating the status quo in the premodern economy of Iceland. The next section analyzes the main components of the equilibrium trap, which prevented large-scale transfer of resources from the farm sector into the fisheries. The section introduces the key players in the economic and political game and identifies their fundamental interests and constraints. The third section has a dynamic perspective and analyzes the demise of the traditional system and the transition to a new structure of industrial organization. The final section summarizes and concludes.

The Poverty Trap

Background

Iceland was settled in the late ninth and early tenth centuries, mostly by Norsemen, and after enjoying a lengthy period of considerable prosperity, the country entered a path of economic stagnation and later experienced serious economic decline.[5] The evidence for stagnation and decline, which correlates with cooling temperatures, is overwhelming.[6] Agricultural technology was virtually unchanged from the Viking age until the nineteenth century, archeological studies reveal shrinking and wasting infrastructures, the annals report famines with increasing frequency (see chapter 4), and the average height of the population shrank, reflecting deteriorating nutrition.

> From the age of the settlement down to the 16th century stature remained more or less constant, or about 172 cm. In the 18th century it fell to 167 cm, and about the middle of the 20th century it rose again to 176.8 cm. In other words in a period lasting 400 years at the outside, or in the course of 16 generations, the mean stature of the population first falls about 5 cm and then rises 10 cm again, a variation of 1 cm a generation on the average. (Steffensen 1958, 44).

The central paradox in Iceland's economic history is Icelanders' failure to develop a specialized fishing industry and exploit on a large scale the country's famous fisheries. From the Middle Ages until the end of the premodern era in the nineteenth century, various institutional arrangements blocked the development of an independent fishing industry. A crucial component of these human-imposed constraints were laws and regulations that prohibited the development of townships with specialized fishers. The law restricted labor mobility by requiring all adults, with few exceptions, to live on farmsteads as farmers or servants and banned cooperation in the coastal fisheries between Icelanders and foreigners. During the period of Danish monopoly trade, 1602–1787, even Danish merchants were not allowed to winter in Iceland.[7] Finally, Icelandic prices were regulated, and the price for fish relative to the price of agricultural exports was kept lower in Iceland than in foreign markets. These regulations reflected the narrow economic interests of farmers, landowners, and the Crown. The Crown's uncertain control of its tax base in Iceland was a major part of the story, as were the farm community's fears of competition in the labor market.

Before examining the property rights of leading economic and political actors in premodern Iceland, it is necessary to provide a short account of the country's industrial organization (Eggertsson 1992, 1998b). Until the late nineteenth century, Iceland was essentially a rural society of farmsteads scattered in coastal and fjord lowlands around the island. The farmers raised livestock, which grazed unattended in mountain pastures in the summer and on home fields in the winter. The main crop was hay. Both by law and in practice, fishing was a secondary activity of (some) farmers and their servants, mainly occupying them during the slack winter season. In winter, the valuable migratory cod was found in shallow coastal waters in the country's southwestern region. As most fishermen used primitive open rowboats, they could travel only a few miles and usually returned to land the same day (Gunnarsson 1980).

Following the Protestant reformation in the mid–sixteenth century, the size and quality of vessels apparently deteriorated. In the civil war of the thirteenth century, the Icelanders fought their only naval battle (Flóabardagi, 1244) with some 680 men on thirty-five ships. The ecclesiastical sees at Hólar and Skálholt owned several vessels, including oceangoing ships that were either built domestically or purchased from foreigners. For example, in 1413 Hólar bought a ship from English merchants to sail between Iceland and England, and in 1567 Hólar bought another large ship, this time from the merchants of Hamburg (Thoroddsen 1924, 51–52, 72–76). Relatively abundant driftwood was the Icelanders' only domestic material for building boats, but timber was imported for boats, dwellings, and even cathedrals. Inability to acquire suitable vessels (at reasonable prices) is not a convincing explanation of the backward nature of the fisheries.

Because fishermen used small open boats that they could pull ashore for protection at the end of a trip, access to a beach in the southwestern region was a precondition for entering a boat in the winter fisheries (Þorsteinsson 1980, 214). Sources indicate that law and custom provided fairly liberal access to the fishing beaches (L. Kristjánsson 1980–86, 3:93). Under the law, landlords on the coast retained property rights to the beach and a narrow strip of coastal waters, but access to the fishing grounds themselves was otherwise open to all Icelanders. Of course, many farmers, even in the southwest, were inland and did not have access to beaches appropriate for fishing, and all such boat owners were charged for the use of beaches and boat sheds. Also, local authorities put a small tax on fish taken out of a district (L. Kristjánsson 1980–86, 3:93–97). Although farmers in the northeastern region and inland farmers could rent beach rights for their boats from the landlords in the fishing stations of the southwest, they generally preferred to buy the fish, either directly or indirectly, by lending boat owners servants for the season in return for a share in the catch. Figures from the nineteenth century, when internal passports had been introduced, show that most of the servants who left the farms to participate in the fisheries came from districts in the southwest, and participation rates from the northeastern region were far lower than in the southwest (A. Kristjánsson and Gunnlaugsson 1990, 25–27). Coastal properties in the fishing regions frequently were operated by tenants but owned by the church, the Danish Crown, or wealthy individuals. Tenants in these regions often paid their rent in part by serving as fishermen on their landlords' boats.

The Uncertain Property Rights of the Crown

The main economic and political actors that influenced the course of events in the premodern Icelandic economy were the Crown, its agents, the church, landowners, tenant farmers, farm servants, foreign merchants, and foreign governments. Yet in many ways, the Crown controlled the fate of the country's fisheries. Figure 1 presents a summary view of the highest political authority in Iceland from 930 to 1904, but here we are primarily concerned with the period from the union with Norway in 1262 until the end of the premodern age, late in the nineteenth century.

During the commonwealth period, the country's foreign trade was regulated by thirty-nine regional leaders (goðar) who held seats in the national assembly (J. Jóhannesson 1974). Following the union with Norway, the Norwegian king acquired property rights to all trade with

Period	Highest Authority	Limits to Authority
930–1262	Chieftains of the commonwealth	
1262–1380	The king of Norway	
1380–1904	The king of Denmark	
1415–1475		The English age. England has strong influence on Icelandic affairs.
1475–1520		Strong German influence. Merchants from Hamburg.
1874–1904		The Icelanders gain power. Home rule, 1904.

Fig. 1.   Political authority in Iceland, 930–1904 (based on Þorsteinsson and Jónsson 1991).

Iceland, including the right to determine (at least formally) what foreign merchants could enter the trade (Gunnarsson 1987, 74). After the union of Denmark and Norway in 1383, control of trade with Iceland remained for a while with the merchant of Bergen but passed eventually to the Danish Crown.

The size of the Crown's tax base in Iceland depended primarily on the value added in farming and fishing, and, of the two, the primitive fisheries provided both more tax revenue and greater potential for long-term growth. To grow, the fisheries required extensive foreign contacts—access to export markets and to vital imports such as timber, fishing gear, vessels, and technology. The small scale of economic activity in Iceland demanded that critical inputs and international marketing services either be purchased from outsiders or be obtained through joint ventures.[8] The Scandinavian connection potentially provided such a contact, but the Crown's failure to develop a strong specialized fishing industry in Iceland is puzzling. I believe that the explanation for why the Crown went along with the local elite, which opposed expanding the fishing industry, involves two related elements: Iceland's peripheral status in the kingdom and perceived threats to the Crown from cooperation between Icelanders and other Europeans outside the kingdom.

The Crown's unwillingness to invest substantial resources to enforce its property rights in distant Iceland suggests that the colony was of marginal interest to the kingdom and that the costs of developing a strong presence there were thought to outweigh the benefits. Through the centuries, Scandinavian fishing fleets, unlike those of many other countries, did not ply Icelandic waters because the Scandinavians had access to relatively abundant fishing grounds closer to home. The Crown's unwillingness to invest in Iceland was reflected in Denmark's low profile in the country and the relative autonomy given the Icelanders. Figure 2 presents a schema of the pre-1770 Danish-Icelandic system of administration. The Crown did not maintain a permanent military post or a regular police force in the country, and the royal administration in Iceland numbered only about thirty individuals (excluding a few inspectors of Crown property and the servants of the church, who became servants of the Crown after the Protestant Reformation). Until 1770, even the Danish governor of Iceland sat in Copenhagen. Finally, the center communicated with the dependency mostly during the summer months; for the remainder of the year, Iceland was out of contact.[9]

The strategy of limited involvement gave considerable autonomy to the local elite. As late as the sixteenth century, Icelandic leaders maintained that the Crown could not set new laws for the country without consent from its general assembly, the Alþing. Similarly, until about 1700, Icelanders were allowed to set new laws by having their courts rule on questions of general nature (Ó. Lárusson 1958, 208). In sum, limited involvement implied royal reluctance to confront the local elite except over fundamental issues, such as sovereignty.

The other element of the explanation is that the Crown, because of limited engagement and no organized defense, was vulnerable to incursions by outsiders onto its remote possession, and Danish leaders particularly feared foreigners attracted by Iceland's rich marine resources. For the Crown, even voluntary cooperation of Icelanders with foreigners over fishing and international marketing posed a potential threat. Events of the fifteenth and sixteenth century, when Copenhagen temporarily lost control in Iceland, convinced the rulers of the need to isolate the island. The English, who around 1400 entered the Icelandic fisheries, were the first foreign power to intrude in a serious way. The British were motivated by strong European demand for dried fish and aided by a technological revolution in shipping.[10] During this era, the English operated coastal stations in Iceland. In 1528, an English report on the Iceland fishing fleet listed 149 ships (doggers), all from the east coast of England, while in 1528 England's entire fishing fleet numbered

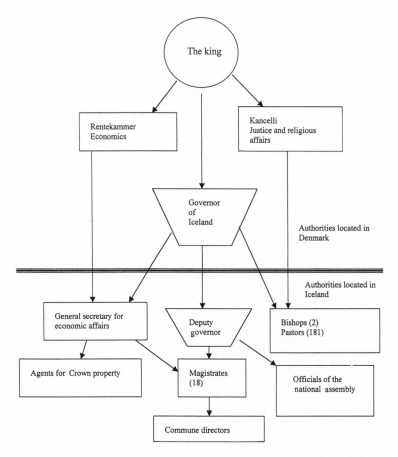

Fig. 2.   The administration of Iceland, 1700–1770 (based on Þorsteinsson and Jónsson 1991, 226).

440 vessels (Þorsteinsson 1976, 49). The Iceland fisheries were of considerable importance for the English economy in the fifteenth and early sixteenth centuries, and the English Crown levied heavy taxes on the fleet (Þorsteinsson 1976, 121–22). For the Icelanders, who at the time had been compelled to trade solely with Bergen, the English connection opened a new and valuable market. In consequence, the fishing sector expanded, and the Icelandic economy blossomed. Yet the period is also known for plunder and violence.[11]

It took Copenhagen about 150 years fully to dispose of the English intruders in Iceland. The Crown met the challenge in various ways: it attempted unsuccessfully to sell licenses to the English fishermen (Þorsteinsson 1976, 121–22), played a game of hostages by closing the Danish straits to the English and thereby eliminating their access to valuable trade in the Baltic Sea, and probably even tried to get rid of Iceland by offering it to Henry VIII as collateral for a loan (Þorsteinsson and Jónsson 1991, 149–77).[12] More effectively, Copenhagen exploited the interest of German traders, particularly those from the city of Hamburg, in the Icelandic fisheries and played the Germans off the English in a competition for Iceland's resources.[13] In the sixteenth century, the Danish Crown assigned German governors to Iceland, and English and German traders skirmished in coastal fishing stations, with the Icelanders now siding with the Hamburgers, who offered more lucrative trade than the English did. Around 1540 the English lost their last posts on the Icelandic mainland, and in 1559, with some help from the Scots, the Danish drove the English from a stronghold in the Icelandic Westman Islands. With the English out of the picture, the Danish Crown turned on the Hamburgers and in 1554–55 confiscated their property in Iceland, including forty-five fishing boats that the Germans had operated jointly with the Icelanders. The boats became the core of the Crown's new fishing fleet. The Danish navy had become a powerful force, and in 1574 the Crown confiscated thirty ocean vessels belonging to the Hamburgers. Toward the end of the sixteenth century, the Danish monarch had regained control over Iceland (Þorsteinsson 1976; Þorsteinsson and Jónsson 1991, 149–77).

The Crown now confronted a dilemma: how to both find cost-effective ways to protect its property rights in peripheral Iceland and provide conditions for a strong economy that would maximize tax revenues. However, the two goals conflicted. The economy was best served by a policy of free trade that allowed the Icelanders to cooperate with whatever foreign party had the most to offer, but events of fifteenth and sixteenth centuries had taught Copenhagen that, in Iceland, free trade without strong defense meant the end of Danish rule. The compromise solution, which put Iceland on a path of decline until the end of the eighteenth century, had four elements: (a) the country and a protective belt of ocean around it were put off-limits to all non-Icelandic vessels; (b) the Crown monopolized trade with Iceland and leased the rights to traders in specific cities in the kingdom; (c) measures were taken to prevent the development of coastal townships that might draw traders from outside the kingdom; and (d) only farmers were permitted to enter the coastal fisheries. In the mid–sixteenth century, the Danish authorities (in cooperation with the Icelanders) began a drive to eradicate foreign fishing interests from the Icelandic coast. From around 1600, the Danes strove to enforce a ban on trade between Iceland and persons outside the kingdom, and in 1631 the Danish Crown claimed an exclusive fisheries zone around the country. At that point, the North Atlantic was an open ocean, mare liberum, except for an exclusive zone around Iceland. However, the enforcement costs were high, and Danish ability to enforce these rights varied with the strength of the outside pressures and with the fortunes of the kingdom (Þorsteinsson 1976, 119–30).

Danish monopoly trade prevailed from 1602 to 1787. The arrangements varied, but the rights to trade with Iceland usually were leased, often for periods of six years, to merchants in Danish cities, mostly Copenhagen. For two periods during the monopoly era, 1759–64 and 1774–87, the royal household directly managed the trade. The value of a monopoly license was related closely to the volume of fish products in the trade—that is, licenses to trade in stations of the northeastern region, which primarily exported farm products, were less valuable than licenses to trade in the more valuable fishing stations of the southwest. Trade in farm products was relatively unprofitable for the Danes because agricultural prices were kept artificially high, which, in effect, made the fishing regions of Iceland subsidize those regions primarily dependent on farming (Gunnarsson 1987, 52).[14]

The Crown also entered the fisheries directly as a landlord by acquiring valuable property in the coastal regions of the southwest during the Protestant Reformation of the mid–sixteenth century. The Danes brought a military force to Iceland for the occasion, confiscated land owned by the monastic orders, and compelled the see in Skálholt to trade much of its best coastal property in the southwest for land in primarily agricultural districts. When the smoke had cleared after the Reformation, the Crown owned nearly 20 percent of the farmland and operated its own small fishing fleet.[15]

The Crown appeared to be satisfied with its compromise solution. Although modernization, specialization, and greater scope could have increased enormously the yield from the fisheries, the Crown did not press for structural change but occasionally tested the resolve of the local elite. These occasional attempts instructed the farmers to improve their boats and gear and pay more attention to the fisheries. Through the centuries, the offshore presence of English, Scottish, Dutch, German, Spanish, and French fishing fleets, along with their occasional incursions and illicit trade with the Icelanders, constantly reminded the Crown of the need to isolate Iceland from outsiders and maintain good relations with the local elite. Powerful interests back home did not demand access to the Icelandic fisheries: various circumstances in the Danish kingdom, such as access to the Norwegian cod fisheries, kept the Scandinavian fishermen mostly in their own region and kept them from chasing the cod to Iceland and later to North America.

Landlords and the Labor Market Constraint

The Danish policy of limited engagement required cooperation from the Icelandic powerful. In Iceland, power was closely associated with landownership, which was concentrated in relatively few hands, as shown in tables 1 and 2. In 1695, 52 percent of all farmland was privately owned, the church possessed 32 percent, and 16 percent belonged to the Crown. The private sector was dominated by a small number of powerful individuals—for example, at the beginning of the eighteenth century, eighty-one individuals owned half of the country's private land.[16]

In the premodern period, nearly all farmers were tenants and did not own the land they inhabited. Tenants were mobile and free to rent farms anywhere in the country. In a total population of 8,191 heads of households in 1703, 96 percent were tenants (B. Lárusson 1967). Farmland in Iceland was scarce, and the number of farmers remained relatively stable at around 6,000 through most of the premodern era. The number of hired laborers was relatively large, with 18–24 percent of the

TABLE 1.   Distribution of Landownership by Type of Owner (in %)

Year	Private	Church	Crown
1540–50	53	45	2
1560	50	31	19
1695	· 52	32	16

Source: B. Lárusson 1967, 60.

TABLE 2.   Distribution of Ownership of Private Land around 1700

Share in Total (%)	Individuals
18.36	richest 13
30.98	next 68
50.66	remaining 1,224

Note: Around 1700, private individuals owned 52.3 percent of all farmland.

Source: Þorsteinsson and Jónsson 1991, 231.

total population listed as farm servants in the eighteenth and early nineteenth centuries. Labor was cheap, and even poor tenants frequently hired one or more workers (Gunnarsson 1987, 35). It was customary to employ servants on one-year renewable contracts, and, during the contract period, employers were responsible for their servants' welfare. As we saw in chapter 4, Iceland's informal social insurance system was based on about 160 communes (*hreppar*), which had considerable autonomy and were the smallest units of the country's administrative system. Indigent individuals had a claim on their local commune for support when neither their households nor their extended families were able to care for them (Eggertsson 1998b).

Two themes united the farmers of the premodern era. One was an obsessive concern that adverse selection and moral hazard might undermine the insurance system of the *hreppar* and drain the taxpayers' wealth. Each farmer was responsible for his or her servants, but independent workers and fishermen might attempt to free ride on their *hreppar* and become strategic welfare recipients (Gunnlaugsson 1988). The other issue was a constant worry about labor shortages (or upward pressure on labor costs), which did not subside even in the second half of the nineteenth century, when the servant-farmer ratio was relatively high (Magnússon 1985, 240). Both issues were related to the tension between the economy's two sectors, the farms and the fisheries.

The productivity of labor in farming was low because of the harsh environment and primitive techniques, whereas marginal productivity in the fisheries was much higher than in farming and the potential for growth far greater. Landlords and tenants realized that the development of a specialized fishing industry would draw farm workers away, substantially increasing labor costs. Indeed, farmers had experienced such developments in the fifteenth and sixteenth centuries at the time of the English and German involvement in the fisheries. Farming provided the typical household with only a small margin beyond mere subsistence, and the yield appears to have declined over time with cooling temperatures (the Little Ice Age), soil erosion, and other factors. Female servants typically received only food, clothing, and shelter, while each male servant received a small additional payment (Thoroddsen 1921). For the farmers, therefore, demand pressures from the fisheries appeared ominous. A substantial upward shift in labor costs would bankrupt tenants on marginal land, they thought, and significantly reduce landowners' wealth.

Yet in a poor country where famine was endemic, the high opportunity cost of ignoring the fisheries was obvious. To solve the dilemma, the Icelanders had developed institutions that allowed farmers to exploit part time the inshore fisheries but also sheltered the agricultural sector and tied down the labor market. Central to the system were institutions that blocked the rise of an independent labor force as well as fishing and trading towns. To accomplish this goal, all workers were required to live on farms, and independent wage labor and nonfarm households were not allowed.[17]

Institutions that compelled all Icelanders to belong to farm households date back to the beginnings of the country's history, but the rules received new meaning and enforcement was intensified in the fifteenth century, when farm servants flocked to the coast to participate in the fisheries and work for English and later German traders who wintered in Iceland.[18] Various resolutions concerning the exclusion of foreigners were made but initially had little effect. For example, in 1480 Icelandic leaders wrote to their king, complaining about foreigners who operated establishments in coastal areas, draining servants away from the farms. The critical regulation of that period, which influenced later developments, was a 1490 ruling by Governor Pining. The Pining judgment, which the Alþing confirmed, forbade foreigners to winter in Iceland except in emergencies; outlawed cottagers unless they met a stringent minimum-wealth requirement; and required others to be either farmers or farm servants (Thoroddsen 1921, 299–301). Restrictions of this nature remained in force during the rest of the premodern era (and into the early modern era), with the Pining judgment frequently reconfirmed by the courts; however, enforcement varied considerably among periods and locations.[19]

The authorities were particularly concerned with suppressing itinerant workers. Legitimate itinerant workers did exist, but they were required to meet a high minimum-wealth requirement, which in the eighteenth century was three times higher than what was demanded of those who wanted to become farmers. The reins were tightened (unsuccessfully) toward the end of the era, 1783–1863, when itinerant workers were outlawed altogether (Gunnarsson 1987, 32–33).

Readers may wonder why most Icelanders tolerated restrictions that bordered on slavery despite relatively weak organized or formal enforcement by the authorities.[20] Two main reasons exist for the lack of public resistance: local and international isolation. Ordinary people had few opportunities to come together and organize opposition. Except for a few trading posts, Iceland had no towns or villages, even the farms were scattered, there were no roads, and distances were long. The public possessed virtually no mobile resources such as money, and all trade was strictly controlled. Second, during the Danish monopoly period, the country was isolated and off-limits to foreigners except for monopoly merchants during the summer. Those who desired to leave the island for Europe did not have many options. They either had to seek permission to sail with the Danish traders or somehow illegally and out at sea contact fishing vessels from other countries. As a result, substantial outmigration to Europe was practically impossible.

Evidence from court records reveals that the various restrictions did not eliminate constant tugs-of-war between the two activities, farming and fishing. The farm community was conscious of latent upward pressures on labor costs and fought those pressures. When the pull of the fisheries was relatively strong, courts reaffirmed the regulations in the labor market, and authorities tightened enforcement. New incentive schemes for the fishermen were seen as a threat to the system and forbidden. For example, in the sixteenth and seventeenth centuries, courts in the western district repeatedly outlawed a sensible incentive system for fishers. According to this practice, the fishers, mostly farm servants, received possession of fish caught on specific hooks on their setlines, which have many hooks (L. Kristjánsson 1980–86, 3:311–12). The farm community also saw improvements in fishing gear and the resulting increase in productivity as upsetting the balance. In fact, landed interests opposed setlines, which had probably been introduced into Iceland by English fishermen. In 1578 and again in 1586, the national assembly ruled that fishing lines with many hooks were not permitted during the main (winter) fishing season. A 1581 letter has survived in which prominent farmers complained to the king's deputy about the common use of setlines in a particular district. The complainants gave as one reason for their grievances the fact that servants preferred to work in fishing stations that used setlines, which incited them to go their own ways and created farm labor shortages (L. Kristjánsson 1980–86, 3:429–31).

Finally, the artificially low relative price of fish must have discouraged investment in the fisheries. Under Danish monopoly trade, the price of exports and imports was fixed according to a royal price list that was revised only infrequently and corresponded to historical price lists for internal trade in Iceland.[21] The Crown appears to have taken advantage of the traditional price structure in internal trade and assigned a low purchase price to the country's most valuable export. The large gap between the world price for fish and the purchase price in Iceland increased the value of the trade licenses sold by the Crown, but the long-run effects discouraged local investments in the fisheries. Available evidence registers a decline in the share of fish product in total exports in the monopoly era, although a number of factors may have contributed to this decline (Gunnarsson 1983, 52–54; Þorsteinsson and Jónsson 1991, 232–33). In the last quarter of the eighteenth century, when the Crown made serious efforts to revive the Icelandic economy, large increases in the relative price of fish were a key element of the reforms.

The Case Revisited

Our main thesis is that the colonial element was essential for sustaining the equilibrium trap that held the Icelandic economy at a very low level of development. Without the colonial component, local barriers would have raised the cost of entry into the fishing industry but could not have prevented the emergence of an independent fishing industry.

To thrive, the fishing industry had to reach beyond the restricted Icelandic market and find lucrative outlets elsewhere in Europe—for example, in England, the German regions, or southern Europe. For a landlord who sought to specialize in fish products for export, Icelandic institutions certainly presented a serious hurdle. The law required a boat owner to operate a farm and tied all labor to a farm. These rules apparently were not enforced rigorously all the time in the fishing communities of the southwest, where some households were only nominally involved in farming. The main fishing areas were not self-sufficient in labor and drew seasonal workers from other districts, where the migration was related inversely to the fortunes of farming. The law made employers personally responsible for the welfare of their permanent workers, even when they lived in separate households.

The barriers in the labor market should not be underestimated. In 1776–87 the trade monopoly, now directly managed by the Crown, unsuccessfully attempted to operate a "modern" fishing fleet in Icelandic waters. The director of the company blamed the failure on the shortage of labor and on Icelandic resistance to innovation (Gunnarsson 1983, 184–98, 253). But there were other factors that made life difficult for the director, including the notorious Famine of the Mist (1783–86), when some 20 percent of the Icelanders perished, and a fall in the price of fish when American supplies reached the European market after the American Revolution (1783). Although the barriers in the labor market were not trivial, the historical evidence shows that the demand-pull of a thriving fisheries sector in the fifteenth and sixteenth centuries and again in the late nineteenth century could overcome restrictive labor market institutions.

Access to money and credit was another obstacle that could restrain prospective entrepreneurs. The local economy essentially was not monetized, although money was not unknown, and the country did not have formal credit organizations.[22] Foreign trade would have gradually brought exporters into contact with more sophisticated credit and exchange mechanisms, but a local entrepreneur initially could have traded fish and other exports for better equipment. In this context, it is interesting to note the price of large oceangoing vessels relative to the value of fish in foreign markets. Þorsteinsson (1976, 67–69) examined accounts of English doggers that operated off Iceland in the first half of the sixteenth century and found that the value of one shipload of stockfish was equal to 40–80 percent of the price of a dogger, plus labor and other operating costs. In other words, a lucky investor in England could almost recover the price of a ship in one fishing expedition to Icelandic waters—at least in this time period when fish prices were high.

Opportunities for setting up a modern fishing operation varied greatly among Icelandic landowners, with the relative advantage going to actors who already had international contacts and experience in the part-time fisheries. Game-theoretic reasoning suggests that in an open economy, defecting from the coalition of landlords would be the dominant strategy for players with relative advantage in the fisheries. As the sole defector, a landlord branching into modern fisheries could ignore the feared downward pressures on the price of land and rising labor costs (because one person's actions would have no noticeable effect in these markets). If a large number of actors were likely to defect, the landlord would have an incentive to be the first. In this game, individual defectors are motivated by private gains in the fisheries, while landlords taking an encompassing view predict that large-scale entry into the fisheries would devastate the farm sector.

Iceland's two powerful and wealthy sees, at Skálholt and Hólar, with their international connections, were prime candidates for defection, and there is evidence to suggest that they may have tried to defect. Both sees maintained oceangoing vessels and relatively large fleet of fishing boats. In 1576 the bishop at Hólar bought a large ship from the Hamburgers and later obtained permission for the ship to trade in northern Iceland and go overseas. The landowners responded in the highest court of the national assembly, which sent a note of protest to the Crown. In the letter, the bishop at Hólar is accused of greed, of placing self-interest above the general welfare, and of damaging the interests of the ruling class.[23]

Defecting from the coalition of landlords and overcoming constraints in the labor market represented only a first step toward setting up an advanced fisheries operation. Developing a viable export industry required foreign contacts, both to acquire inputs and to find outlets for the product, a situation that raises two fundamental questions: (a) Did the Icelanders enjoy relative advantage in fishing? And (b) could they have found foreign markets for their products?

With regard to the first question, proximity creates valuable opportunities for processing the fish ashore and for organizing the fisheries from a nearby land base. In historical times, foreign fishermen put much value on access to Icelandic shores, which the policy of isolation denied them. After discovering the Newfoundland fisheries, the English set much store by the availability of a land base.[24] The importance of a base near the fishing grounds also is evident from an 1855–56 French attempt to obtain permission for a large settlement on the Icelandic west coast.[25] Finally, during the twentieth century, location proved extremely valuable for the Icelandic economy. Economic growth led by the export of fish products created living standards comparable to those of Scandinavia.

The counterfactual question of developments in the absence of the royal trade monopoly and related colonial policies, especially concerning Iceland's access to international markets, is a complex matter. In the fifteenth century, the world market came to Iceland in the shape of English fishermen and traders, and various forms of cooperation (and conflict) ensued. The Hamburgers, who emphasized trade and sold the highest-quality Icelandic *skreið* in central Europe, followed the English. After losing their foothold in North America, the Dutch became more interested than before in the Iceland fisheries and in trade with the Icelanders, filling the vacuum when wars in Europe kept the Danes at home. The Danish merchants of the monopoly sold about half of the fish from Iceland in Denmark but contracted with Hamburg and Amsterdam to sell high-quality fish in their markets, again mostly in central Europe. Finally, late in the eighteenth century the Danes began to venture directly into the markets of southern Europe, which in the nineteenth century became very important outlets for Icelandic exports.

In short, the Icelanders faced a large number of potential collaborators, but the Danish policy of isolation and monopsony prevented any cooperation except for temporary illegal exchanges. Under ideal conditions, the merchants of Copenhagen were relatively unattractive partners in the fish business—as recognized by a number of Denmark's leading civil servants in a 1787 report in which they ruled against opening trade and relations with Iceland to actors outside the kingdom:

> Several foreign nations could not only sell several products [to the Icelanders] at a lower price than His Danish Majesty's subjects are able to do, but the profitable Icelandic fisheries will always be so tempting for them that excluding them (i.e. the foreigners) from the trade and the country would be impossible if its inhabitants were to be allowed to come into contact with them. (cited in Gunnarsson 1983, 149)

The Danish merchants also operated under less than ideal conditions: in the long run, the institutional framework created perverse incentives for Danes and Icelanders alike. The low price for fish offered by the monopoly gave the Icelanders little incentive to invest in better equipment and increase their supply. The merchants had even less incentive to invest because (a) the returns would be appropriated by the Crown, which extracted most of the rent by selling licenses and by taxation; (b) renewal of the (six-year) licenses was uncertain; and (c) regulations forbade Danish participation in the fisheries. It is not surprising that until the last years of the monopoly period, the merchants rented but did not own their ships and typically used them both as living quarters and for storage during their summer visits to Icelandic ports. Nor did the merchants invest substantially in international marketing. Instead they relied on intermediation, primarily by merchants in Hamburg and Amsterdam. Only toward the end, when the Crown directly managed the monopoly, do we see substantial investments in vessels, housing, storage facilities, and marketing (Gunnarsson 1987).

Why did enlightened members of the Icelandic elite not lobby the Crown to change its policy toward their country? The answer is that some of them did. As I discuss in the next section, a number of Icelanders lobbied for an open economy and modernization, but they were a small minority. A string of statements and resolutions extending into the nineteenth century demonstrates that for the most part, Icelandic leaders supported the various restrictions that held back the fisheries.[26] I contend that the elite relied on a partial model of social change and did not recognize the potential general equilibrium consequences. I return to these issues in the chapter's concluding section.

The disintegration of the premodern system and the evolution of an independent fishing industry had to wait for the Crown to change its strategy and allow free trade, an impulse that in itself was sufficient to unsettle Iceland's traditional social equilibrium. The institutional change leading to the modern era is a large topic that I briefly sketch in the next section.

The Game Unravels

The Collapse of the Traditional System

In the last quarter of the nineteenth century, incipient urbanization and a modern fishing industry put the premodern system in Iceland to rest, but the seeds of its destruction had been sown a hundred years earlier. In the first part of the eighteenth century, Copenhagen made several halfhearted attempts to lower entry barriers and expand the Iceland fisheries, which were of considerable economic importance both to the Crown and to the Danish community. Yet the peripheral status of Iceland and the policy of limited engagement made the Crown hesitate to impose its will on the Icelandic elite.

In 1701 the Crown decided to permit Danish merchants of the trade monopoly to winter in Iceland, but the Icelandic leaders protested, and the Crown yielded in 1706. The trade charter of that year states, "The merchants are not allowed to have any fishing boats in the country nor hire any laborers for working in the fisheries nor have any fishing lines close to the coast" (Gunnarsson 1983, 24). In 1759 the Crown allowed a single merchant to spend the winter in the country, and, in a trade charter of 1763, the merchants were allowed to station people in Iceland throughout the year but were still forbidden to employ Icelanders in fishing (Gunnarsson 1983, 24). By a decree issued in 1762, Copenhagen appointed a special inspector for fisheries in Iceland; ordered that catch statistics be collected for the country; and forbade inland farmers from buying fish from the fishing stations as a means of compelling the farmers to do their own fishing. The magistrates in Iceland and others opposed the measures beginning in 1762, and in 1763 the Crown withdrew the regulation (Gustafsson 1981). In this instance, the proposal was impractical because fish were a key component of the Icelandic diet, and many farmers did not have easy access to the sea (Rafnsson 1983). In spite of minor confrontations, the evidence shows that in matters of institutional change, the administration in Copenhagen was sensitive to the wishes of the Icelandic elite, especially the magistrates, who usually were wealthy Icelandic landowners (Gustafsson 1985).

Beginning around 1770, the Crown changed its strategy and took a much firmer position on economic reforms. The virtual collapse of Icelandic society, to which the policy of isolation and monopoly trade had contributed, is a key factor in explaining the new approach. It had become clear in Copenhagen that Iceland, weakened by the policy of isolation and limited engagement, lacked the reserve and resilience to cope with cold spells, natural disasters (particularly volcanic eruptions and epidemics) that savagely plagued the country in the eighteenth century, which saw three major population crises. In Copenhagen, there were discussions about moving all or some of Iceland's population off the island (A. Kristjánsson 1977).

In 1770 and again in 1785, the Crown appointed a royal commission of high officials to study the economic situation in Iceland and to recommend economic reforms. Both commissions paid special attention to the fisheries, and many important reforms of the late eighteenth century were based on these recommendations (Þ. Jóhannesson 1950). In 1770 the office of the governor was moved to Iceland from Copenhagen; in 1771–72 the Crown subsidized the monopoly trade company to bring Norwegian boat builders and timber for eighty vessels to Iceland; in 1776 the Crown took over and directly managed trade with Iceland and began operating a fleet of decked fishing vessels in an effort to introduce new technology to Icelandic fishers (Þ. Jóhannesson 1950, 265–67). Other developments in 1776 included a new royal price list that doubled the export price of fish (Þ. Jóhannesson 1950, 275). In 1787 the Crown abolished the trade monopoly and opened trade with Iceland to all subjects of the kingdom, and the merchants were allowed to employ Icelanders in fishing, but free trade with all nations was not permitted until 1855 (Þorsteinsson and Jónsson 1991, 256–60). When the trade restrictions were lifted, the price of fish increased even further because of a shortage of food in Europe (Þ. Jóhannesson 1950, 230). Finally, on the recommendation of the 1785 royal commission, the Crown attempted to establish a number of townships in Iceland and to provide subsidies and tax exemptions for traders and artisans who might choose to live there (Þ. Jóhannesson 1950, 223).

The disasters of the eighteenth century jolted not only the Crown but also the Icelanders themselves. A number of modernists, including many members of a growing colony of Icelandic intellectuals in Copenhagen, supported efforts to liberalize the Icelandic economy and lobbied the Crown to that effect. Yet even among the intellectuals, modernists were in a minority. As early as 1757, for example, and again in 1767, an Icelandic intellectual, entrepreneur, and the Crown's general secretary for economic affairs in Iceland, Skúli Magnússon, made proposals for ending the trade monopoly but did not receive general support from Icelandic leaders (Þ. Jóhannesson 1950, 209–11).[27] Rather than providing support for these attempts to liberalize the economy, the landed interests pushed in 1781 for the introduction of internal passports for people crossing county boundaries (L. Kristjánsson 1980–86, 2:393). Two years later, the small and restricted but potentially threatening category of independent workers was outlawed altogether, giving the workers six months to find employment as farm servants. The ban remained in effect until 1863 (Thoroddsen 1921, 342–44). In retrospect, the opposition by most of the country's leaders to an open economy and other reforms may sound unreasonable and may raise the question of whether the opposition was genuine or whether Denmark pressured the Icelanders to support the status quo. The evidence indicates, however, that the leaders generally spoke their minds.

Population Pressures and the Dynamics of Institutional Change

The dynamics of institutional change in Iceland, from the early reforms in the late eighteenth century until the emergence of a modern fishing industry 100 years later, is a complex story in which demographics played an important role.[28] It is clear that population pressures interacting with strict limits on new farmland contributed to the softening of traditional labor regulations long before the rules were formally removed. Figure 3 shows that Iceland began the eighteenth century with a population of about 50,000, but by 1785 the population had fallen to less than 41,000. Sustained population growth subsequently began, and the population reached 47,000 in 1801, 59,000 in 1859, and 72,000 in 1880. Improved living standards and rapid population growth were in part related to various reforms in the country's fisheries. In fact, Iceland almost quadrupled its exports of fish products in the first forty years of the nineteenth century (Þorsteinsson and Jónsson 1991, 268). In its response to the debacle of the eighteenth century, the Crown did not stop at the fisheries but also introduced various piecemeal reforms in agriculture, including fencing, and the restructuring of property rights, which included selling churches and Crown land to private owners (Þ. Jóhannesson 1950; G. Jónsson 1991). The agricultural reforms helped the country sustain a larger population, but reforms took place within the old institutional frame-

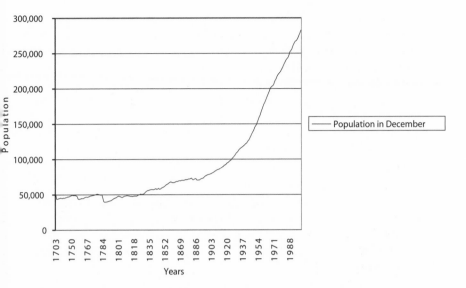

Fig. 3. Population of Iceland, 1703–2000 (Census Bureau of Iceland, www.hagstofa.is).

work, although they undermined it. Formally, the fisheries did not receive free access to manpower.

Weakened by a disastrous involvement in the Napoleonic wars, Copenhagen still did not directly challenge Iceland's landed interests' resistance to reforms.[29] For example, in 1808 the Royal Financial Bureau in Copenhagen stated "that in the future, no one will be allowed to settle by the coast, unless he proves that, in addition to the house he rents or purchases, he has access to enough land to support at least one cow or six ewes" (cited in Hálfdanarson 1991, 67).

Until the last decades of the nineteenth century, bondage in the rural labor market slowed down but did not prevent the development of urban communities in coastal areas. In 1801 about 0.6 percent of the population lived in Reykjavík, the country's main urban center, but by 1850 the proportion had grown only to about 2 percent and to 3.5 percent in 1880. By 1930, however, resistance to urbanization had been overcome, and more than a quarter of the population lived in Reykjavík (*Statistical Abstracts* 1984, 7). The rapid nineteenth-century increase in the Icelandic farm population put great pressure on the farm community, which responded by subdividing existing farms, setting up new farms on marginal land, and increasing the ratio of servants to farm households. As the informal institutions of the labor market prevented farm servants from marrying each other, the proportion of (disgruntled) unmarried men and women grew rapidly (Gunnlaugsson 1988, 108–18).

In the last quarter of the nineteenth century, the dam burst. Periodic cold spells devastated many subdivided and marginal farms, and now the Icelanders had a new option: they could vote with their feet. In the last quarter of the nineteenth century, some 15,000 individuals, about 20 percent of the population, left the country, mostly for North America.[30] Others drifted into urban areas, ignoring restrictions on labor mobility. The traditional system had received its coup de grâce, but the remnants of the formal institutional structure lingered. Historians frequently date the advent in Iceland of a specialized fishing industry around 1870, but the Icelandic Parliament finally removed labor bondage in 1894 and restrictions on cottagers only in 1907 (Þorsteinsson and Jónsson 1991).

This chapter has addressed a puzzle: why a nation that lived for nearly 1,000 years on an island next to some of the best fishing banks in the world did not develop an independent fishing industry until toward the end of the nineteenth century but gave priority to low-productivity subarctic farming, suffering extreme poverty and famine. While a number of European nations, beginning in the 1400s, maintained large fishing fleets off Iceland, the Icelanders organized their fisheries as part-time activity, mostly using inferior technology and small open rowboats. Because of Iceland's relative backwardness, small population, and isolation, local entrepreneurs would have required cooperation from foreign entrepreneurs and financiers to develop an efficient export-oriented industry. In particular, Icelanders needed assistance in international marketing and in the acquisition of high-quality inputs and capital assets. The country was a dependency of the Danish-Norwegian kingdom, which could have cooperated in such efforts.

The chapter's main argument is that Iceland was stuck in a pernicious equilibrium trap that had both domestic and foreign components. It is further argued that the domestic component alone would not have sufficed to maintain the status quo. The internal component was related to the economic self-interest of landlords and farmers, who feared that the development of high-productivity fisheries would raise the cost of labor in the low-productivity farm sector and reduce the value of land. A compromise evolved, therefore, where labor was tied to the land but tenants and farm servants could be used as part-time fishermen, especially in the winter. Under this arrangement, which provided modest insurance against periodic setbacks in farming, the possibility still remained that enterprising Icelanders might defect from the coalition of landed interests and join foreign interests in developing a specialized fishing industry. The external element of the equilibrium trap, however, effectively constrained potential defectors.

The Danish Crown followed a policy of isolating Iceland from foreign influence and taxing the Icelanders by selling monopoly rights to trade with Iceland to cities in the kingdom, particularly Copenhagen. The Danish merchants of the monopoly trade were forbidden to participate in the country's fishing industry or even to spend the winter in Iceland. Denmark did not invest in permanent military presence in the country and relied on a small number of administrative agents, usually Icelandic landlords. The country did not have a police force or an army.

The Danish policy of limited engagement and isolation was motivated partly by the experience of the fifteenth and sixteenth centuries, when English and later German interlopers drawn by the valuable fisheries eclipsed Danish rule in Iceland. Similarly, many local measures for tying labor to the land originated in the English-German era and were intended to stop and reverse the growth of coastal fishing communities during that period. Under the monopoly-trade system, the Icelandic elite derived most of its wealth from the land, whereas the Crown profited more from the part-time fisheries (Gunnarsson 1987, 47–49). The purchase price of fish was set artificially low relative to prices in foreign markets, but agricultural products received fair prices.

The Crown pursued two conflicting goals: maximizing its revenue from the fisheries (and from the colony in general) and ensuring the support of the local landowning class, which opposed productivity growth and expansion in the fisheries. The outcome was a social equilibrium involving primitive, low-productivity, and nonspecialized fisheries. The dominant landowners based their opposition to an efficient fisheries sector on an incomplete partial equilibrium model. They focused solely on adverse supply effects caused by the anticipated increase in the opportunity cost of labor inputs. They did not allow for positive demand effects for farm products that would emerge from a growing fisheries sector and rising national income.[31] Modern economists would evaluate these issues with the help of a general equilibrium model. They would consider a shift in the economy's production possibilities frontier, reflecting productivity gains in the fisheries; shifting supply and demand curves in the farming sector (with a negative substitution effect and a positive income effect); the scarcity of new farm-land in Iceland; and the natural protection against many farm imports.[32] Without empirical studies, modern analysis could not have conclusively reassured the landlords that structural change would leave intact their wealth. Yet adding positive demand effects to the negative supply effects at least reduces the expected loss and introduces the possibility of net gains. General equilibrium models, however, were not part of the mental apparatus of Icelandic landlords.

Economic actors in Iceland evaded the premodern system's constraints on various margins, with negligible consequences. Small-scale illegal trade with foreign fishers was known to exist, especially when events on the continent of Europe kept the Danes busy at home.[33] Some farmers in the chief fishing districts in the southwest set up on their homesteads cottagers whose primary activity was to fish rather than farm, assuming responsibility for the welfare of these families. Yet high transaction costs and isolation held back the fishing industry.[34]

The equilibrium trap finally came apart when the Crown, responding to deteriorating conditions in eighteenth-century Iceland, revised the policy of isolation and monopoly trade. The slow transition to a new economic system that would be based on an independent modern fishing industry with a specialized labor force lasted almost a century. Economic forces gradually overcame the restrictive regulations in the labor market, which usually were formally abolished only after they had become obsolete. The economic actors that destroyed the status quo were not empowered by sophisticated social models of structural change. Rather, they found themselves in an environment where the pursuit of personal gain initiated long-term economic growth.

PART III

Institutional Policy

CHAPTER 8

Applying Social Technologies
Lessons from the Old Theory of Economic Policy

In the 1980s, after decades of neglect, academic economists rediscovered that social institutions matter and that useful ways of analyzing them could be found. In part I of this book, I introduced some of the theoretical vistas that the new institutional economics has opened up. I am particularly interested in what we have learned about imperfect institutions and economic decline. The scholarly literature initially focused on the origins and functions of institutions, but scholars have also recently turned their attention to issues in institutional policy, perhaps partly because of prodding by reformers and policymakers and unexpected problems with transitions in various parts of the world. Roland's *Transition and Economics: Politics, Markets, and Firms* (2000) provides an outstanding example of rigorous analysis of institutional transformation that challenges the so-called Washington consensus and the belief that market institutions will invariably emerge in a nonmarket economy when prices are deregulated and standard measures of macroeconomic stabilization are introduced.

The purpose of a normative theory of institutional policy is to design strategies for repairing dysfunctional institutional environments. Although fundamentally distinct, institutional policy shares a common vision with macroeconomic policy and planning. Both fields are concerned with the general environment of economic activity (which in the case of institutional policy is not only the national/international environment but also the local environment of various industries and even organizations). Both macroeconomics and institutional economics have a strong interest in explaining unwanted economic outcomes, whether unemployment and inflation or industrial decline and economic stagnation. Unlike the new institutionalism, however, macroeconomics immediately developed an explicit policy perspective. The rise of modern macroeconomics is associated with the publication of Keynes's *General Theory of Employment, Interest, and Money*

(1936), which is essentially his attempt to make sense of the Great Depression. The Keynesians put policy issues on the front burner from the beginning.

In chapter 1, I set the stage for the theory section with a discussion of modern growth theory and its evolution through three phases; then, in chapter 2, I defined a role for institutional growth theory and located its sphere of competence. Here I similarly begin the book's policy section by discussing macroeconomic planning and how three broad waves of theorizing—Keynesian macroeconomics, rational-choice macroeconomics, and bounded-rationality macroeconomics—created new perspectives for policy. My aim with this foray into the world of macroeconomic policy is to draw lessons for institutional policy and to contrast the two forms of policy. The pioneers of macro-economic policy developed and sought guidance from what they called the theory of economic policy. The theory of economic policy was originally an attempt to use the logic of mathematical decision theory to design strategies for macroeconomic policy based on Key-nesian economics. The section that follows introduces the basic elements and concerns of the old theory of economic policy. The subsequent two sections briefly describe how the evolution of macroeconomics created new perspectives on policy, both by suggesting new strategies and by shrinking the planners' set of available choices. The chapter concludes with a general discussion of what practitioners of institutional policy can learn from more than half a century of macroeconomic planning.

The Old Theory of Economic Policy: Basic Elements

The old theory of economic policy emerged mainly from the work of Ragnar Frisch and Jan Tinbergen, a Norwegian and a Dutchman who were influenced by (and contributed to) Keynesian macroeconomics and received the first Nobel Prize in economics.[1] Tinbergen's (1956) classic study, *Economic Policy: Theory and Design,* deeply affected and reinforced the way economists thought about the policy implications of their work. The volume and related studies did not propose new economic theories or explicitly evaluate the state of economics science but contributed at a different level. Tinbergen's decision models have the flavor of systems analysis in engineering, and his aim was to show how economic knowledge could be organized to regulate and guide economic systems. The theory of economic policy uses general assumptions about the structure of economic systems to derive various rules for the optimal design of policy, and specific economic theories are cited only for illustration.

The theory of economic policy emerged in an era of great expectations about the promise of social engineering, reflecting the hopes of welfare economics (Bergson 1938; Samuelson, 1947, chapter 8), the Keynesian revolution, the new field of development economics (Kindleberger 1958), and the central planning literature (Johansen 1977). Although Tinbergen, Frisch, and other early contributors to the theory were well aware that policy goals are shaped by political forces and that policy is often dominated by uncertainty, they did not emphasize such complications, and the economics profession initially absorbed a mechanical version of the Tinbergen framework. In the 1950s and 1960s, mainstream policy studies usually made the following assumptions, either explicitly or implicitly:

1. The *goals* or *targets* of economic policy (embodied in what was alternatively referred to as *target preference function, objective function,* or *social welfare function*) are given or correspond to standard concepts of efficiency in economic theory and to recognized notions of justice in ethics and related fields.
2. The basic structural relationships of the economic system are known. Structure may limit the scope of policy and put certain targets out of reach, but limited knowledge and inaccurate policy models generally do not cause policy failures.

In the last quarter of the twentieth century, unexpected difficulties emerged in manipulating Western economic systems both at the micro and macro levels (Lucas 1976; R. A. Posner 1986, part III). Furthermore, mainstream economic thought had begun to doubt the viability of socialist central management and development policies in the Third World, although lone critics had appeared much earlier. These setbacks undermined the optimism of the early postwar era and helped create new and more skeptical perspectives on economic policies, as I discuss subsequently, but I will begin by outlining the traditional view of economic policy and planning.

The brain of the old theory of economic policy, metaphorically, was a policy model that laid down the structure of the economic system in terms of two critical subsets of variables, the instruments of policy and the targets of policy. Johansen (1977, 55–64) provides an excellent compact summary of the traditional view, using a formulation that accords with Arrow's (1956, 440) four components of any decision problem.[2]

1. A *policy model* that specifies empirical relations, $x = f(a, z)$, where a vector of outcomes, x, depends on policy measures, a, and exogenous factors, z (such as climate and export market conditions).
2. A set of *policy instruments, A.*
3. An *objective function, $W = W(x)$.*
4. Computational methods for finding values for policy instruments that maximize the objective function.

Given the structure of the policy model, the prevailing exogenous factors, z, specify the set of outcomes, x_z, that are within the reach of the policymakers, who compute and apply optimal policy measures, a^*, that maximize their objective function—the social welfare function—reaching $W^* = f(x^*)$. In this world of planning, the role of economists or "analytical experts" is one of both helping to specify the policy model and computing the optimal solution in accordance with the preferences of the policy authority, $W = W(x)$, which in turn is consistent with the popular will or the public good.

In their quiet moments, the pioneers contemplated how politics and information problems might complicate the planning process (Johansen 1977, 104–9). Frisch was concerned, for example, that analytical experts might find it difficult to establish $W(x)$ in a form usable for the decision problem. Johansen ([1974] 1987, 542–44) reports that in working on this problem, Frisch identified five different approaches to acquiring information about the policy preference function: (1) experts directly ask political decision makers to specify the decision functions; (2) experts interview decision makers; (3) experts conduct imaginary interviews with political leaders; (4) experts draft inferences about preferences from policy statements; (5) experts rely on revealed preferences of policymakers derived from their observed behavior. Frisch also recognized that politicians might hesitate to reveal their preferences, either for strategic (political) reasons or because they are uncertain about elements in the planning process.

The divide between economics and politics shows up in Frisch's distinction between selection analysis and implementation, and in Tinbergen's (1959) notion of the optimal economic system. Frisch defines selection analysis as the task of finding optimal outcomes, W^*, in a world free from political constraints; in practice, however, political constraints often place W^* out of bounds.[3] If W' represents the highest value of W that social realities permit, then $(W^* - W')$ measures the cost of political constraints in terms of the social welfare function. Similarly Tinbergen (1952, 1959) recognizes that social and political forces often support suboptimal economic systems. Tinbergen refers to measures aimed at reforming the economic system as "qualitative policy" and distinguishes them from "quantitative policy" that leaves basic structures intact. Johansen (1977, 147–48) makes a distinction between minor and basic qualitative policy: Basic qualitative policy implies radical change in power structures, "which will generally not be contemplated by any central authority under the prevailing power structure" (Johansen 1977, 148). Minor qualitative policy measures in Johansen's sense have some correspondence with Lucas's (1990) well-known notion of regime change, in contrast with policy action within a regime, and Buchanan's (1975, 1987) policymaking within a constitution versus constitution making. Tinbergen believed that in the long run, policymakers would select comparable social welfare functions and optimize over all known institutions (social technologies), which made him predict that all economic systems would converge toward a common basic structure. Tinbergen's convergence hypothesis drew worldwide attention, and the neoclassical growth model, discussed in chapter 2, embodies a similar notion of convergence.

But let us put these speculations aside and return to the traditional prescriptions for standard quantitative macroeconomic policy. The instruments of policy include such variables as exchange rates, tax rates, base money, price ceilings, import restrictions, plan indicators, and agricultural production quotas. The structure of the policy model defines what target values are attainable and what instruments of policy are most effective in reaching the desired goals. Policy targets can be absolute (policy success depends entirely on a specific value for each target variable), or the policymaker can weigh target variables together in a target preference function, $W(x_1, \ldots, x_n)$. The aim of economic policy is either to reach absolute targets or to maximize a target preference function.

When targets are fixed (absolute) or when target preference functions are maximized without limitations, basic logic suggests two well-known rules of thumb: First, in general "the number of instruments should be (at least) equal to the number of targets" (Hansen 1963, 7). Think, for example, of a market where, in terms of a supply and demand diagram, quantity and price (P_1, Q_1) are determined by the intersection of the supply and demand curves. The authorities now set a new target, (P_2, Q_2). A single instrument that moves only one of the two curves or shifts both of them along some fixed path would only by chance reach the new target, (P_2, Q_2). A general solution to this policy problem requires at least two instruments, one each for shifting the supply and demand curves.

The second rule of thumb advises against decentralized policymaking where each policymaker controls an instrument that is assigned to a specific target variable. Instead, all available instruments should be coordinated and directed jointly toward the set of target variables (Hansen 1963, 7). To extend the previous example, imagine that policy actor A controls one instrument and has P_2 for a target and that actor B controls a different instrument and has Q_2 as a target. It can be shown that, without coordination, the efforts of the two actors to reach their separate goals can generate oscillations around the overall target, (P_2, Q_2), that do not necessarily converge on the target. It follows from this line of reasoning that as a rule, centralized policymaking is necessary.

Finally, the structure of the policy model has important implications for policy. The structure describes the interrelationships among the vectors of variables in $x = f(a, z)$ and determines whether the model can be divided into autonomous departments, which has critical implications for policy. Following Simon (1953), all endogenous variables and instruments in a policy model can be arranged according to causal ordering from the first order to the highest, Nth order. Instruments of the Nth order influence targets of the Nth order without affecting lower orders of the system. The use of first-order instruments, however, has repercussions not only for first-order target variables but also for endogenous variables at higher levels, potentially throughout the system (Hansen 1963, 18–22). Unlike policy action within a regime, structural policy or regime change must rely explicitly on a theory of institutions and institutional change, but causal ordering in the social system determines how complex theory and complex measures are required for particular changes in the structure of an economic system.[4] For example, designing the transition to markets in Russia and Eastern Europe becomes a relatively simple task if desired market institutions would emerge autonomously once "the prices are set free," which was (roughly) the position initially entertained by many mainstream economists who advised these countries on their transition strategies (Murrell 1995). The notion of structurally ordered variables suggests that policymakers who have uncertain knowledge of social structures may get unexpected results at other levels of the system than their instruments were planned to affect.

Private Policy Models and Rational-Expectations Macroeconomics

It is only a slight exaggeration to say that the old theory of economic policy is an engineering manual for implementing the social technologies suggested by Keynesian macroeconomics, which aggregates individual behavior into stable mechanical relationships for the whole economy, thus appearing to provide a favorable environment for central control. Yet the mechanical image is not truly representative of the master himself. Unlike many of his disciples, Keynes was preoccupied throughout his life with changing expectations and quirky responses by individuals to their uncertain environments (Skidelsky 1994). The initial mathematical formalization of Keynes' general theory (which was primarily the work of his colleagues) set all such fuzziness aside by presenting snapshots of the economic system, freezing and stabilizing structural relationships. The image of stable aggregate relationships implies that new policy measures will not call forth responses from the public that change the relationship between instruments and targets in the policy model, $x = f(a, z)$, and in some circumstances totally undermine the measures. The so-called rational expectations revolution of the 1970s created a brand-new perspective by recognizing that economic actors often have the incentive and ability to ease the burden of new policy measures and that these responses can change the structure of the policy model (Lucas 1976, 1990).[5]

In its initial form, the rational-expectations paradigm made rather extreme assumptions about the information and knowledge available to representative economic actors. The theory assumes that economic agents base their decisions on correct models of the macroeconomy and that private economic agents know how the policy authority is going to respond when desired values for target variables differ from their actual values. The introduction of educated counterpolicy by the public, based on private policy models, can significantly shrink the set of outcomes, X, available to policymakers.

Policy Models as Dependent Variables and Bounded-Rationality Macroeconomics

When theorists build models of social systems, they must decide how much the various types of actors should know, what they do not know, and how they learn (Sargent 1993, 165). Rational-expectations macro-economics, in its pure form, makes a very strong assumption about how much the actors know. The theory is essentially static, in our sense, because it assumes that all actors have done their homework and already know the structure of the game. Relevant actors share a reliable (social) model of their environment and have adjusted their behavior to coherent rules and expectations. As Sargent (1993, 21) remarks, these models endow representative economic actors with more knowledge than their creator, the model builder, possesses. The model builder—the economist or econometrician—must statistically estimate and infer information about policy models, which these procedures assume that the agents already know.

A well-known early result of rational-choice macroeconomics is that smart counterpolicies by economic agents neutralize and rule out government policy aimed at exploiting the so-called Phillips curve, which involves trading unemployment for inflation or vice versa.[6] Consequently, public policy cannot be used to lower the rate of unemployment below its equilibrium (or natural) rate and keep it there by stepping up demand pressures and raising the rate of inflation. What is puzzling here is why in the 1960s and early 1970s governments and their experts in many parts of the world did pursue such policies. One might be tempted to interpret their actions as cynical maneuvers intended to fool the public, but to fool whom—agents with full knowledge of the system? One branch of the literature offers a solution to the puzzle by (implausibly) claiming that during this episode, private agents were endowed with correct models, whereas the policy models of governments and their experts were based on erroneous economic theory (Sargent 1993, 160).[7]

Strict rational-expectations macroeconomics is closely related to general equilibrium theory in microeconomics. In their purest versions, both theories assume complete knowledge, but when knowledge is not complete, we immediately encounter the question of how actors learn. When economists attempt to understand a social system, they construct a theory, collect data, and use the data to test the theory. In an analogous manner, Sargent (1993, 23) sees regular economic actors constructing theories and models, which they coordinate and share, and rational-expectations equilibrium prevails only when the actors have solved their "scientific problem." A regime change involves a shift of policy models, but economics lacks a generally accepted theory of the dynamic path between the old and new regimes. The research agenda of bounded-rationality macroeconomics is to analyze the learning involved during the adjustment to a new policy regime. An obvious way to proceed is to model social agents as behaving like economists and scientists when they acquire new knowledge, but Sargent (1993) recognizes that little is known about how scientists actually learn about the world, although, of course, their statistical estimation techniques (such as classical or Bayesian econometrics) are known.

Lessons for Institutional Policy

The experience of half a century of theorizing about the process of macroeconomic intervention offers many lessons for institutional policy, but each stage in the development of macroeconomics sends a different message. Classic macroeconomic planning teaches two lessons: (1) the importance of being clear about the preference function of the ruling policy authority and (2) the need to specify the policy model, $x = f(a, z)$, and to identify the available policy instruments, A. In chapter 5 I discussed various attempts, mostly by political scientists, to explain why the target preference functions of many (seemingly rational) political leaders do not give priority to economic growth. Economists recently have developed an interest the political dimension of economic reforms, as evidenced by the field of political macroeconomics (Alesina 1988, 1995).[8] To allow for pure political preferences for economic outcomes, we add politically valued outcomes, $g(x)$, to the target preference function, which now becomes $W = G(g, x)$, implying that economic alternatives sometimes play little or no role in policy-making independent of political preferences.[9] Although many studies in the new institutional economics are sensitive to political factors, the field needs to pay more attention to the implications of politics for institutional reforms.

The main lesson of rational-choice macroeconomics for institutional policy is the insight that outcomes from public policy depend not only on government policy models but also on the private policy models of individual social actors. All social equilibria reflect individual actors' perceptions of their environments, and the actors' policy models embody these perceptions. Accordingly, the particular models that individuals entertain about prevailing social technologies and government decision rules limit available choices in public policy. An early recognition of the significance of incomplete and variable policy models is found in Steven Cheung's (1975, 1976) investigation of rent control in Hong Kong. Cheung provides a striking image of a regulatory process that involves revisions and updating of both private and pub-

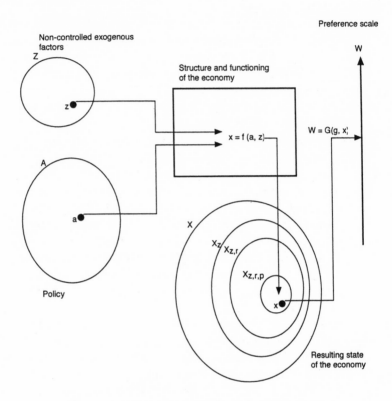

Fig. 4.   The policy process (based on Johansen 1977, 58).

lic policy models, which brings us to bounded-rationality macroeconomics.

Bounded-rationality macroeconomics directs our attention to the quality of public and private policy models and the role of experience, learning, and imagination in updating these models. Substantial institutional change requires that various types of actors adopt new policy models, which introduces yet another dimension in policymaking: attempts to influence learning and interpretation by targeted actors. In other words, policy models now become intermediate targets in the policy process. In its present state, institutional economics usually treats incomplete knowledge as a problem arising from scarcity of data (due to measurement costs) or from a human inability rapidly to process data rather than as involving incomplete social models (shaped by mental path dependence) that limit the capacity to select and interpret data.

Figure 4 summarizes the discussion in this chapter by extending a diagram from Johansen (1977, 58) to incorporate rational expectations, political outcomes, and political constraints. The figure shows how rational expectations, r, reduce the choice set from X_z in the traditional (Keynesian) policy model (where a set of exogenous variables, z, limit possible outcomes) to $X_{z,r}$ in a model with strategic private responses or counterpolicy. Political constraints (for example, constitutional rules or insufficient parliamentary support) can further restrict a government's choice set by putting certain outcomes, p, off limits, which in figure 4 reduces available outcomes (the choice set) to $X_{z,r,p}$. Economic outcomes, x, can also have valued political consequences, $g(x)$. If certain economic outcomes are still preferred in themselves (rather than for political reasons), the policy preference function now becomes $W = G(x, g)$ which further limits the ability of economists and other experts to influence the goals of public policy.

Our journey through the intellectual history of macroeconomic policy and planning has brought two key issues to the fore: the concept of policy models as dependent variables and the idea of endogenous policies. When taken to the limit, the concept of endogenous policy appears to suggest policy determinism, leaving no role for reformers who face a world where all decisions are made by maximizing actors. The following chapter discusses the limits for institutional reform and makes the case that the idea of policy determinacy implicitly assumes stable policy models. Although it is not necessary to give up the concept of social equilibrium, policy determinism is not absolute when policy models are incomplete, variable, and endogenous.

CHAPTER 9

Degrees of Freedom in Institutional Reform

In this chapter, I look at three basic issues in institutional policy. In the second section, I argue that the concept of optimal regime or optimal economic system (see chapter 8) is too elusive to be of practical use. In neoclassical economics, however, it is customary to define inefficiency as deviation from an optimal state, such as perfect competition. The third section suggests two related definitions of "imperfect institutions" that are amenable to comparative institutional analysis. I refer to one of the definitions as exogenous and the other as endogenous. My third topic concerns limits to institutional reform. After concluding that particular social institutions are imperfect and advocating reform, politicians, advisers, and others often discover that there are few degrees of freedom. Limits for reform follow directly from the modern interpretation of social institutions as equilibrium outcomes in games involving decision makers who maximize their utility functions and have economic, political, and social interests. When a social system is in equilibrium, the usual assumptions of the social equilibrium literature leave zero degrees of freedom for institutional reform. These issues are discussed in the fourth section, which argues that limits for reform are real, while complete determinacy is a theoretical construct that should not be taken literally. In the fifth section and in the following chapter, I discuss two sources of large-scale institutional reform. First, unexpected exogenous shocks frequently change relative prices and other variables, knock the system off balance, and open a window for reforms (discussed in chapter 10). The other source of reform is adjustments in policy models or the rise of new models (discussed in the fifth section of this chapter). Actors change their social models in response to persuasion in the market for ideas, through learning by doing, and via interactions in social systems. I refer to a study of policy models and policymaking at the Organization for Economic Cooperation and Development (OECD) in the early 1970s to illustrate struggles in the market for ideas, and I use the dynamics of the European welfare state to explain adjustments in personal and public policy models.

The Elusive Search for an Optimal Regime

In this section I argue that policymakers, with their incomplete social models, lack the necessary knowledge to set up an economic regime that is optimal for achieving their particular economic goals. They cannot systematically carry out what Frisch labeled *selection analysis* and Tinbergen called the choice of an *optimal regime* (see chapter 8). Conceptually, the transition to an optimal system requires that policymakers complete two superhuman tasks, which I describe. To simplify the discussion, I assume that the policy preference function involves only economic growth.

To discover the optimal economic regime, reformers need to estimate the ultimate growth potential of different economic systems by comparing how well each would function under optimal management. The task calls for working out optimal policy, $x_j^* = f_j(a^*, z)$, for all (known) economic systems—for all j's in J. For example, the policymakers must establish whether a Soviet-type economy would outperform all versions of the market system if the authorities used optimal central management policies rather than, say, the methods of the former Soviet Union. The discovery process also involves finding the legal, social, and political foundations for each type of economic regime necessary for realizing its full growth potential. In other words, the reformers must identify the most effective social technologies for maintaining cooperation, coordination, and communication for each system, j, in J.

The second task pertains to transitions. When preparations are made to transform the current policy regime $f_j(a, z)$ into the chosen optimal policy regime $f^*(a, z)$, it is necessary first to establish whether the transition is feasible in view of prevailing political and cultural conditions. If a feasible transition path does not exist, the reformers are compelled to settle for a second-best solution.[1] When a transition is feasible, the planners must find the optimal or least-cost transition path, allowing for the relevant social, political, and economic factors. This second task corresponds partly to Frisch's implementation phase of the planning process (see chapter 8). When large-scale structural change is planned, it is often impossible make all the changes at once, which necessitates piecemeal reforms. Piecemeal economic reforms, however, are risky because some transition paths can create interim periods of severely malfunctioning "incomplete" economic systems. Reformers must, therefore, discover the optimal sequence—for example, by examining whether the introduction of Y (free international capital flows) prior to X (mature domestic market for securities) will destabilize the system (McKinnon 1991; Roland 2000). The design of an optimal transition path must likewise recognize political constraints. In the transition to markets in Eastern Europe, advisers have disagreed about whether it is appropriate to respond to a "window of opportunity" with (1) "big bang" measures, (2) gradual introduction of reforms, or (3) hybrid strategy mixing the two (Dewatripont and Roland 1995; Roland 2000). An optimal sequence can also involve sociological factors. The culture of a low-income country may readily accept only select elements of a Western legal code. Similarly, particular economic reforms may fail in "collectivist" societies, in the sense used by Greif (1994), but function properly in "individualist" societies.

Finally, there is the difficult issue of long-term social dynamics, which preoccupied Marx, Schumpeter, and several other pioneers of social science. Ideally, the search for an optimal economic system cannot ignore long-term social dynamics, including systemic propensities to create and use new knowledge or tendencies to for systems to regenerate or degenerate. Does a growth-oriented authoritarian system of type Y contain the seeds of its own destruction; will rent seeking and economic sclerosis eventually strangle a market system of type Z?

Obviously, full-scale selection analysis—a successful search for the optimal policy regime—is beyond the pale of any group of policymakers. The making of comprehensive institutional policy is usually a walk in the dark or at least in poor visibility; modern social science is far from having a reliable theory of social change. The walk-in-the-dark metaphor is an appropriate characterization of the initial advice that many economists offered in the early 1990s on the transition to markets in Eastern Europe. Predictably, the advisers selected aspects of the transition problem for which their tools appeared suitable. Their tools, however, were designed primarily for analyzing the operational properties of posttransition market systems.

Benham, Benham, and Merithew (1995) have inventoried and classified studies dealing with transitions to markets in Eurasia that appeared in economic journals between 1989 and 1994.[2] The authors report that macroeconomic topics (stabilization policy) dominate this subset of the literature. These studies usually apply standard macroeconomic analysis directly to the stabilization problems of the transition economies. When the literature of 1989–94 is directly concerned with structural change, methods for selling (or transferring) public capital assets to private owners is the most popular topic, perhaps because of a recent concern in the West with privatization of public enterprises. Finally, the early transition literature contains strong opinions, with little scientific backing, concerning the timing of reforms, especially the relative merits of shock treatments (big bang) and gradual approaches in the transition.

In the early years, the literature paid little attention to theoretical and empirical issues regarding the institutional foundations of a modern market systems—topics such as legal reforms, economic organization, and public administration (Murrell 1995). This has now changed. In recent years, interesting new theoretical work dealing explicitly with economic transitions has appeared, and the literature pays more attention than before to interactions between the economy and the wider social system (Roland 2000). It is no longer surprising to come across first-rate studies by economists examining such issues as the substitution of private rules and private enforcement for formal legal arrangements and how private rules would affect the operations of firms (McMillan and Woodruff 2000). A new multidisciplinary, hybrid approach to structural or institutional change is emerging, reminiscent of other hybrid disciplines such as business administration or public administration. Yet it would be an exaggeration to say that a unified theory of institutional change is on the horizon.[3]

Defining "Imperfect Institutions"

Neoclassical welfare economics does not provide policymakers with tools that are helpful for thinking about institutional policy. We have seen that the notion of an optimal economic system is not helpful, and the concept of inefficient institutions makes no sense in the absence of opportunities for Pareto improvements (or, indeed, structural changes). By assumption, all actors, including policymakers, maximize utility and have already made what they consider the best available choices. An economist who finds room for improvement in such a world has simply ignored some relevant constraints, costs, or benefits (Eggertsson 1990, chapter 1).[4] Yet a theory of institutional policy cannot avoid dealing with inefficient or imperfect institutions, the topic of this book. Hence, we must look for a definition beyond the Pareto criterion of neoclassical economics.

I propose a definition of imperfect institutions that is in the spirit of comparative institutional analysis. According to this definition, institutions can be imperfect either in an exogenous or endogenous sense. A set of institutions is exogenously imperfect (or inefficient) in the eyes of an observer if he or she believes that an alternative bundle of institutions would provide a superior outcome, as defined by the performance criterion used by the observer (his or her target preference function). For example, in the eyes of an individual who uses the wealth criterion (as I do in this book), the institutions in country X are imperfect if she concludes that they generate less wealth per capita than another set of institutions known to her in theory or practice (such as the institutions of some other country).

Institutions are said to be endogenously imperfect when actors downgrade institutions that they previously judged as effective and conclude that an alternative set of institutions (including reformed institutions) would generate superior outcomes. Abstracting from knowledge falsification, downgrading of institutions occurs when actors adjust their policy models. Various factors give rise to such adjustments, including investment in new information, persuasion, gradual emergence of unexpected institutional dynamics, and random shocks to social systems.

These definitions bypass both complications posed by the idea of universal optimization and the question of available degrees of freedom in reforming imperfect institutions. The observers believe, rightly or wrongly, that alternative institutions would give better results, as defined by the observers, when the new institutions have been installed, but they may or may not conclude that social forces will block reforms.

The Determinacy Paradox

When actors of all types maximize their objective functions, formally institutional policy is endogenous to the social system, which leaves no room for outside experts to influence policy.[5] In this world, even destructive policy reflects the choices of rational actors—for example, as Bates (1981) explains.[6] The old theory of economic policy (see chapter 8) makes room for reform and expert advice by banishing rigorous optimization of personal utility functions from the political and social spheres, restricting such behavior to the economic domain.

Government leaders who follow their political noses are more likely to oppose qualitative institutional policies than quantitative policies within an existing policy regime; of the two, quantitative institutional policy, which amounts to structural change, is more likely to upset the political balance.[7] Quantitative policy usually involves marginal adjustments of one policy or another, holding approximately constant the underlying distribution of power and wealth. In a stable policy regime, the functions of those who control and coordinate the key instruments of quantitative policy are usually well defined and clearly established. There is little uncertainty about the policy space of functionaries at the central bank, the finance ministry, the environmental protection agency, or the central planning bureau. A set of permissible and politically sustainable policies has been institutionalized, the latitude of each functionary has been established, and the digression of each agent is part of the social equilibrium.[8]

Fundamental structural change differs from quantitative policy in that the former usually occurs in times of political instability or major institutional failure because guardians of the status quo must be either overruled or in the throws of a deep crisis before they allow radical reforms. Advocates of major institutional reform typically must wait for the social equilibrium to dissolve before they can act and then must carefully adjust the measures to the social and political environment.

The literature has long recognized the limits to reforms. Bhagwati (1978) refers to the implications of endogenous policy as the "determinacy paradox," and a passage by Johansen (1979) in a review essay vividly highlights the problem.[9] Johansen is reviewing the report of an official committee in the United Kingdom that had been appointed to examine whether application of optimal control techniques to macroeconomic planning might improve the overall performance of the British economy. Feeling that the Committee on Policy Optimization is "almost apologetic" about past performance of British policymakers, Johansen makes the following observation ([1979] 1987, 569).

One might so to speak ask what degrees of freedom the Committee has assumed for the comparison of possible alternatives. If all sorts of constraints referring not only to strictly economic aspects, but to problems of information, political pressures etc. are introduced, then one might end up with the sort of overall social theory in which the government is endogenous rather than an autonomous decision-maker, and there will not be much point in discussing hypothetically what would have been the outcome if the government had behaved differently. On the other hand, one may consider the government as a rather free decision-maker with a wide scope for choice between alternatives.

The new literature on institutions obviously lies closer to the deterministic end of Johansen's scale than the free-choice end, as Dixit (1996, 2) confirms in his survey of "transaction-costs politics." Dixit rejects the common argument that economists have a duty to make "sound" economic judgments and leave political considerations to others. "This argument appears to assume that economic and political aspects are additively separable in their effects—that one can analyze each separably and then find the total effect by adding together the two calculations," says Dixit (150). Not all scholars agree with Dixit's dictum, and many economists still argue for partial analysis of the social system, with the economy treated in isolation from other sectors. Lucas (1986, 405), one of the greatest economists of our times, states, for example, "that the problem of controlling inflation has been 'successfully solved' in a scientific sense." Lucas then adds a footnote for skeptics: "Obviously few societies have solved the problem of inflation in a political sense. I do not see this fact as qualifying my claim in the text, any more than I would view the current popularity of 'creationism' as qualifying the scientific status of the theory of evolution."

The various approaches in the new literature on institutions, which were examined in the first part of this book, all support the notion of limits for reform, whether the theories focus on interest groups, the state, or culture. Let us summarily outline the implications for institutional reforms that are embedded in these approaches.

Interest-group and rent-seeking theories demonstrate how incomplete information, rational ignorance, free riding, and costly collective action make it possible for well-organized small interest groups, even in democracies, to pressure the government to create institutions that transfer wealth to these groups. These measures typically reduce aggregate wealth.[10] Yet interest-group theories do not explicitly tell us how society can escape from the clutches of special interests and avoid their negative-sum games. No group of actors seems to have the ability and the incentive to neutralize these forces (or they would have done so already). Olson (1982) suggests that relief is most likely to come in the wake of powerful exogenous impulses, such as wars, that upset the social equilibrium and (temporarily) dissolve these groups.

Another set of theories makes the state rather than interest groups the force behind imperfect institutions. The state is modeled as an enterprising actor with an agenda of its own (Almond 1988). Political leaders, both in democracies and autocracies, form coalitions of supporters and design institutions to create new client groups (Bates 1990). All other things being equal, governmental leaders would prefer to build growth-supporting political coalitions, but, as chapter 5 explained, the circumstances frequently make imperfect institutions and bad economics good politics (in terms of survival for the leaders) (Bates 1981; Fernandez and Rodrik 1991; Weingast 1994). The point here is that theories of coalition politics usually do not identify a practical escape from a destructive political game.[11] The players are locked in a general social equilibrium.

Theories that explain the origins of imperfect institutions in terms of cultural factors also offer little help to reformers. One way that adverse cultural factors hinder economic growth is by raising the cost of enforcing rules of "good conduct" in various arenas of social exchange. Game-theoretic explanations of how countries build "commercial morality" and other institutions that underpin specialization, exchange, and economic growth typically appeal to social structures that serve as focal points in repeated games. Although these focal points vary greatly and include ideas or shared beliefs (Weingast 1995), culture (Kreps 1990), ethnic networks (Landa 1994; Greif 1995), or ideology (Hinich and Munger 1992; Bawn 1996), they usually share the feature of not being a policy instrument of the government. We may then ask whether cultural resistance to growth-friendly institutions would disappear if governments found ways to shape cultural variables according to their policy needs. The answer is no. If governments could create norms, culture, and ideology by proclamation, these informal institutions would become equivalent to laws and regulations, and governments would promote specific norms to please interest groups and coalitions of supporters. Only when these interests seek economically efficient property rights would growth result.

Degrees of Freedom: Disequilibria and Divergent Policy Models

Many economists and statesmen have discovered the political and social limits to reform the hard way. Yet these limits are not as absolute as they appear in the literature. As chapter 10 discusses, shocks that destabilize the social system sometimes create opportunities for institutional reform. This section examines how the incompleteness of policy models provides another exit from the determinacy paradox.

Uncertainty about policy models, as manifested in the notion of endogenously imperfect institutions, undermines the determinacy paradox, as some scholars have recognized. Dixit (1996, 30) underscores the role of both shocks and incomplete models when he states that "one should admit that there are some degrees of freedom for policy making at almost all times, more at some times than others." In particular, the opportunity to recommend regime changes "generally arises at times of 'breaks' in the system, when major flaws in the previous arrangements are apparent" (153). In addition, noting that public policy spans a spectrum from specific operational issues to constitutional questions, Dixit argues that politicians can be more open to expert advice on constitutional rules than on rules lower in the hierarchy. Constitutional rules typically involve greater uncertainty, which provides relief from policy determinism.

I will discuss five aspects of policy models (and the social models from which they are derived) that are relevant for institutional policy. The five points are:

1. Policy models are typically incomplete.
2. Firms, households, and other actors rely on their private policy models when responding to public policy measures.
3. Actors adjust their private policy models for various reasons. These adjustments can change the properties and effectiveness of social institutions.
4. Manipulation of private policy models is an instrument of public policy.
5. Competition among contending policy models is a frequent feature of the policy process.

Experts influence institutional policy and promote reforms either by persuading those in power to alter the government's target preference function, $W = G(g, x)$, or by trying to obtain their support for a new more effective policy model, $x = f(a, z)$. In the latter case, the experts act as salespersons for particular social technologies—for example, when economists advocate competing models for macroeconomic management, as leading economists did in 2003 when they publicly debated, sometimes acrimoniously, whether a proposed reduction in federal taxes would strengthen or paralyze the U.S. economy.

The winning side in the "model wars" sometimes takes over and temporarily dominates policymaking organizations and even professional groups. In a daring study, Fratianni and Pattison (1976, 78) seek to uncover the policy model "that is used by the [Paris-based] OECD in the formulation of hypotheses for testing as well as for policy making." To discover the OECD policy model prior to 1976, the authors search both published and unpublished organizational documents. Fratianni and Pattison, monetarists of the Brunner-Meltzer persuasion, conclude that a British-Keynesian approach to macroeconomic stabilization policy dominates the OECD's advice.[12] In commenting on their study, Hansen (1976, 142), who partly faults the authors' methods and findings, agrees that the OECD Department of Economics and Statistics was dominated in its thinking by British Keynesianism and "was always firmly anchored in British institutions and tended to think that policy that is good in Britain must be good for any other country."

Reflecting on the OECD Committee on Fiscal Policy, with which he had been associated, Hansen (1976, 152) stated, "It would hardly be wrong in this instance to characterize the OECD as an overseas missionary post for British Keynesianism trying to reform continental budget policies." To this he added in a footnote, "I recall once having seen an internal OECD document where France and Germany were called 'overseas countries!'" The struggle between proponents of contrasting policy models, of course, is not limited to macroeconomics. Rodrik (1996) reports on conflicting policy models for reforming the economic systems of low-income countries.

Modern economic history provides many examples of countries suddenly changing their policy regimes for either the whole economy or individual sectors. Sometimes such changes in direction are correlated across regions of the world. Siegmund (1996) provides empirical evidence showing alternative waves of nationalization and privatization in the 1900–1995 period in Europe and select Asian and Latin American countries. These and other examples suggest that perhaps at times the state changes its mind, as I discuss in chapter 3, which identifies three sources of new policy: new policy models, redistribution (usually involving a shift in political power), and system repairs (for example, following exogenous shocks).

To this we should add that the introduction of new policy models or continued support for old ones sometimes involves knowledge falsification (Kuran 1995). In their study of the OECD, Fratianni and Pattison (1976) are of two minds about why OECD experts peddled British Keynesianism rather than, for example, the authors' favored Brunner-Meltzer monetarism. On the one hand, according to the authors, the OECD experts were genuinely committed to the Keynesian view. On the other hand, there was evidence of knowledge falsification. The latter conclusion is based on the assumption that the personal utility functions of the OECD experts, with their basic goals of self-preservation, underlie the organization's bureaucratic preference function. In particular, the authors claim that the OECD is inclined toward eclecticism and avoids falsifiable hypotheses, which they interpret as a strategy of self-preservation (Fratianni and Pattison 1976, 122–24). Fratianni and Pattison suggest that a switch by the

OECD from an old to a new regime of policy recommendations might simply reflect a decision by the bureaucrats to update their strategy for survival in response to changes in the political and ideological environment. Along the same lines, the evidence indicates that especially toward the end, knowledge falsification was common among policy-makers and advisers in Europe's former Soviet-type economies (Kuran 1995, chapter 16; Hollander 1999).

Private Policy Models

We have discussed disparate public policy models and how changes in institutional policy sometimes emerge from competition among diverse models. I now turn to the role of private policy models, which guide the behavior of individual actors. I first discuss the general human propensity to model complex phenomena in simple terms and then examine the propensity of actors living under a new institutional regime to initiate, usually with a lag, cumulative and interactive adjustments in their policy models. Over time, adjustments in private models and corresponding behavioral changes sometimes undermine social institutions that previously had functioned well; the institutions become endogenously imperfect. As dissatisfaction grows, experts pushing alternative models get a wider audience, including the policy authority. I use the modern welfare state of northwestern Europe to illustrate the internal (endogenous) dynamics of institutional regimes.

All individuals face unavoidable scarcity of information, knowledge, brainpower, and time, forcing them to economize on these resources. Research in several scholarly fields finds that people respond by employing a series of schematic, simplifying models when they interpret their social and physical environments.[13] Considerable empirical evidence supports the theory that both experts and ordinary people rely on schematic models. DeNardo's (1995) important study of how Americans model deterrence in the nuclear age is a good example of recent work in this area. DeNardo examines whether there are qualitative differences in models and beliefs of everyday people (novices) and experts (corporate managers in the aerospace and defense industries, professional defense analysts, senior government officials, and academic specialists). Although detecting differences between novices and experts—the latter group, for example, thinks more abstractly and knows more about weapons' systems—DeNardo concludes, "Experts rely on the same heuristic rules of thumb that novices use, and they combine them in the same intuitive, understandardized, unprogrammed way" (240).[14]

The introduction in the twentieth century of the modern welfare state is a massive social experiment, reflecting new social models and untested social technologies. Lindbeck (1995a, 9) describes the welfare state as "as a triumph of western civilization," but in a series of papers he has analyzed dynamic adjustments to welfare-state institutions that are sometimes benign but in other instances are hazardous (Lindbeck 1994, 1995a, 1995b, 1997; Lindbeck, Nyberg, and Weibull 2003). I focus here on hazardous dynamics.

Lindbeck makes roughly the following argument. A sustainable, generous welfare state presupposes a productive economy with a large share of the population at work. The system must also effectively control strong economic incentives for cheating by taxpayers and beneficiaries who face high taxes and generous benefits. Effective enforcement requires not only strict administrative control but also a high degree of self-enforcement through social norms to overcome hazardous economic incentives. In the workplace prior to the emergence of the welfare state, there was a relatively close match between economic incentives and social norms. In the past, a decision not to work normally invited severe economic hardship, and cheating on taxes was not very tempting because marginal tax rates were low.

Various social mechanisms can be evoked to explain why hazardous adjustments come with a lag and do not occur immediately. The gradual weakening of social norms when they conflict with strong economic incentives plays a fundamental role in this process.[15] Weakening of enforcement is another factor. As the number of recipients of social benefits increases and taxes are raised, administrative control is not always expanded commensurably. With enforcement falling behind, cheating becomes easier and more common, especially in social groups over which traditional social norms have relatively weak influence. As time passes and new generations enter working life, the new entrants, with no direct memories of the old system, may be less responsive to traditional norms than were previous generations. A major macroeconomic shock that suddenly increases the number of those receiving social benefits can also act as a catalyst undermining the system. As the number of violators increases, potential violators of social norms feel less threatened by social sanctions. According to Lindbeck (1995a, 11), after the process takes off, an abrupt "ketchup effect" in chiseling and cheating becomes possible.

The hazardous dynamics that Lindbeck describes reflect sequential updating of private and public policy models, to use our terms. When private actors adjust their models and behavior, aggregate outcomes eventually will change. In a welfare state, these adjustments may lead to a decline in private saving and a subsequent reduction in the stock of national wealth, and the resulting economic difficulties can move the authorities to update their models and introduce institutional reform. Political competition is another possible reason why the welfare state reaches a crisis. Instead of aiming for benefits and taxes that are sustainable in the long run, in each election round politicians compete by offering their voters greater benefits (and implicitly higher taxes) until the system crashes.[16]

If hazardous dynamics run out of control and substantially shrink the economy—for example, by reducing the supply of saving and labor—the government may lower its social benefit levels. Various groups of citizens, such as the elderly, now face political risks. The welfare state was originally seen as an efficient way to insure the public against economic risks that private insurance schemes handle poorly or not at all. If the welfare state is hit with homegrown economic stagnation and a substantial reduction in the tax base, the government will cut social benefits, and the public will experience unpredictable changes in benefit levels. For ordinary households, an unexpected curtailment of public services is a new type of risk, political risk, that is particularly costly because most people have not made other plans for dealing with contingencies (Lindbeck 1995a, 13–14).

Lindbeck's work on hazardous dynamics in social systems is not unique. The literature contains countless examples of serial interplay between public and private models. In pioneering studies, Krueger (1978, 1993) and Bhagwati (1978), for example, analyze hazardous adjustments that undermine foreign trade regimes. At the industry level, there is Vietor's (1994) examination of federal government regulation of the U.S. commercial airline industry. Airline regulation initiated a sequence of actions and reactions between the regulators and the industry, giving rise to inefficient operations and steadily increasing costs. Higgs (1982) presents a vivid picture of regulation dynamics in the salmon fishing industry of the U.S. Pacific Northwest that involved technical regress and depletion. And, as a final example, there is Krueger's (1990) fascinating study of long-term institutional dynamics in the U.S. sugar program.

In this chapter, I emphasize an obvious conclusion: When social science assumes that (intended) rational and goal-oriented behavior extends beyond the market to all social spheres, the structure of the economic and social system is endogenous, implying that experts and reformers have little or no scope to initiate institutional reform (other than changes already planned). My second major point concerns the neglected role of incomplete knowledge in social change. In this context, I introduce a subjective definition of "imperfect institutions" that is compatible with comparative institutional analysis. Further, I argue that explanations of institutional change that rely solely on state finances and changing political equilibria are seriously incomplete if they ignore the role of incomplete knowledge. It is unreasonable to assume that people's ideas about the nature of social and economic systems are stationary or unchanging or to assume that changing social models, private and public, are not an independent force in institutional change.

The concept of a general social equilibrium has a useful role in drawing attention to the limits of reform. I argue that opportunities for reform are created by real factors that upset the political balance, by real shocks and exogenous impulses that induce actors to revise their models, and generally by the spread of new social ideas and models. These factors often interact; moreover, a community's historical background plays a key role in selecting the new social equilibrium that emerges during reform.

CHAPTER 10

Eluding Poverty Traps, Escaping History

Introduction: Forces of History and a Handful of Heroes

As we saw in chapter 1, modern growth theory pinpoints world knowledge as the primary source of economic growth. According to new or endogenous growth theory, leading countries forge ahead by developing and applying new production technologies, and growth laggards fall behind because they are unable to adopt and apply knowledge that already exists. The main point of this book, however, is that the technical and even financial problem of copying and applying new production technologies is not the fundamental factor blocking progress in developing countries. DeLong (2000) is close to the truth with his half-serious comment that a poor country needs only a handful of engineering graduates to copy advances in foreign production technologies. My thesis is that poor countries lack social institutions that are necessary complements of modern production technologies.

The previous chapter, which dealt with the concept of policy determinacy, introduced the idea that internal dynamics, evolving policy models, and external shocks sometimes dislodge entrenched social equilibria and create opportunities for institutional reforms. This chapter examines in more detail various catalysts that upset social equilibria and initiate reform processes. But when such opportunities emerge, I argue, reformers cannot build from scratch: history limits available choices.

The capacity to initiate major institutional change—for example, to introduce a new system of property rights—usually lies with governmental leaders and the politically powerful. A country's government sets laws and regulations, codifies social practices, and manages the police as well as other enforcement organizations. In terms of the concepts introduced in chapter 8, there are four reasons why a government might fail to introduce the social institutions necessary for growth.

1. The leaders' target preference function, $W = G(g, x)$, gives growth-promoting social institutions a low rating because they are thought to threaten the leaders' personal wealth or power.
2. The leaders lack political authority to introduce certain institutions necessary for growth; political constraints exclude the institutions from the leaders' choice set.[1]
3. The leaders' policy model, $x = f(a, z)$, lacks the policy instruments, a_j, necessary for creating institutional conditions for growth. For example, tools for replacing certain social norms may be lacking.
4. The leaders rely on policy models, $x = f(a, z)$, that misrepresent the links between institutions and growth.

We can use the historical case of chapter 7 to illustrate the four reasons why public authorities tolerate imperfect institutions. In the case study, I claim that premodern society in Iceland could have escaped dire poverty and starvation if the country's leaders had promoted new technologies and organization in the fisheries. Instead, Iceland relied on medieval farming technology and lingered in a low-income social equilibrium. A breakthrough would have required cooperation with European fishing nations, but condition 1 precluded cooperation with foreigners (the Germans, the English, the French, or the Dutch) to develop a state-of-the-art export industry. The supreme authority, the Danish Crown, (correctly) saw direct foreign investment as threatening Denmark's control of the colony, and Icelandic landlords believed that a high-productivity fishing industry would undermine their wealth and status, which was based on primitive farming. Condition 2 was relevant in the eighteenth century, when the Danish Crown gradually became willing to reform but was not yet ready to override political opposition by the Icelandic elite. Condition 3 was of secondary importance. Iceland had ancient legal traditions of secure property rights, and traditional legal norms were not in fundamental conflict with a modern legal code. Developments in the late nineteenth century demonstrate that traditionalist ideology, with its opposition to new industries and social change, was capable of slowing but not preventing change. Finally, condition 4, misleading policy models, apparently played a significant role in sharpening local opposition to reforms. The historical evidence indicates that Icelandic landlords interpreted the country's development strategy in terms of a partial rather than a general equilibrium model that exaggerated the threat to farming and landlords from independent fisheries. The fears that a prosperous fishing industry would bankrupt the landlords via high wages and lack of farm workers ignored the demand effects from rising incomes. Rising incomes and greater demand for farm products would increase in the value of land, and higher living standards would create a sustainable increase in the supply of labor. Moreover, in the labor market, a common wage rate in farming and fishing would have equaled the marginal product of labor in the farm sector. In other words, the fishing industry could have attracted labor with rewards comparable to what workers were receiving in the farm sector.[2]

When hazardous endogenous dynamics and external shocks create a window for institutional reforms, various advocates and experts play a prominent role in propelling the reforms forward and influencing the direction they take. Many observers perceive the opportunity for reform as always having been present; all that was needed was enthusiastic reformers willing to make themselves heard. Thus, one finds no uneasiness about limits to reform in Harberger's (1993) well-known account of his "handful of heroes" and their large role in successful policy reforms. Drawing on his experience as an economic adviser to countries in Latin America, Harberger describes how a small number of high-powered experts have profoundly affected economic reform in the region, proclaiming "This paper has its origins in my long-standing conviction that successful economic policy in developing countries is very far from being the product of pure forces of history—something that happens when it happens because its time has come. Far from it, in every case about which I have close knowledge, the policy would in all likelihood have failed (or never got started) but for the efforts of a key group of individuals, and within that group, one or two outstanding leaders" (343).

By profession, these reformers and experts were central bank governors, directors of economic institutes, and cabinet ministers (especially of planning and finance), often educated at foreign universities and with extensive foreign contacts. Using their superior skills, personal magnetism, and abundant energy, the experts persuaded their governments to introduce better macroeconomic policies, deregulate, and liberalize trade and payments, sometimes over violent opposition from those who expected to lose from such changes or did not believe in their effectiveness.[3]

No one disagrees with the claim that only human beings, experts and reformers, are capable of designing, promoting, introducing, and implementing institutional reform. Without human effort, no structural change will occur. I assert, however, that perverse social equilibria undermine all well-meaning reform efforts until new features in the political landscape, unexpected economic shocks, or erosion of old social models make officeholders revise their strategies. And even when the political elite supports reform, the culture of a country may prove incompatible with the new institutions. Yet hyperoptimistic reformers who possess useful knowledge and strong determination to promote their ideas often have useful roles. One reason is that the tipping point where new policies become acceptable to a large number of pivotal actors usually is uncertain or unknown because the actors' social models are subjective and not directly observable. Moreover, as Kuran (1995) has examined, actors often falsify their preferences to accommodate social pressures.[4] It follows that tireless reformers are sometimes in luck. Moreover, reformers and the rest of society may be caught by surprise when they succeed in pushing community opinion to the tipping point, thus initiating institutional reforms.

Once again, let us return to the case of premodern Iceland. When the country finally saw effective institutional reforms, it was an external shock that upset the country's perverse social equilibrium: stepwise introduction of international free trade in Iceland, beginning in 1787 and culminating in 1855 with free trade with all countries. Free trade emerged in Iceland because of the defeat of Denmark in the Napoleonic Wars and the destruction of the Danish navy, British domination of the North Atlantic, and the ideological and political move to free trade in Europe. Although "forces of history" created the conditions for change, human agents of the Harberger type—various leaders, ranging from businessmen to politicians and poets—actually fought for and introduced the new social technologies, pulling the country in a new direction.

Using a very large scale, this chapter and the next map the journey that begins when some forces undo a country's perverse social equilibrium and, if all goes well, lead it into the realm of sustained economic growth. This chapter first discusses various impulses and shocks that upset the social equilibrium, emphasizing their exogenous nature. The remainder of the chapter illustrates with the help of three cases how history limits national policymakers' choices. The following chapter looks at legal transplants and the "transplant effect" before examining various questions concerning minimal property rights for growth.

Escaping Poverty Traps

In an interesting study, Acemoglu, Johnson, and Robinson (2000) provide striking evidence for the longevity of perverse social equilibria and ineffective social technologies. They also explain about three-quarters of the variation in current per capita income in former colonies by using a theory that assumes that current social institutions reflect the nature of initial colonial institutions.[5] In some colonies, the European powers set up extractive states; in other colonies, the settlers tried to replicate European property rights, and, according to the study, current institutions typically reflect the initial path chosen in the colonial context. These findings are based on an econometric estimation that uses as statistical instruments historical data for the mortality rates of soldiers, clergy, and sailors visiting the colonies and European settlements. The authors "document empirically that (potential) settler mortality rates were a major determinant of settlements; that settlements were a major determinant of early institutions (in practice, institutions in 1900); that there is a strong correlation between early institutions and institutions today; and finally that current institutions have first-order effect on current performance" (2).

The authors claim that their "findings do not imply that institutions today are predetermined by colonial policy and cannot be changed" (Acemoglu, Johnson, and Robinson 2000, 29). Institutions can be improved, and the study shows that the gains will be substantial, but the evidence also strongly supports the idea of institutional path dependence—implying that in many countries one or more of the four conditions discussed earlier block institutional reforms. Demsetz (1967) presents a more optimistic picture that advances the argument that all communities respond to new economic opportunities by introducing or refining exclusive property rights whenever they expect such agreements to increase aggregate net wealth. My presumption is that opportunities are lost because hard social constraints often hold back wealth-maximizing producers, consumers, and politicians, sending their countries into relative backwardness. Not all countries live by Demsetz's dictum; his theory of property rights is not a general theory but a special case.[6] I subsequently discuss various events and developments that sometimes soften the constraints that hold back the evolution of property rights that Demsetz envisioned. I find it useful to distinguish between the forces that initially trigger change and exogenous factors that shape the reform process itself. This section discusses the triggers, leaving the determinants of the reform path for later.

Many contributors to the "how the West grew rich" literature (North and Thomas 1971; North 1981; Rosenberg and Birdzell 1986; Mokyr 1990) agree with this view of the growth process, assigning an important role to extraneous circumstances and historical forces. Some of these authors, for example, emphasize the consequences of rivalry between states or the evolution of new domestic political forces that challenge absolute rulers and gradually introduce separation of powers and democratic constraints, raising the opportunity cost of exploitative policies. The discussion that follows identifies six categories of impulses that often challenge low-income social equilibria and destabilize regimes.

External Politics

The removal or addition of foreign political constraints can upset a country's social equilibrium and create openings for reform, which in the long run may or may not be realized. Examples of such changes include events that put an end to foreign domination (colonial or Soviet-type), foreign involvement in coups toppling a domestic dictator and his or her coalition, or foreign military occupation and the imposition of a new legal code and other social institutions. Foreign intervention or withdrawal, however, has an uncertain impact on institutions and reforms. The end of colonial domination has not always put countries on a reform path; domestic political leaders sometimes continue a new version of the exploitive policies of the former foreign masters.[7] Also, the thesis has been advanced that foreign support, such as structural adjustment loans from the World Bank for poor African countries, in some cases has sustained rather than upset perverse political equilibria and stabilized dictatorial regimes (Ndulu and van de Walle 1996).

Domestic Politics

The social science literature offers convincing insights into the forces that maintain a low-income social equilibrium, where no pivotal actor has both the incentive and the ability to defect. To explain why actors do not leave poverty traps, the theory relies on theoretical mechanisms such as the prisoner's dilemma, free riding, or open access and uses these tools to explain the consequences of disruptive factors such as diverse and hostile ethnic groups, weak states that are not fully in control of their territories, rulers with short time horizons and narrow power bases (see chapter 5), or well-organized special interest groups. Our understanding of undesirable social equilibria, however, is not matched by comparable understanding of the dynamic path from an undesirable equilibrium point to a more desirable one.

Many historical accounts suggest that transitions from perverse to benign social equilibrium are often associated with various autonomous domestic (and also external) developments that alter the balance of power. These forces include the gradual rise of a new religion or political ideology, diminished hostility between ethnolinguistic groups, the rise of a new social class, and other comparable developments that usually are not under the direct control of government policy. Such slowly evolving changes in the environment of key decision makers eventually make it logical and feasible for them to solve previously intractable problems and, for example, to establish democratic constraints and separation of powers, to arrange credible commitments by ethnic groups to cooperate with each other, to consolidate state power over all its territory, and to coordinate ideological beliefs of major social groups concerning legitimate state behavior.[8]

The next four impulses on our list—discovery of natural resources, sudden economic crises, declining relative economic status, and new social models—are not clearly distinct from the previous two categories (external and domestic politics), but I list these forces separately because they often have a life of their own in the literature.

Natural Resources

It is tempting to conclude that unexpected discoveries of abundant natural resources, such as rich diamond mines or oil reserves, will jolt countries into reforming their structure of property rights.[9] The new resources might ease financial constraints that previously blocked reforms or activate the Demsetz cost-benefit process and justify costly investments in extending and improving property rights and their enforcement. However, the relationship between growth and natural resources is complex and ambiguous. Abundant natural resources sometimes enable countries to reach relatively high levels of per capita income while continuing to rely on inferior social institutions. In other words, abundant natural resources economize on social technology, which is the case in many oil-producing countries. For example, a government may share the resource rent with foreign companies that it employs to extract, process, and market the raw materials, and outsiders who leave few traces in the host country provide expert knowledge. Prosperity based on natural resources but relying on stagnant inefficient social structures is unlikely to lead to sustained economic growth. The initial spurt will not last because the countries lack flexibility to cope with adverse developments, such as depletion of the resources, fall in demand when substitutes become available in the world market, or domestic struggles regarding distribution of the resource rent. If a resource-based economy lacks the capacity to develop social institutions for supporting modern industries, it will eventually enter a path of decline.

The scenario that I have presented does not necessarily support the currently popular concept of the "resource curse," if the term is taken to mean that a discovery of abundant natural resources necessarily impede social progress, driving otherwise capable countries off their growth paths (Sachs and Warner 1995; Gylfason, Herbertsson, and Zoega 1999).[10] I simply argue that abundant natural resources may temporarily boost the economies of countries that generally lack the social capacity to import and apply modern production technologies. Two other possibilities also exist: (1) the resource curse, where the discovery of abundant natural resources destroys a country's existing or nascent political and social capabilities and blocks their future development, and (2) the Demsetz case, whereby such discoveries create incentives to build effective social institutions for growth. Historical cases probably support all three hypotheses—for example, the economic history of North America appears to fit the Demsetz theory about the origins of effective property rights.

In sum, the discovery of abundant natural resources often upsets the prevailing social equilibrium, but we cannot generalize about the effects of resource abundance for long-run growth.

Sudden Economic Crises

In modeling impulses that trigger policy reversals, the political economy literature (which typically deals with reforms in macroeconomic policy rather than with major institutional change), gives pride of place to sudden economic setbacks or crises such as hyperinflation, massive unemployment, collapse of export markets, and balance-of-payments problems. In a study of eight countries, Bates and Krueger (1993) find that reforms were always undertaken when economic conditions had deteriorated. Economic shocks sometimes initiate policy cycles with alternating phases of reform and crisis-generating policy packages. Such cycles can foster long-term economic stagnation. In a contrary manner, severe economic setbacks can also create strong disaffection with current policies and institutions, mobilizing an effective reform movement. Chapter 4 examines different responses to economic shocks and refers to an empirical study by Rodrik (1998) that uses variation among countries in latent social conflict and effective institutions of conflict management to explain their different responses to shocks. Again, prior conditions determine how countries respond to external events.

Declining Relative Economic Status

For individuals, families, and nations, few social developments have stronger psychological impact than the experience of a decline in economic status relative to one's reference groups. For nations, relative decline brings not only a sense of humiliation but sometimes also fears of political and military aggression by other countries. In social science, the best-known formulation of the relative wealth effect is Gerschenkron's (1962) thesis that relative backwardness has positive effects on latecomer economic development by inducing reforms. Gerschenkron bases his theory on the development experiences of Russia, Germany, France, Italy, Austria, and Bulgaria. He concludes that the greater the degree of backwardness, the greater the state's role in creating conditions for growth. Fishlow (1989, 146) rightly criticizes Gerschenkron's relative-backwardness thesis for its inadequate attention to political constraints, claiming that Gerschenkron "pays too little attention to the domestic classes and groups whose interests the interventionist state must adequately incorporate if it is to play the central role required."

For our purposes, the relative-decline explanation has the familiar disadvantage of not explicitly telling us what conditions eventually make growth laggards respond to their sinking status. The European countries in Gerschenkron's sample responded much sooner to relative decline than many Third World countries have done. The relative-wealth impulse is undoubtedly important, but without knowing more about the underlying social structure, its impact is not predictable.

New Social Models

Social models are the carriers of new ideas and new knowledge about social technologies—the organization of society—so it is not unreasonable to expect that shifting social models sometimes upset low-income social equilibria by changing strategies and behavior at various societal levels, from the household to the national government. Most modern scholars tend to discredit Max Weber's thesis that the "Protestant ethic" was the driving force behind the rise of modern growth.[11] The roots of the rise of the West go further back than the Reformation. Yet the idea that earlier religious forces contributed to the rise of Europe remains alive. Moreover, erosion of antimodernist religious movements (for example, the collapse of theocracy in early twenty-first-century Iran) can create conditions for growth.

In addition to ethical and practical models underlying daily household and work routines, there are grand policy models that try to capture the essential properties of economic and political systems. Combined with unexpected shocks, uncertainty about the properties of the social systems can lead to wholesale rejection of particular social models, acceptance of new models, and fundamental revision of government policy, even when basic policy targets remain the same (see chapters 3 and 8).

The pervasive uncertainty about the nature of social systems explains why nations sometimes seem stumble onto growth-promoting social technologies. Recent work by Weingast and his coauthors, analyzing what they call market-preserving federalism, illustrates my point.[12] Weingast and his colleagues argue that during the past 300 years, market-preserving federalism has characterized the political organization of the growth leader in each period (the Dutch Republic, England, and the United States). Furthermore, these scholars contend that impure initial versions of this constitutional arrangement probably are on the verge of turning China, India, and Mexico into emerging economic giants.

The theory of market-preserving federalism builds on Tiebout's (1956) model under which dissatisfied actors vote with their feet and leave their local communities. The Weingast (1995) market-preserving constitution combines an unrestricted federal market for inputs and outputs, local self-financing and control of economic organization, effective local financial responsibility (no bailouts by the national government), and credible commitments by all units of the federation not to undermine but to preserve the system and its constitutional arrangements. In such an environment, competition among lower governments for inputs and tax revenues compels them to provide growth-friendly environments and to experiment with best available social technologies.

Market-preserving federalism is a perfect example of what I referred to earlier as grand policy models providing visions of national development under particular social technologies. As far as I can tell, however, in many or most cases, market-preserving federalism emerged without the key players being fully aware of the economic properties of the system—they did not purposefully plan a new system with the aid of clear-cut policy models.[13] Consider England during the Industrial Revolution. At the time, England was not a federal state de jure; de facto, however, it met the conditions of market-preserving federalism.[14] The important role of circumstantial forces is particularly evident in accounts of political developments in India, China, and Mexico toward the end of the twentieth century, which may represent initial steps toward full-blown market-preserving federalism (Montinola, Qian, and Weingast 1995; Parikh and Weingast 1997; Careaga and Weingast 2000). In these three cases, leaders of subnational units who believed that they could perform better than the federal government took the initiative to reform their local structure of property rights. Although these subnational units did not belong to free federal markets (one of Weingast's conditions), they have compensated by trading in world markets.

Parikh and Weingast (1997) argue that in India, a small group of states recently have exploited the slim majority and the political weakness of a new federal government (which has replaced the perennial Congress Party), claiming power to reform their local economies. In a federation, the demonstrated effects of outstanding economic success by a few reforming subgovernments can incite reformers throughout the system.[15] But ripples of reform are only one of many possible outcomes. Very little is known about the origins and maintenance of credible commitments to market-preserving federalism. What forces, for example, will prevent a federal government from intervening to protect unsuccessful local economies with subsidies or by allowing them to raise trade barriers? Sooner or later, coalitions pressing for protective measures are likely to emerge and threaten federal systems of the Weingast (1995) variety.

The foregoing discussion of the six overlapping categories of impulses and their effects does not imply that anything at all may happen. Rather, it establishes that history matters. Both game-theoretic work on comparative institutions (Aoki 2001; Greif, forthcoming) and historical institutional analysis (North 1981) emphasize how the preexisting structural context selects equilibria, constraining the choice set available to a community. Social systems have evolved along different historical paths, so the consequences of comparable shocks or events need not be identical across countries. The heterogeneity of the past makes it all the more difficult for social science to generalize about social change. Of course, in the context of particular structures, it may be possible to make sound predictions.

Political Histories and the Reform Path

This section uses three cases to illustrate how the political history of a country affects the direction and speed of institutional reform after pressures for change have built up. I consider three types of political environments. First, I look at circumstances in which subnational governmental units pressure a reluctant national government to reform. Second, I consider the reverse situation, in which a willing national government meets opposition to reform from its entrenched lower units. Finally, I discuss circumstances in which policies promoting modernization challenge the interests of neither central nor local governments. The cases of China, the former Soviet Union, and Botswana will be used to illustrate each of these three historical circumstances.

Reluctant Center, Willing Districts (China)

After suffering two episodes of monumental economic setbacks, each attributable to perverse economic policies by the center (the Great Leap Forward, 1958–60, and the Cultural Revolution, 1966–76), in 1979 a process of sequential reform got under way in China that over the next twenty years generated one of the world's highest growth rates (more than 9 percent annual rate of growth in per capita income) and raised the country from poverty to middle-income levels (Qian 2000a, 2000b, 2002; Roland 2000). There are many ways to tell a story of such profound importance and complexity, but here I focus on only one aspect, basic political forces behind the reform process (Henning and Lu 2000).

The fiasco of the Cultural Revolution, coming on top of the Great Leap Forward, left China's leaders (of the Party and the nation) with an awkward choice between the status quo and economic reforms. Without institutional reform, China seemed to be headed for relative economic and military decline, and grassroots pressures for reform were growing. China's economic experience and lessons from other countries suggested that effective reforms required greater reliance on economic incentives and competitive pressures instead of plan indicators and bureaucratic control. The substitution of prices for command, however, would create uncertainty for many party functionaries about their social and economic positions and in the long run possibly release hard-to-control cascades of reforms leading toward capitalism, with unforeseen consequences for the Communist Party. In the uncertain environment of the late 1970s, the relative autonomy of China's regions and districts had a crucial impact on the reform process.

In the 1970s, China's structure of central management reflected its early (agricultural) stage of development and the huge size of the country and its population, as well as recent reckless episodes of decentralization beginning in 1958. These circumstances gave subnational governmental units considerable autonomy, involving far greater local control than prevailed at the time in the Soviet Union (Granick 1990; Qian and Xu 1993). The reforms that began around 1979 grew out of defiant acts by farmers, workers, managers, and local government and party leaders in regions where the power of the national government was relatively weak. The local initiatives involved incentive-based adjustments in economic organization that initially transformed China's agriculture and later its manufacturing sector. Following decades of upheaval, the soil was ready for economic reforms, and local experimentation and reorganization rapidly and dramatically increased productivity in the reforming agricultural areas, which in turn had demonstrable effects in other locations.[16] Subsequently, stepwise local initiatives in manufacturing created similar ripple effects. The power elite at the center realized that the cost of opposing reforms was rising rapidly and decided after considerable internal struggles that the best choice was to legitimatize and shape the new developments (Qian 2000b).

Although the Cultural Revolution had upset China's social equilibrium, strengthened local leaders vis-à-vis the political center, and created an opening for structural change, various forces nonetheless could have blocked growth-promoting institutions. In particular, during major restructuring of property rights, potential losers have strong incentives to sabotage the reform. When expected losers are politically powerful or hold strategic positions in society, transitions are likely to fail unless compromises are reached about adjusting the new structure of property rights to meet the interests of the losers but without removing (all) its growth-promoting potential. Economists who evaluate such second-best solutions in isolation from political factors are unlikely to be impressed, but other transition paths simply are not available. At one level, the complex reforms in China can be viewed as a series of successful compromises that preserved growth and protected potential losers. In a series of studies, Qian (2000a, 2000b, 2002) describes the details of these compromises. At the local and enterprise levels, reliance on economic incentives and market forces leaves little or no role for functionaries of the old system, who therefore have much to lose. Yet the bottom-up nature of reforms in China provided these potential losers with an opportunity to protect their interests. Township-village enterprises (TVEs) became the crucial vehicle of growth in China's economic miracle, appearing initially in agriculture and later in manufacturing and other sectors. TVEs have a nonconventional ownership form, neither state nor private firms but local government firms, a structure that provided rewarding opportunities for displaced functionaries of the central management system.

Moreover, the country's legal framework has defied the conventional wisdom. The move away from state control of the economy toward market relationships took place in a legal environment that did not define or defend private ownership and contractual relations. The state has also been ambiguous in its support of private property, and private firms until recently have developed slowly.[17] In this environment, the thriving TVEs have relied on protection from local government and local power brokers, but recent trends toward privatization have impressed on the Chinese leaders the need for a modern legal code.

In China the so-called dual-track approach has also provided a temporary shield for potential losers from the reform by allowing organizations designed for central planning to operate alongside market-based firms. According to the dual-track approach, economic agents must first meet basic obligations in the planning sector (where planners set the prices) and are free thereafter to produce for the market at free-market prices. The arrangement protects potential losers in planning sector while increasing efficiency and incomes all around. The relationship of local governments to the national government has a comparable structure: The collection of taxes and provision of local public goods remains with local governments (owners of the TVEs), which are required to pass a fixed amount of revenue to the central government but are allowed to keep the residual.[18]

The scholarly literature has debated whether it was wise for China to select a gradual dual-track approach instead of attempting a swifter and more radical transition, as some of the former Soviet countries of Europe have tried. Sachs and Woo (1997) assert that China has harvested rapid economic growth not because the country followed a gradual approach but in spite of it. The authors claim that retaining inefficient state enterprises and letting them operate alongside the emerging nonstate sector slowed growth. Although its economic logic is clear, this argument overlooks the social obstacles to change. Historical and political accounts of China's path indicate that its economic reforms are the outcome of a tug-of-war between a reluctant national government (the party leadership) and willing subnational governments (Henning and Lu 2000). The fundamental impulse driving the reforms is centripetal, notwithstanding Beijing's efforts to legitimatize and coordinate local initiatives, anticipate and channel new developments, and modify the national institutional environment to accommodate the reforms. If this account of the bottom-up nature of the reforms is correct, the debate, whether the Chinese were wise or unwise in choosing gradual instead of big bang reforms is immaterial. The Great Leap Forward may have been Mao's choice in some sense, but nobody "chose" the current gradual approach. The counterfactual hypothesis that big bang reforms would have produced even better economic results for China is not of practical interest because we cannot ignore the historical political context.

The future of China's economic reforms is a puzzle of monumental importance but remains clouded by uncertainty. Since the early 1990s, the direction of economic change has been from second-best transition institutions to best-practice institutions (as defined in purely economic terms). The dual track in production markets has been gradually phased out, while potential losers have been carefully compensated. Moreover, throughout the 1990s, the TVEs have been privatized, and a constitutional amendment has given privately owned firms more legitimacy. In spite of their very useful role in the transition, TVEs involve high transaction costs and relatively weak managerial incentives (Qian 2002, 40). Privatization of the TVEs has been relatively successful, indicating that transition institutions and piecemeal reforms do not necessarily lead to a reform trap. Attempts to reform state-owned enterprises (SOEs), however, have generally failed, with many reform measures working either poorly or not at all (Qian 2002, 44). The party's control of appointments of managers is the major source of failed attempts to reform the SOEs (Qian 2002), which is reminiscent of failed reforms in the Soviet economies of Eurasia (see the following section).[19] In China, however, the fast growth of the nonstate sector has so far mitigated failures in the state sector, which has shrunk in relative importance (Qian 2002, 47).

At the beginning of the twenty-first century, the success of economic reforms in China had aggravated the obvious friction between capitalism and communism or more generally between economic and political forces. If China is to maintain sustained growth and catch up with the West, the country must successfully neutralize potential sources of conflict. In particular, the ongoing diffusion of market relations and exclusive ownership will undermine the party elite's position of power, and much depends on the leaders' responses. Growth-friendly outcomes are certainly possible. China may undertake a smooth transition either to democracy or to noncommunist form of autocracy, in each case without interference with long-term economic growth. At least three unfavorable outcomes are also possible. First, the leadership may attempt to protect the political status quo by discontinuing the transition to markets. Recent history indicates that political leaders who succeed in diverting attention from economic reform must instead offer their people new highly salient focal points, such as fears for the country's security. Second, struggles at the top over the direction of economic affairs could bring political chaos and economic breakdown. The third issue of concern is adverse social consequences of rapid growth. When extremely rapid growth affects regions and social groups unequally, which it almost always does, spontaneous unrest or conflict may spread from disaffected local units and throughout the nation. In other words, market-preserving federalism may backfire: instead of generating orderly competition among institutional arrangements, rapid uneven growth can fan the fires of civil unrest.[20]

The future economic and political direction of China in the twenty-first century is of paramount importance, yet we know little about the likely course of events. Indeed, rapid economic growth in China during the last quarter of the twentieth century startled most economists, including experts in the economics of property rights, and our forecasting skills for predicting major social change have not substantially improved. Still, the most unlikely future development in China that I can think of is the combination of continued transition to private ownership and markets, rapid growth, and a stable role for the communist state.

Willing Center, Reluctant Agents (USSR)

When people praise or blame China for taking the slow road to reform, they sometimes forget that prior to their collapse, the former Soviet Union and the Soviet economies of Eastern Europe attempted gradual economic reform. These experiments, which went on for decades, failed miserably, and many people came to believe that the internal logic of centrally managed economies made the systems irreparable (Nove 1986, 1992; Kornai 1992). In this view, plan indicators, commands, and party control did not mix with partial liberalization of prices. Winiecki (1990 [1996]) argues, however, that the reforms in Soviet Eurasia never succeeded in replacing bureaucratic control with market forces because midlevel state functionaries, the potential losers from reforms, always found surreptitious ways to retain their control of the production process.

Soviet economic decline is a classic example of hazardous internal dynamics, a process that made Soviet-type economies increasingly more inefficient relative to market-based economies (Nove 1986; Winiecki 1986). The passage of time accentuated several fundamental problems in the Soviet world. Positions of leadership were filled with people who showed outward signs of loyalty to the regime rather than professional competence, and this practice gradually lowered the level of efficacy in Soviet organizations. In another development, the central management system became increasingly dysfunctional in a world of rapid technological change. When enterprises implemented new technologies, their production flows were temporarily interrupted, creating suspicions of mismanagement and disrupting the planning system. Moreover, the system itself was not a fertile source of new technologies. The task of centrally coordinating the economy became more difficult with time because production relationships in new and technologically advanced industries were often more complex than those of traditional industries such as coal and steel. These and other time-related problems put the Soviet economies on a path of long-term decline, which had adverse consequences for the rulers. Falling and even negative growth rates weakened public support for leaders, giving domestic rivals an opportunity to challenge the leadership, and undermined national defense and geopolitical ambitions. The Soviet leaders, therefore, eagerly sought reforms that would raise industrial productivity and economic growth. Rather than suffer economic collapse, the totalitarian Soviet leaders probably were ready to sacrifice state ownership for private ownership and a market-based economy in an autocratic state. In a market-oriented dictatorship, certain branches of the top leadership—namely, top politicians and administrators, the police, and the military—would still prosper, but there was also an important group of probable losers.

The economies of the Soviet Union and its European satellites were more centralized and hierarchal than the Chinese system, in spite of other similarities.[21] To operate the economic system, Soviet leaders relied on two chains of agents reaching from the highest ranks of government to the enterprise level: a chain of administrators and managers and a chain of Communist Party functionaries for monitoring the managers. To discipline the central management process and for other reasons, Soviet-type management was characterized by planned shortages (taut planning), including shortages of consumer goods. In this environment of shortages and rationing, the authorities provided favored groups with informal access to scarce goods and services, which became the chief source of privilege. A transition to markets would gradually remove the administering and monitoring roles of Soviet managers and apparatchiks, depriving them of their various privileges (Winiecki 1990 [1996]). While top bureaucrats had a good chance of surviving in a new system, mid-level agents had few good opportunities and would become the most significant group of losers. Midlevel managers and apparatchiks were selected from a shallow pool of actors who claimed loyalty to the system but had few marketable skills. Their system-specific human capital would depreciate rapidly in a market environment, giving these actors a strong incentive to sabotage economic reforms.

In the Soviet Union and Eastern Europe, economic reforms originated with the leadership at the top and then were passed down the chain of command to be fine-tuned, implemented, and enforced by midlevel operators—the potential losers from successful implementation. The reforms began on a small scale as early as the 1950s, and Winiecki (1990 [1996]) documents how functionaries reshaped the measures to retain in some manner valuable control over the production process. The nature of the resistance varied. Reforms were at times effectively aborted at the outset while the functionaries pretended otherwise. Another strategy involved making the reforms, deliberately but secretly, internally inconsistent, which made the measures fail and provided an excuse for abandoning them. When reforms initially succeeded, the functionaries reversed them, claiming that the measures had gone too far and were disrupting the economy.

Governments are usually needed to initiate and implement large-scale institutional reforms, but the two cases of the Chinese and Soviet economies should remind us that governments are not monolithic. Divided interests and conflict among levels and branches of governments often decisively influence institutional reform. When a government attempts reform, it does not start from scratch. It must cope with an endowment of political factions and interests of varying strength.

We turn now to a final case, a unique African success story in which national leaders are supportive of growth-oriented reform and lower governmental units are cooperative.

Willing Center, Willing Districts (Botswana)

Africa's sub-Saharan region had lower per capita income at the end of the twentieth century than in the mid-1960s. Most countries of the region lack social capacity to update their production methods and apply new technologies, and the problem is quite severe compared to other parts of the world.[22] A common alternative explanation blames African economic decline not on inadequate social institutions but rather on natural factors and geography (climate, disease, resources, and transportation costs for goods and knowledge) (Bloom and Sachs 1998; Gallup, Mellinger, and Sachs 1998; Sachs 2001). The natural environment, it is said, influences the productivity of agriculture and the quality of human resources and thus the level of income. A third explanation identifies trade as the engine of growth and explains poor growth performance by a country's limited integration into international trade networks (Frankel and Romer 1999). In this study, I claim that institutions rule, although ultimately the answer is an empirical issue. Rodrik, Subramanian, and Trebbi (2002) have tested the relative influence of institutions, geography, and trade on income levels around the world. The authors employ recently developed statistical instruments for geography and trade to separate direct and indirect effects on incomes from the three explanatory variables. They also allow for reverse causality.[23] The authors find that, when institutions are controlled for, geography and trade have at best weak direct impact on incomes, whereas the quality of institutions has a strong impact on incomes.[24] Geography and trade, however, have substantial indirect effects by influencing the quality of institutions.

If we do not accept the geography and trade explanations, we need to show how political, social circumstances have prevented poor countries from upgrading their social technologies. Why have African leaders failed to built property rights for growth? Do national governments fail to carry out effective reforms because they lack the necessary incentives or political authority? What about local and regional units—why do they not compel their national governments to reform?[25] The usual institutional explanation of economic stagnation in sub-Saharan Africa emphasizes political history. National borders, often artificially drawn in the nineteenth century by the European colonial powers, typically engulf an arbitrary collection of ethnolin-guistic groups that previously had not formed an organized political entity (Easterly and Levine 1997).[26] Attempts by national governments to introduce modern systems of property rights often challenge the wealth and status of leaders in traditional subnational groups, who then oppose such measures. To further complicate efficient national governance and modernization in the postcolonial period, so-called colonial indirect rule, which relied on traditional leaders such as para-mount chiefs, had strengthened traditional authorities that oppose the new order. When independence arrived, many African countries were in dire straits: they lacked infrastructure and human capital, yet their considerable mistrust of the West and its ways often made them reluc-tant to borrow Western knowledge and use Western advisers.[27]

According to Bates (1981), the most effective political strategy for capturing and maintaining power in many parts of newly independent Africa has been to form a narrow winning coalition of the urban elite, including civil servants, the military, and captains of the incipient urban industrial sector. The narrow support base made it both possible and effective for the rulers to reward their followers not with public but with semiprivate and private goods, either through direct resource transfers or indirectly by granting them various monopoly rights.[28] In these primarily agricultural economies, the agricultural sector became the target of destructive exploitation by the state, thereby creating powerful disincentives for producers. Infrastructure projects, when they were not outright neglected, were used as chips to pay off political clients and divide and rule the countryside. In this environment, the constitutional structures that evolved put few restrictions on abuses of power, and the lack of democratic constraints raised the stakes in the political game.

These accounts of the political economy of decline in Africa do not assume that the leaders in the region are necessarily incompetent or immoral. Rather, they are seen as the product of particular historical circumstances that did not allow them to form legitimate, encompass-ing, and growth-oriented political coalitions. Sitting in the middle of this growth tragedy, Botswana, which was in dire straits at the time of its independence in 1966, is the great African exception. During the last third of the twentieth century, Botswana enjoyed the world's highest rate of per capita growth (over 7 percent per annum).[29] In a study that contains both their personal analysis of "how Botswana did it" and also literature and history surveys of the case, Acemoglu, Johnson, and Robinson (2001) argue that at independence, Botswana was favored

by a political history that enabled its leaders to lay the social foundations of growth.

Virtually no scholar claims that Botswana has been successful
because its leaders discovered and pursued novel and unconventional
economic policies (Acemoglu, Johnson, and Robinson 2001). On the
contrary, Botswana established a modern system of secure property
rights and a well-functioning market system and displayed discipline
and restraint in macroeconomic management. The puzzle concerning
the country's economic success centers on the social and political foundations of the policy choices made by its leaders. A look at the historical facts reported in Acemoglu, Johnson, and Robinson (2001), however, reveals such abundance of favorable background factors that
explanations of Botswana's high growth rate tend to become overde-
termined. My purpose here is not to provide new explanations for the
"Botswana economic miracle," which is already the subject of a large
literature, but to emphasize that the basic causal factors typically
involve autonomous features of the social environment at the time of
independence. Consider the following background factors

> As Botswana was only of peripheral interest in colonial times,
> Britain did not fully activate its "indirect rule" or take other
> measures that strengthened traditional leaders. Therefore, tra-
> ditional leaders were relatively weak when Britain left, and the
> national government could easily consolidate its hold on the
> country. Botswana's modernization efforts did not meet
> significant local resistance (Acemoglu, Johnson, and Robin-
> son 2001).
> As Botswana is relatively homogenous ethnically and linguisti-
> cally, its government did not face the challenge of dealing with
> sectional hostility and lack of cooperation among heteroge-
> neous groups, which is a major problem in many African
> countries (Easterly and Levine 1997).
> The political structure of traditional Botswana included advisory
> assemblies of adult males at local and national levels. Scholars
> debate whether these assemblies, which are not characteristic
> of precolonial African society, were rubber stamps or nascent
> form of democracy, but they seem to have contributed to polit-
> ical stability and democracy in the independence era (Ace-
> moglu, Johnson, and Robinson 2001, 23).[30]
> In Botswana, the traditional urban-rural political split and the
> usual African exploitation of the rural sector was not an invit-

ing political strategy. Agricultural interests were a dominant force in the winning coalition, with cattle owners holding up to two-thirds of the seats in the National Assembly (Acemoglu, Johnson, and Robinson 2001, 22).

These and perhaps other environmental factors apparently made it possible for the government of independent Botswana to survive while building institutions for economic growth. At independence, the country's formal educational level was dismally low.[31] Faced with initial lack of educated manpower, in an unusual move, the government sought out highly skilled but foreign-born civil servants and obtained various technical advice from abroad while giving highest priority to investment in education at home. For building its manufacturing sector, Botswana relied primarily on direct foreign investment, which has meant that domestic manufacturers demanding protection did not become important players on the political stage.

Finally, the case of Botswana and its favorable political environment enables us reject the "resource curse" hypothesis, at least as a general rule. The discovery after independence of enormously rich diamond mines did not throw the country off course. The diamond resources (which yearly account for about 40 percent of gross national product) have been used to support economic growth; elsewhere in Africa natural resources, have fueled civil wars rather than growth.

The experience of Botswana seems to confirm that the conventional wisdom concerning the appropriate mix of policies and property rights for growth also holds true for sub-Saharan Africa. But this case offers no lessons at all for the rest of Africa, because other countries cannot re-create their history. In their search for growth, the example of Botswana's political structure may of course help other countries to better formulate their targets for political development. However, the ability of nations to consciously reform their fundamental political structure in a relatively short time often appears to be limited, which is not the same as saying that reformers in these countries should give up. Finally, the Botswana case underlines our limited ability to recognize growth-friendly social conditions and predict where institutional reforms will succeed. In the 1960s, for example, many development economists were optimistic about African countries, such as Nigeria, but had little hope for South Korea. Indeed, our social models are incomplete.

Minimal Property Rights and Legal Transplants

Assuming that the reform measures have already passed through the formal political process, we focus here on problems with implementation. The question of failed reform is examined in the context of legal transplants.

The transfer of legal institutions between countries has had mixed success, indicating that production technologies travel better than social technologies. The transfer of legal rules is actually an attempt to transfer patterns of behavior, which requires that actors in the target country adjust and coordinate their policy models to a new institutional environment. Successful legal transfers also require that the authorities allocate sufficient resources to the "production of legality"—in other words, that they provide necessary infrastructure and inputs for the legal system. I will discuss some of the reasons why legal transplants fail. The other concern in this chapter lies with the minimal (formal or informal) legality required for supporting growth. In this context, I raise several questions. Is a weak or a strong state a greater threat to growth? Is there only a single appropriate structure for growth-promoting property rights? And can a low-income country take cost-reducing shortcuts when trying to provide minimal property rights for growth?

Diffuse Opposition to Institutional Reform

In chapter 1, I argued that the fundamental reason why some countries are poor and unable to use foreign production technologies is their inability to apply new social technologies necessary for supporting a modern economy. These countries do not set up growth-supporting institutions because their leaders lack incentives or political support to introduce reform or because their reform measures fail when they are tried. Institutional reform fails for many reasons, all of which involve incomplete social models. In this section we are concerned with diffuse social resistance rooted in incompatibility between old and new social technologies.

In the social sciences, perhaps the best known empirical case of incompatible social technologies is the study by Putnam with Leonardi and Nanetti (1993), which examines the attempt initiated in 1970 by the Italian authorities to reform the country's regional governments. The reform did not equalize the administrative performance of the northern and southern regions. The study attributes the failure in the south to the region's lack of social capital or civic capacity, which it measures by using communal traditions of association and civic engagement as indicators.[1] The Putnam study is both celebrated and controversial. In a review essay, Tarrow (1996), while praising the study, argues that Putnam's bottom-up model overemphasizes socio-economic and cultural factors and neglects the political dimension, especially relations between national and regional governments (see chapter 10).

There are three obvious analytical modes of theorizing about individual opposition to new laws and regulations. The first mode, common in standard political economy, focuses on strategic choices by rational actors who rely on policy models that correctly represent the nature of the game. It is usually assumed that the actors maximize their personal wealth and value new social rules only as instruments for reaching goals. The actors resist growth-oriented laws and regulations only when the rules conflict with their goals—for example, because the actors will not partake of the new prosperity or receive satisfactory compensation.

The second mode of diffuse resistance to reform retains all basic features of the first except that actors differ in how they model social structures. With uncertain knowledge of social structures, some people may oppose new rules and refuse to live by them because they do not believe that these rules will produce the intended results. The second mode emphasizes disagreements over means to a common end.

In the third mode of resistance, actors are still goal oriented but they value certain rules for their own sake and not only as means to an end, such as greater wealth. Valued rules reflect worldviews and moral codes and are stickier than ordinary (nonvalued) social rules, which actors readily reject when the rules unambiguously fail to yield expected outcomes.[2] Yet valued rules are not of infinite value. Most people stop living by valued rules if the opportunity cost of observing them becomes high enough—for example, they would rather break a dietary rule than starve to death. According to the third mode, social resistance to legal codes and other rules can arise when they conflict with social values.

When governments try to foster growth by introducing new social rules, people's responses are likely to reflect all three modes: pure (economic) strategy, uncertainty about means and ends, and valued rules, but the relative importance of the three modes will vary with circumstances. As a further complication, the transition to a new social equilibrium for an entire nation involves learning as well as complex coordination of changing individual expectations. The processes of learning, revision, and coordination are far simpler when an individual actor transfers from a dysfunctional social equilibrium in her home country to a foreign country with effective rules. The adjustment of a whole community to a new social equilibrium is comparable to interactive adjustments in a complex game with multiple potential equilibria, whereas the adaptation by a single individual to a new community is similar to adjustments by households and firms to fixed parameters in a competitive market. Not only is the task of coordination relatively simple, but also an individual who moves to a new society and brings with her a set of valued norms that are unknown and highly dysfunctional in the new setting probably will gradually ignore the old norms if the cost of compliance is transparently high.

The Problem with Legal Transplants

Thorough understanding of successes and failures of legal transplants, which are prime instances of international diffusion of social technologies, would greatly aid our understanding of social barriers to growth. As long as laws have existed, transplant countries have copied or had forced on them legal rules from source countries. Nevertheless, the literature is in fair agreement that we lack a robust theory with practical applications for what makes legal transplant succeed or fail. We do not lack evidence, theoretical or empirical, of positive links between secure property rights and economic performance. And although the law and economics literature provides valuable insights into the economic effects of modifying various aspects of modern legal systems, these are marginal adjustments within a stable system. Less is known about conditions of success when foreign legal systems or major parts thereof are planted in countries with traditional or dysfunctional systems. In a survey of the issues in judicial reform and economic development Messick (1999) identifies several unresolved puzzles, including the following:[3] Is a fair judicial (and legal) system a cause of good economic performance, or is there some third factor (beliefs, social capital) that affects both the quality of the legal system and economic performance? Does the success of judicial (and other legal) reforms depend on the order in which the various elements are introduced? Is it vital for success to integrate judicial reforms in developing countries with informal enforcement mechanisms, and how should that be done? Stephenson (2000) voices similar skepticism in his discussion of the current U.S.-China initiative for promoting the "rule of law" in China, a concept that the two governments define in different terms. He suggests that weak theoretical foundations may contribute to the failure of the initiative. When discussing current programs of legal reform, scholars often look to the failed law and development movement of the 1960s, when the United States made a concerted effort to provide legal assistance to countries in Asia, Africa, and Latin America to contribute to their economic development.[4] Much has been written to explain why the movement did not reach its goals. Messick (1999, 126–27) reports the following themes, among others: Law reform does not lead but adjusts to social change—the law is not an engine of social change. To close the gap in developing countries between the law on the books and the law in action requires more than better education for lawyers. The target countries did not find particularly attractive the unique American legal style—for example, lawyers' ability to influence changes in policy through litigation.

In fact, legal history provides examples of all degrees of success for legal transplants, from fully successful transplants to utterly failed ones. Modern comprehensive legal order for nations with market-based economies emerged in several European countries in the late eighteenth and early nineteenth centuries and eventually became one of Europe's most significant exports (Berkowitz, Pistor, and Richard 2000). The main transplants were English common law, the French law code, and the German law code. In our times, most countries that possess a comprehensive legal order have borrowed one of these three codes, which now constitute the core of the borrowers' legal systems, with the transplants mostly taking place in the late nineteenth and early twentieth centuries.[5] Recently, of course, there has been a rush of transplant activities in the former socialist countries of Europe and Asia.

Berkowitz, Pistor, and Richard (2000) estimate the relationship between (a) legal families and transplant methods and (b) levels of legality (security of property rights). The authors also estimate the statistical relationship between levels of legality and levels of economic development (measured by per capita income). With a sample of forty-nine countries—ten source countries and thirty-nine transplant countries—Berkowitz and his colleagues make an ambitious effort to classify the transplants (of the English, French and German codes) according to the nature of the transplant.[6] Using econometric methods, the study then attempts to estimate the transplant effect. The transplant effect measures the success in transferring a legal code (a social technology) from a source country to a transplant country. Berkowitz, Pistor, and Richard compare indexes of legality (legal security, or the effectiveness of institutions that enforce law) in source and transplant countries to empirically estimate the effect. A negative value for the transplant effect indicates that attempts to transfer a particular social technology were not entirely successful. The study finds that the transplant effect lowers a country's level of legality on average by about one-third compared with the source, which in turn is related to lower gross national product (GNP) per capita.[7] The econometric analysis shows that the "transplant effect can explain roughly 69 percent of the variance in legality, which in turn . . . explains 83 percent of the variance in GNP" (Berkowitz, Pistor, and Richard 1999, 3).[8] The legality variable in the study is a weighted index of five subjective proxies for the quality of the legal system.[9]

A transplant country's level of legality is determined largely by the methods used to acquire and apply the foreign code, but the actual legal family of origin (English, French, or German) is of little significance. The study develops somewhat complicated proxies for representing how law has been transplanted and received, but the basic distinction is between receptive and unreceptive transplants. The negative transplant effect on legality is associated only with unreceptive transplants. The basic assumption here is that domestic demand for the new legal order is required to make it effective. Countries receive involuntary transplants only as colonies (but not, for example, through defeat in a war). Involuntary transplants are always unreceptive, except when the inhabitants of the target country are familiar, for cultural and historical reasons, with the new legal tradition. Voluntary transplants are receptive when target country is either familiar with the new law or makes significant adaptation of the foreign law to its (formal and informal) preexisting legal order. Voluntary transplants are defined as unreceptive when there is neither significant adaptation nor prior familiarity.[10]

Let us pause to take a closer look at these concepts. Consider a voluntary unreceptive transplant—for example, the case of Turkey, which scores 11.84 on the legality index (where Switzerland has the highest score, 21.92). Turkey acquired the French law code in the years 1850–1927 but had relatively little familiarity with the French legal tradition and did not adapt the foreign legal system to Turkish traditions (according to Berkowitz, Pistor, and Richard's classifications).[11] Berkowitz, Pistor, and Richard analyze why many countries introduce new laws and keep them on the books if the new laws fail to produce a reasonably high level of legality. We can argue that deep changes in its structure of property rights apparently were inconsistent with the country's social equilibrium, but the question of why voluntary but unresponsive transplants persist remains. One possible answer is that the leaders keep ineffective law on the books in the hope that the laws will turn into an engine of social change.

Finally, the statistical coefficients of the study allow the authors to test (perhaps not too reliably) various counterfactual hypotheses.

For example, Ecuador received the French law during 1831–1881, without significant adaptation. Moreover, the citizens of Ecuador were not familiar with the transplanted law. Had Ecuador been in a position to develop its own legal system internally or to adapt the transplanted law better to its local conditions, back of the envelope calculations suggest that its 1994 GNP per capita would have increased from $1,200 U.S. to roughly Ireland's level ($13,000 U.S.). (Berkowitz, Pistor, and Richard 2000, 3)[12]

The study tells us that unreceptive transplant is not fate. Some countries reverse the transplant effect, implying that the econometric model underpredicts their legality performance. In the data set, Hong Kong, Taiwan, Singapore, Spain, and Portugal have higher levels of legality than the model predicts (Berkowitz, Pistor, and Richard 2000, 27).

Analyzing the Transplant Effect

Transplant effects—incomplete transfers of social technologies—such as Berkowitz, Pistor, and Richard (2000) attempt to estimate, are key elements in the puzzling behavior of growth laggards—why they seem to be unable to benefit from world knowledge. As a theoretical assessment, the Berkowitz study suggests that cognition and demand considerations must account for the transplant effect. People who use a particular legal code must understand and accept the principles on which it is based, and they must in some sense demand such a legal system.[13]

The literature is strongly divided on the relative importance of decentralized cultural factors (belonging to the third mode of analysis discussed previously) and political strategies (the first mode), with relatively little attention paid to problems of comprehending new systems (the second mode). These distinctions are of considerable practical importance. If the third mode of response (diffused defense of traditional valued rules) is the primary force behind major transplant effects, growth laggards face particularly dim prospects for rapidly upgrading their social technologies and catching up with high-income countries. A national government that introduces a modern legal code does not have many policy options available when society at large rejects the new laws because they conflict with valued rules. In contrast, if the opposition to the legal code is political and based on material interests, the government can at least contemplate economic, political, and legislative responses; to counter the second mode of resistance, the government can launch an educational campaign to try to convince the public of the good properties and effectiveness of the new legal order.

How, then, do we explain the puzzle of the transplant effect? Do new legal codes fail because of values and cognitive processes that are present in the culture of some countries but not in others? Are there more down-to-earth practical and political explanations of the transplant effect? How are cognitive and practical considerations linked? Should we perhaps ask whether cognitive adjustments in values and strategies will be forthcoming when practical and political conditions are met. Let me first briefly explain what I mean by practical and political considerations.

A legal system is more than the law on the books: it is a service industry that produces legality. Like other industries, a well-functioning legal system requires start-up investments, the services of skilled workers, various other inputs of reasonable quality, and informed consumers. A transplant country will not reach a high level of legality if it only acquires a new legal code but does not properly attend to start-up investments (such as buildings, recording systems, and diffusion of knowledge about the system) or fails to provide quality inputs for current operations. Such failures of a legal system are analogous to the failure of a firm that neglects plant and equipment, input quality, and marketing.

By political factors I am referring to the role of a legal system as a manifestation of the power structure in a community and to legal changes as tools in the struggle for control in a polity. When a modernizing Third World national government introduces a Western legal code, the measures, if they take hold, are bound to weaken or even destroy the power base and eventually the sources of wealth of influential segments of the local elite. A new official legal system can also change the relative wealth and power of regions and ethnolinguistic groups. As an illustration, consider a traditional legal system that gives power and legal authority to clans, does not allow women to inherit property, and restricts transfers of land to specific social groups. In this setting, when the national government introduces Western laws and judicial systems that, for example, encourage free sale of land, more is at stake for the rural community than clinging to valued rules for sentimental reasons. The new legal regime challenges the power base of traditional society. Those who stand to lose from the new system have strong economic incentives to use all available means to oppose and undermine the new order. Their response sometimes involves threats intended to prevent people from taking their cases to official courts and to induce people instead to send the cases to tribal councils for traditional arbitration. Another strategy is to overburden an understaffed, fledgling official court system by flooding it with new cases and then withdrawing them before a verdict is reached. Creating delays by deluging the courts or by using injunctions, local power brokers can crush weak opponents, including widows who seek to enforce their new inheritance rights, and later force an arbitrated solution on their own terms. Such situations make it difficult to distinguish the separate roles of valued rules, naked material interests, and confusion about the true properties of the new legal system.

Selective introduction of modern legal codes is a time-honored strategy for minimizing disruption and social resistance and protecting the interests of those who control the state. In Africa and elsewhere, the European colonial masters recognized that their laws might conflict with the material interests and values of traditional society, which made Europeans in some instances apply their laws only to European settlers. In other situations, the imperialists avoided implementing legal categories that were particularly likely to clash with traditional values but were of limited economic interest to the colonial power (Stephenson 2000). For example, a Western commercial code could be introduced but traditional family law could be left alone.[14] Selectivity is also a strategy used by China's contemporary leadership, which has tried to build fire walls between sectors of the legal system. The regime avoids categories of Western laws that are especially likely to undermine its autocratic rule but favors modern laws of ownership and contract that will make China a safe country in which to do business. Authoritarian Spain under Franco saw the advantage of a comparable strategy and gave great deal of independence to its judiciary but made sure that the courts handled only politically innocuous cases (Stephenson 2000, 18–19). In their attempts to modernize, democratic governments in the Third World might want to minimize confrontations with the traditional sector by initially seeking only those changes in the legal system that are essential for producing growth.[15] Such strategies for minimizing political frictions, however, raise questions about minimal property rights for growth, which is the subject of the sections that follow.

A new legal code is unlikely to function properly if, prior to its introduction, the government has not established reasonable degree of control over its territories and harmonized or contained deeply conflicting social interests. The new legal system is unlikely to be effective when criminal gangs run loose or when the state is unable to settle factional disputes, create a broad political base, expand its time horizon, and lower the stakes in the political game to make it less tempting to cheat. Some scholars and reformers turn the causal relationship around and argue that a modern legal code is a first-order policy instrument that affects target variables throughout the social system (see chapter 8). According to this view, a new legal code will shape social norms, harmonize material interests, consolidate a weak and fragmented state or tame a predatory one, and launch economic growth. I disagree with this view and find it unlikely that new formal laws per se can accomplish such changes.

Minimal Levels of Legality for Sustaining Growth

The question of minimal levels of legality necessary for sustaining economic growth involves both legal content and degree of enforcement. First, we must to ask what form of legality or property rights is most likely to create growth-promoting incentives and behavior. Market arrangements along a broad spectrum are growth friendly provided that they are well managed. The second issue is the security of exclusive property rights. Property rights are insecure either because the state exploits its subjects and violates their ownership rights or because private actors prey on each other and the state provides insufficient protection. The remainder of this chapter makes the case that growth-friendly market institutions often deviate from the ideal-type criterion of standard economics. In addition, I briefly consider whether a weak or a strong state is better for growth. The third issue concerns the division of labor between public and private organizations in protecting property rights and enforcing contracts: if the government does little to protect ownership rights, can private organizations define and protect these rights to a degree that is sufficient for growth—assuming that the government is weak or incompetent but not predatory? Finally, the chapter introduces the neglected issue of how to minimize the cost of supplying secure property rights in a poor country. Because swift introduction of a modern legal system imposes heavy burdens on a poor country that lacks human and physical capital, the cost-minimizing strategy may be to start by producing the minimal property rights required for growth, assigning refinements of the system to later stages in the country's development.

The Diverse Institutional Foundations of Growth

When mainstream economists evaluate different regimes of property rights, they tend to rely on neoclassical models of general equilibrium and welfare economics. These images of optimal allocation of resources in a stationary economy, where the actors have complete information and property rights are fully defined, have limited relevance in a world of incomplete markets, fundamental uncertainty, learning, and technical change and where social and political constraints circumscribe choices and affect outcomes. For example, most economists would expect dire results and give a failing grade to government policy that invites huge conglomerates to monopolize a developing country's key industrial subsectors and rewards the monopolists with subsidized loans from a government-controlled, repressed financial system. Yet Korea used such methods in the 1970s to build from scratch its heavy and chemical industries, which helped generate the so-called Korean growth miracle that was driven by the mammoth *chaebol* conglomerates (Woo-Cumings 2001).

Context matters when government policymakers stray from the laissez-faire model, encourage monopolies, and interfere in market and industrial affairs. In the Korea case, government-sponsored monopolies were an integral part of a hard-nosed general policy of growth carried out by a strong government that initially did not suffer serious agency problems that could undermine its policy. In many other countries, when the state favors firms with monopoly rights, influences their production plans, and subsidizes their loans, the measures are unrelated to any systematic strategy for achieving growth but rather rewards for political support.

The Korean case tells us not only that context matters but also that economic regimes, far from being static, are comparable to organisms that grow and develop through interactions with their environment. In Korea, the top-down strategy of symbiosis between the government and the *chaebol* conglomerates gradually became dysfunctional, requiring difficult reforms (Woo-Cumings 2001). The two lessons that context matters and that internal dynamics gradually change economic regimes have general validity. Economic miracles are also economic mysteries, as illustrated, for example, by the various contributions to Stiglitz and Yusuf 2001, which documents (not always consciously) our general confusion about the interpretation of growth miracles and their changing fortunes.[16]

If any generalization is possible, it is perhaps that the many variants of growth miracles have one feature in common: a growth-friendly political equilibrium. A state where all levels of government support or at least accept a strategy for growth, whether imposed from the top down or growing from the bottom up, is likely to discover through trial and error some approach to economic transformation that suits its particular environment. Such market-oriented but mixed strategies often seem unorthodox according to standard economic theory, but standard theory really does not deal with structural transformations. The other part of this generalization is that in organizing property rights for growth, there are no final solutions. All regimes contain endogenous dynamics, which, along with exogenous shocks, are the main factors responsible for bringing down or temporarily tarnishing economic miracles of various kinds. No institutional setup is insulated from the forces of decline, whether it is the one supporting the industrial revolution in England; the Gold Standard; the early Soviet Union growth miracle; the post–Second World War German growth miracle; miraculous incomes policies (for jointly achieving stable prices and low rates of inflation) of some European countries in the 1960s and 1970s; Scandinavian welfare systems; and undoubtedly some of the twenty-first century miracles. Only societies capable of continually renewing their property rights structures and adjusting them to new technologies, external shocks, and internal dynamics are able to sustain growth indefinitely. The institutional environment of a country loses effectiveness when the authorities fail to adjust the system to new economic developments or when new political forces change the country's institutions for the worse. New developments include new technologies, new economic opportunities (for example, in foreign trade), and gradual deterioration of social mechanisms. Entrenched interests often block necessary adjustments to new circumstances, although ignorance about appropriate responses is also to blame. A new political balance often emerges through changes associated with economic growth, including the rise and fall of regions and industries or population changes. Political forces that emphasize redistribution at the expense of growth may replace previous growth-oriented coalitions.

Which Is a Greater Threat to Growth, a Strong or a Weak State?

A discussion of minimal levels of legality necessary for growth cannot avoid mentioning the possible threat to growth from the state itself; indeed, much has been written about the relative merits of weak versus strong states. The main point of this section is that we cannot generalize about the growth-friendliness of weak or strong states. Not only does context matter, but also we must distinguish between growth-oriented and predatory states or governments.

When they prey on economic agents, governments lower the expected rate of return on private investment. Predatory state behavior involves outright confiscation of assets or arbitrary taxation, bribes in exchange for essential business licenses and monopoly rights, and corrupt courts. Cross-country regressions show that insecure property rights adversely affect growth when the quality of property rights is represented by an index composed of various indicators of corruption and uncertainty (J. Svensson 1998). The findings of such cross-country regressions are supported by a recent microlevel study of firms in five former socialist countries in Eastern Europe and the former Soviet Union that shows that even firms already in operation respond to insecure property rights by reducing new investment (Johnson, McMillan, and Woodruff 1999). Johnson, McMillan, and Woodruff find that entrepreneurs in the same country but in different industries or firms do not share identical expectations concerning the security of property rights, which is not surprising. Not all industries or firms are equally vulnerable to exploitation because of their different locations, physical features, and other factors.

A strong, well-organized state can be good or bad for economic growth, depending on its orientation. A powerful predatory state is bad for growth, but a strong growth-oriented state promotes growth unless its policymakers are guided by dysfunctional policy models and fail to learn from their mistakes. When governmental weakness brings about disorder, rebellion and chaos, strengthening of either growth-friendly or predatory states may help growth, because even predator states attempt to uphold some social order, if only to protect their rule and revenue from private predators. Yet when the government is weak, private actors and organizations sometimes fill the vacuum to create private order and build tolerably effective institutional environment. Therefore, no simple generalizations can be made about the implications for economic performance when a weak state becomes even weaker.

History shows that economic progress is sometimes possible even during revolutionary times. In their careful microlevel study of revolutionary Mexico, Haber, Razo, and Maurer (2003) find that new investments and entry of new firms did not dry up during the 1918–34 period of political instability and social turmoil. The growth rate of the Mexican economy in this period did not differ substantially from that rate during 1890–1905, when the country was stable and the economy booming. The Haber, Razo, and Maurer also find that outright warfare in Mexico 1914–17 interfered with production and new investment by disrupting communications, although physical destruction of plant and equipment was less than many scholars have believed. In contrast, Albania of the communist period demonstrates how strong and stable predatory states stifle growth. In 1990, Albania was the poorest country in Europe with GNP per capita of about $1,250, although this small country is endowed with rich reserves of chrome, nickel, copper, natural gas, iron, coal, lignite, and oil and is located close to some of the most developed countries in the world (Biberaj 1991).

Can Private Order Provide Minimal Property Rights for Growth?

The previous section introduced the question of whether private actors and their organizations are able provide minimal property rights for growth when the state fails to do so. Both in modern and historical times, specialized production and trade are found in many countries that have dysfunctional or virtually nonexisting official legal systems and rely in instead on private order. Furthermore, private-order property rights are found also in countries, such as the United States, that have highly developed systems of public order.

There exists a substantial body of literature with an empirical bent that examines how private-order mechanisms enforce ownership and contractual rights. In an important study employing a game-theoretic approach, Greif (1994) analyzes two forms of private-order organization of Mediterranean trade (individualistic and collectivistic) in the Middle Ages. Landa (1994) examines how firms in twentieth-century Asia relied on ethnic ties to support transactions, and Milgrom, North, and Weingast (1990) study the role of the medieval law merchant and the champagne fairs in protecting long-distance trade. Finally, in an often-cited study, Ellickson (1991) examines how private order governs relations among ranchers in modern California's Shasta County, and Bernstein (1992) does the same for the diamond trade in her study of the New York Diamond Dealers' Club.

In advanced market economies, reliance on private order is most common in groups with restricted membership because in some such groups the transaction costs of securing complex exchange are lower under private arrangements than public ones. In those cases, however, private order is nested in an effective public legal system. In the developing world, there is evidence to suggest that certain countries, such as China, have been able to move through the early stages of modernization and industrialization without the support of modern law, relying instead on private or local order (see chapter 10). These countries usually do not have outright predatory governments, but their legal systems are antiquated or dysfunctional.

To analyze private order and private enforcement, the literature typically relies on noncooperative game theory as well as the economics of property rights. In the economics of property rights, the cost of enforcing contacts depends on transaction complexities, characteristics of traders, problems with measuring quality, and the time path of transactions. Private enforcement is effective when two parties are locked into a long-term trading relationship because switching to other traders is costly. When each trader estimates that the (present value of) expected net benefits from future transactions will outweigh the gains from cheating in current exchanges (which would put end to the relationship), enforcement is spontaneous. Self-enforcement of contracts can also emerge in personalized multilateral exchanges in closely knit groups where information flows freely. Reputation and social norms protect trade in these environments, and in groups based on ethnicity and religion, disapproval and expulsion usually carry greater weight than do sanctions in groups based entirely on commercial relationships (Landa 1994).

Bilateral and multilateral exchange based on spontaneous private order within networks of close-knit groups has a useful role in all societies, but is dysfunctional as the general social technology for exchange in developed economies. With greater specialization, expanding markets, and growing need for impersonal transactions, rising information costs block trade because informal trading networks are not practical in such circumstances. In reputation-based trade, new firms find it difficult to enter the market, and traders, fearing high enforcement risks, often turn down offers of low price and high quality when actors outside their networks offer these bargains (McMillan and Woodruff 2000).

When economic development and scale effects have made informal exchange institutions ineffective (at the margin), private trade associations and other business organizations sometimes can effectively replace informal networks (McMillan and Woodruff 2000). Well-functioning private associations standardize commercial practices, collect information about contract violations, and coordinate punishments. Enforcement through business organizations is effective if, prior to contracting, members always check whether their prospective trading partners have a history of breaching contractual obligations with other organization members. If the organization refuses to help in enforcing contracts of members who neglect to seek advance information about their trading partners, the members have less incentive to free ride on the organization (Milgrom, North, and Weingast 1990).

Enforcement through private business organizations has an important disadvantage: the organizations have a common propensity to monopolize the market and even block technological change, especially when the organizations represent only one side of the market, particularly the sellers (Mokyr 1990). According to McMillan and Woodruff (2000, 43–44), neutral intermediaries include medieval law merchants, Taiwanese trading companies, and the New York diamond-traders association. One-sided organizations, usually on the sellers' side, are the medieval guilds, the Japanese bank clearinghouse, and the U.S. Fur Dressers' and Fur Dyers' Association. In the early stages of modernization, business organizations, in place of the government, often supply tolerably secure property rights for their industries. Although business organizations tend to monopolize trade and limit technological change, these problems can also occur under public order. The state, as it becomes stronger, is likely to react to private organizations that have assumed quasi-governmental roles in supplying property rights. To protect their prerogatives, governments will to deprive private organizations of this power and upgrade the legal infrastructure of the state or, in the worst case, suppress private law and create a vacuum.

The purely economic choice between public and private order ultimately depends on the relative cost of each system. To function properly, private order requires rather strenuous collection of information, which the alternative of having recourse to an efficient judicial system will modify. McMillan and Woodruff (2000) find in their study of transition firms in Eastern Europe and the former Soviet Union that public order and private order complement each other. When the two are complements, the value of a marginal unit of private order institutions increases with the development of the formal legal system, and efficiency requires that the two forms grow together. McMillan and Woodruff also find that informal networks and formal legal systems are substitutes, which means that the importance of enforcement through informal networks should fade as the legal system matures.

Minimizing the Costs of a Legal System: Clear Rules or a Sophisticated Judiciary?

The complementary relationship between private-order institutions and the law suggest that at some point in the economic development process, a modern law code, especially laws of ownership and contract, will be needed. Toward the end of the twentieth century, for example, the national leaders of China felt that its development process required modern commercial laws and that the reliance on locally supplied rights could not continue indefinitely. Building a modern legal system makes heavy demands on the resources of a poor country, especially on its human capital. In some low-income countries, a sophisticated legal system would require a substantial share of the country's stock of high-quality college graduates. Therefore, we can ask whether in building its legal system, a poor country profitably could make shortcuts and refine the system at a later date.

The least-cost strategy for building an effective legal infrastructure in stages is largely a matter of speculation. R. A. Posner (1998) and Hay, Shleifer, and Vishny (1996) make a case for a rules-first strategy. They believe that a poor country faces a fundamental choice between using its scarce resources for costly reforms of the legal system and using those resources for a much less costly investment in revising its legal rules to make them relatively efficient, clear, and simple. In many cases, the reform of laws and regulations will require throwing out inefficient rules that survive from a previous period. Posner distinguishes between the substantive efficiency of rules, which refers to their direct economic impact (the extent to which they improve the allocation of resources), and the procedural efficiency of rules, which depends on how they affect the cost or accuracy of using the legal system.

In legal systems, open-ended standards are the alternative to clear and simple rules. Standards involve concepts such as bad faith, negligence, or unreasonable restraints of trade, and sound decisions based on standards tend to require sophisticated lawyers and judges and a solid body of past cases to provide legal precedents. When the cost of hurriedly upgrading the judiciary is very high, investing in the provision of clear and simple rules may be the best choice. The disadvantage of simple substantive rules is that they almost always are incomplete in that they do not cover all possible situations and states. Decisions based on ill-fitting rules can be inefficient, but when the fit is reasonably good, somewhat unsophisticated judges will find it easy to detect violations and come to sound decisions because they do not require sophisticated legal reasoning. Furthermore, it is easy for outside observers to evaluate whether or not judges are following the law. Well-designed procedural rules can increase the productivity of a struggling judicial system—for example, by recognizing only written contracts or by requiring that claims of alleged infringement of rights be filed within three years. Rules that require certain disputes to be referred to binding arbitration will lower he judicial workload and encourage the establishment of trade and other business organizations (R. A. Posner 1998).

Those who advocate a rules-first strategy for developing a legal system in a poor country hope that a simple start will encourage economic growth and initiate a virtuous cycle of growth, more wealth, and new demand for a better legal order. If the quality of the judiciary is initially below a certain level of competence and honesty, however, the judicial system may simply ignore clear-cut rules, no matter how efficient they are, suggesting once again how difficult it is to generalize about minimal property rights for growth.

Conclusion
The Subtle Art of Major Institutional Reform

The new institutional economics has made good progress in analyzing the role of institutions in shaping economic outcomes, but the field has made less headway formulating clear principles of institutional policy in many crucial areas.[1] Throughout the world, reformers, convinced that institutions matter for growth, increasingly seek ways to improve their institutional environment. In this book, I discuss opportunities and limits for major institutional reform when relative economic backwardness or imperfect institutions are sustained by social equilibria, when exogenous shocks and new social models are the chief forces destabilizing such equilibria, and when history, political economy, and incomplete knowledge constrain the potential reform path. The main novelty in my approach is an emphasis on incomplete and variable social models that guide decisions by policymakers as well as other actors. My concept of social models is directly related to the idea of mental models in the work of North (1990).[2] In the foregoing chapters, I explained what I mean by social models and attempted to make the concept relevant for the study of institutional reform.

Rather than rehashing the main argument of the previous chapters, this conclusion employs an empirical example to summarize my views. The example concerns the problem of introducing effective institutions for managing ocean fisheries. Institutional failure in ocean fisheries has become a major problem worldwide for both rich and poor countries, leading to overfishing and even the disappearance of fish stocks. I argue that the governance problem in ocean fisheries illustrates how economic progress often depends jointly on new production technologies and matching advances in social technologies. The common-pool characteristics of ocean fisheries imply that improved production technology as well as greater demand for fish can have destructive consequences if these developments are not matched by appropriate social technologies. In the last fifteen years of the twentieth century, Iceland borrowed and modified a new social technology for managing its 200-

mile fisheries zone. The experience vividly demonstrates how exogenous shocks, political economy, and incomplete social models shape large-scale institutional reform.

A Modeling View of the World

Institutional reform is a game involving players with incomplete knowledge who cope by basing their actions and strategies on incomplete social models of varying quality. Social technologies are models that explain—not necessarily accurately—how various elements of social institutions interact, creating particular regularities in behavior and aggregate outcomes. Policy models, also a subcategory of social models, describe the relationship between goals of public or individual policy and the instruments for reaching the goals. All actors, both public and private, use policy models to formulate their strategies.

As the previous chapter reports, reformers have often failed to transplant social institutions from one country to another and to make the institutions work equally well in the new setting. Modern political economy provides several explanations of failed reform and the perseverance of imperfect institutions. The incentives of the ruling political coalition in a target country are sometimes incompatible with the new institutions, powerful special interests may ensure that only scaled-down or unsatisfactory versions of the new social technology are introduced, or unorganized, decentralized resistance can undermine the reform effort. To complete this list of obstacles, I have added social models as an important variable. Social models incorporate visions of how the social world works, in both practical and ethical terms. Institutional reform can fail when authorities or the public lack practical understanding of new social technologies or when critical social groups see new arrangements as illegitimate.

Recognition of incomplete models modifies our views of the process of reform. We are not surprised to see unexpected outcomes, uninformed responses to shocks (such as ill-advised rejection of workable systems), interactive learning, and confusing feedback from major social experiments, as well as problems with embedding alien institutions in a new environment. The introduction of social models as a variable in the policy process also draws attention to public and private strategies aimed at promoting particular models.

Imperfect Institutions and Ocean Fisheries

Modern industrial countries usually rely on well-defined and secure property rights in all major activities, thus restricting to tolerable levels

unproductive and wasteful activities. There are two important exceptions to this generalization: the property rights guiding the use of environmental resources and ocean fisheries. In all parts of the world,
ocean fisheries are exploited in a wasteful manner. Until the Law of the
Sea Convention in 1976 created a 200-mile exclusive economic zone for
coastal states, multinational open access regimes typically prevailed in
valuable fishing grounds. The fishing nations were not willing or able
to jointly manage ocean fisheries in an effective manner. In addition to
political considerations, high transaction costs as well as new entry by
third parties thwarted regulatory attempts. The consequences of open
access for valuable natural resources are well established in the literature. They involve overuse and depletion of the resource rent as well as
wasteful races to be first to capture the resource (Gordon 1954). It was
initially expected that with a 200-mile exclusive coastal zone, fishing
countries would effectively manage their domestic fisheries. These
hopes have not been realized. Current technologies and high transaction costs make it impractical to enforce individual exclusive rights to
specific migratory schools of fish, and traditional government regulations of ocean fisheries have very often failed to protect stocks and
keep costs down.[3]

In an article lamenting the poor state of deep-sea fisheries (Broad
and Revkin 2003), the *New York Times* argues that Iceland's recent
experiment with a new social technology may point the way to effective
institutional reform in fisheries management: "The most important
recovery strategy of all is simply to fish less, experts say. This can be
managed in many ways. Harvest limits can be set with quotas allotted
to individuals in a fishery who can then trade them. Iceland has set the
standard for this approach, which has also been adopted in a few
American fisheries. . . . Environmental and conservation groups,
including Cato, support the practice." I now sketch the turbulent history of institutional reform in the Iceland fisheries, emphasizing the
role of political economy and social models.[4]

The Icelandic Fisheries: Shocks, New Social Models, and Institutional Reform

In Iceland during the process of modernization, the fisheries lubricated
the country's engine of growth. Although their importance is declining,
the fisheries remain crucial for the country's economic performance,
accounting for 40–50 percent of total exports of goods and services.
The institutional environment of the fisheries affects not only the effectiveness of the industry but also economic growth, the distribution of

wealth, and various other macroeconomic properties of the national economy. In a mature democratic country, a pivotal role for a single industry has two important implications: It is very costly for the authorities to tolerate grossly inefficient institutions in this industry, and the industry lobby is very powerful, but its interests tend to be encompassing and to overlap somewhat with the national interest.[5]

In Iceland, an unanticipated series of supply shocks in the fisheries upset the social equilibrium and created opportunities for reform. The first shock occurred toward the end of the 1960s, when the herring fisheries collapsed.[6] By the mid-1970s scientists had issued warnings about the precarious state of various species of groundfish, especially the cod. In the 1980s, these reports became more strident, the catch was falling, and an inefficient rat race generated by a fishing-days regulatory system raised costs.[7] Falling total catch, increasing costs, and huge industry losses were unacceptable for Iceland. The authorities, influential segments of the industry, and the public gradually came to judge the institutions managing the fisheries as imperfect. Pivotal actors were now ready to consider new social technologies for governing the industry.

The reformers had few choices. E. Ostrom (1990) documents cases where local actors who share common-pool resources self-organized and set internal governance rules for effectively using and managing their resources—for example, the utilization of a pasture or a lake. But ocean fisheries in Iceland lack most of the characteristics required for spontaneous self-management, according to the theories and evidence provided by Ostrom. Libecap's (1989) work on fisheries regulation also supports this conclusion. In particular, the industry's strong commercial orientation, heterogeneity of operators and the means of production, and the scattering of the industry all over Iceland hamper self-organization. As for a conventional market solution, simply leaving an unregulated and scarce common-pool resource to market forces will bring perverse results (Gordon 1954). Finally, the experience with direct government regulations had been unsatisfactory: the regulatory regime that the government introduced for managing the new 200-mile zone had malfunctioned. The problems were partly caused by inherent contradictions in the system, which created incentives for excess capacity, and partly caused by weak enforcement of both government targets for total catch and fleet size. By the mid-1980s, reform had become unavoidable, and both government and industry were ready to revise their models and consider a new social technology, individual transferable quotas (ITQs), which introduce elements of exclusive property rights into the common-pool regime of the fisheries.

In the mid-1980s, ITQs were best known internationally as innovative and effective instruments for limiting the cost of industrial air pollution and had found application especially in North America. A market in tradable pollution permits has the advantage of assigning the task of cleaning up industrial processes to firms that can do so at least cost. Favorable experience with tradable pollution permits readily suggested that the method (social technology) could be extended to other common-pool problems. A smooth market in tradable fishing quotas obviously would assign fishing rights to the most efficient fishing firms. In Iceland, small-scale experiments with individual quotas had begun when herring fisheries were resumed in 1976 and had been added for capelin in 1980. A 1985 law extended the system to the vital groundfish, such as the cod, and 1990 legislation completed the system. ITQs became the management system for all of Iceland's ocean fisheries, except that small boats had their own system.

The Limits to Reform

Although fear of collapsing fish stocks had induced authorities to revise their models of fisheries management and created a willingness to experiment with radical reform, policymakers did not have a free hand when the ITQ experiment began. The structure of an ITQ system can take many shapes, each with its particular efficiency and distributional properties. Icelandic policymakers faced several important choices when they implemented the system, but the political economy of their choices is fairly obvious. I focus here on four central issues:

1. A system of individual quotas is possible without trading or with various restrictions on trading in the quotas. Forbidding or limiting trade dilutes the efficiency properties of an ITQ system but may protect high-cost operators, which can be politically expedient—for example, as part of regional policies.
2. The government can initially give the quotas away, sell them, or rent them. The authorities must decide between free quotas and some form of fishing fees.
3. The government must also decide which social groups should initially receive quotas and which ones should be permitted to

buy or rent them at later stages. Possible candidates for these rights include owners of licensed fishing vessels, fishers, the processing industry, economically depressed regions, the public at large, and foreigners.

4. To be healthy and economically successful, ocean fisheries requires management that takes an encompassing view and attends to biological conditions. The responsibility for overall management can be divided in various ways between the industry and government agencies.

Faced with these choices, Iceland's policymakers made the following decisions: They permitted and encouraged trade in quotas but limited trading rights to domestic owners of licensed vessels.[8] In the first round, the government handed out individual quotas for free. Initial allocation was tied to active fishing vessels, with each vessel receiving quota shares in proportion to its catch history in previous years. Fishing rights are restricted to Icelandic citizens. The government manages the resource, setting total allowable quotas for each species, monitoring the operators, organizing marine biological research, and taking action to protect the resource, for example by temporarily closing breeding areas. I will now consider these decisions and their significance.

Compared to other private industries, the government is deeply involved in the fisheries under Iceland's ITQ system, handling issues that usually lie with the firms themselves or with industrial associations. The management and protection of fish stocks rests almost entirely with the government. The government sets and enforces rules determining mesh size and fishing gear, puts sensitive locations off limits to fishers, and regulates the size of fish that can be harvested. Moreover, government agents monitor the location and catch of every vessel. These factors underpin a hybrid ownership structure that combines both private and state property rights. Under the arrangement, a clearly defined set of private operators has exclusive rights of access and use of a share in total allowable catch (TAC) as well as transfer rights, but the state has taken over various ownership roles, especially the ones of maintenance and protection. The law further complicates the ownership structure by specifying that the Icelanders collectively own the resources in the 200-mile zone, explicitly stating that fishing rights acquired under the quota system are temporary and can be withdrawn without compensation.

When a government gives away valuable rights, such as pollution quotas, fisheries quotas, or licenses to operate taxis, and permits trade in these rights, the initial recipients receive windfall gains, whereas subsequent owners who purchase these rights from the original beneficiaries make no such gains: In a well-functioning secondary market, the purchase price of quotas or licenses equals the expected net future gain of acquiring the rights.[9] The decision in Iceland to grandfather the quotas and hand them out for free is not unique. When governments issue formal user rights—quotas—to long-established industries that already have made substantial specialized investments, the most common method of allocation is to grandfather the rights and hand them out for free. In contrast, for relatively new activities with short user history and where previous specialized investments are not important, quotas or licenses are more likely to be sold or auctioned off. Iceland is a special case, however, in that its chief resource-based industry is of vast significance for the national economy, which usually is not true of developed countries.

Delayed Reaction

In modern Iceland, few public measures have evoked such outrage as the "free quotas." The interesting problem for us to explain is not why the government followed a grandfather rule and initially allocated free quotas but rather why the outrage came with a substantial delay and, when it came, why its intensity was so great that outsiders find it hard to understand.

The legislation of 1985 and 1990 that established the ITQ system was not particularly controversial. At the time, institutional failure had wrecked the fisheries, creating alarming and well-publicized losses. In the public mind, the industry was broken. When deciding how to allocate the individual quotas, the government faced a broken industry that had a "first possession" claim on the resource and major political muscle. Both political and practical consideration ruled out levying user fees on the industry.

The reason that negative reactions to the "free quotas" came with a delay is related to the problem of incomplete models. In economics, Coase's (1960) theorem (a social model) provides the standard explanation for why tradable quotas would gradually increase profitability in the industry and raise expectations about the market price of quotas. According to Coase, free exchange allocates property rights to actors who most value the rights, except when high transaction costs prevent trade. In a fishery, quota trade would eventually lower cost curves (through reorganization of the industry), raise output price (because of more effective marketing), and increase profits. It took most members of the international economics profession several years to fully appreciate Coase's contribution, and it is still debated. In Iceland of 1985–90, only a few experts saw the dynamics of tradable fisheries quotas in terms the Coasian model.[10] Most people typically associated future recovery in the industry with restoration of fish stocks, such as the cod, and even the market for quotas initially did not anticipate that a sizable portfolio of fishing quotas would within years be worth millions of dollars. At the time of this writing (2003), the fishing industry is booming, but relatively little progress has been made in restoring the valuable groundfish stocks.[11]

Before discussing the outrage explosion, a few words are needed about the problem of evaluating major institutional reform. The feedback from comprehensive reform is often uncertain because all other things are not equal. Mixed signals from a social experiment, however, muddle the debate and set the stage for "modeling wars." In Iceland, much confusion has resulted from the fact that the primary economic benefits from the ITQ experiment to this point have been caused by radical reorganization of the industry rather than restoration of fish stocks. To further complicate matters, evidence and theory suggest that rising profits in the fisheries have resulted not only from the new ITQ system but also from two additional factors: major improvement in production technologies and radical reform of the financial system (a new social technology). New production technologies include general-purpose and large-scale fishing vessels that process the fish on board. In recent years, several small communities that specialize in fish processing have lost their businesses.[12] Those affected often put the entire blame on the ITQ system. The financial reform of the 1990s was another turning point. Prior to the reform, politically appointed managers controlled the financial system, the real interest rate on loans was negative, and a loan was equivalent to a subsidy. In this environment, the granting of credit often reflected political motives or cronyism. Financial reform deprived the fisheries of hidden subsidies and compelled the industry to rationalize its operations. As they overlap in time, the effects of the three factors—ITQs, new production technologies, and financial reform—are not separable. Incomplete models and the confluence of explanatory factors have muddled and prolonged the quota debate: Some critics focus solely on restoration of fish stocks and do not consider restoration of the industry. And when industry performance or regional dislocation is under consideration, those debating often feel free to focus on only one of three closely correlated variables.

Lord Perry's Question and Regulatory Overfishing

Broad and Revkin (2003) note that the most important recovery strategy is simply to fish less, which requires selecting an appropriately low value for total allowable catch and enforcing that target. With the recognition of 200-mile fisheries zones, valuable fisheries are usually under government regulation, which implies that overfishing is a failure of regulation or regulatory overfishing. In an ITQ system, if the government sets excessively high targets for total allowable catch or is unable to enforce its TAC target, the effect on fish stocks is more or less identical to what would happen under any other regime, given the same level of excessive fishing.

Eagle and Thompson (2003) report that in 1995 the House of Lords held a series of hearings on the distressed state of the British fishing industry. At the inquiry, Lord Perry of Walton asked why (almost) all fisheries management systems have failed to stop gross overfishing. Lord Perry wondered which of three factors was mostly to blame: wrong advice from scientists about total allowable catch, the propensity of politicians to set larger targets than scientists recommend, and failure by fishers to obey the regulations.[13] "Those to whom the question was posed, the Fisheries Secretary and the Deputy Director of the Directorate of Fisheries Research, did not answer it" (651). Experts apparently do not have a ready answer for Lord Perry's question. Again we face incomplete models and data. Eagle and Thompson, scholars at the Stanford Fisheries Policy Project, take up the challenge using data from two federally managed overfished fisheries in the United States. The authors identify a subtle research question: "While some research has previously been done on the potential political and social *causes* of overfishing in regulated fisheries . . . , there is little to none on the question of *how these forces actually manifest themselves* in fisheries management (e.g. to what extent do fisheries managers ignore scientific advice or refuse to enforce rules?)" (651). In other words, we possess only very uncertain and incomplete social models of the subtle relationship between management systems and the behavior of politicians, administrators, and fishers.[14] In Iceland, many experts believe that the ITQ system has modified the behavior of scientists, government, and fishers. Overfishing is less extreme under ITQs than under prior regulatory regimes, but fears of the consequences of overfishing may have increased over time and independently constrained behavior.[15]

Incomplete models of marine biology also undermine fisheries management. Policy models for fisheries management are of little value unless they can draw on reliable knowledge about fish stocks. Uncertainty about the dynamics of life in the ocean, however, complicate fisheries management, including enforcement. Unexpected developments of fish stocks provide fuel for peddlers of alternative theories about life in the ocean and about appropriate management techniques.[16]

Fighting over the "Free Quotas"

In Iceland of the 1990s, the quota debate heated up until it became red hot and dominated the social discourse. The system has its supporters, but the opposition has been fierce. The bulk of the opposition comes mainly from two sources. The first group consists of people who believe that economic life in some small communities (usually including their own) has been adversely affected by the ITQ system, which they blame for a growing concentration of the industry in a few regional centers.[17] These critics typically want to abolish the system in its entirety and replace with some form of direct regulation, such as a fishing-days system.[18] Their opposition is best characterized as protection of personal material interests. From our viewpoint, the other main class of opponents is theoretically more interesting because here the opposition is essentially ideological and rests on models of legitimacy. The core belief is that the fisheries are the property of the Icelandic people, and parliament essentially committed theft when it initially gave free quotas to the industry. The most visible advocates of the purely moral view are intellectuals, both of the Left and of the Right. The struggle is primarily ideological because the material circumstances of these critics would not significantly improve if the government were to heed their proposals.[19] Their actions instead represent social models at war (and perhaps utility functions where increases in the wealth of "undeserving others" enter with a negative sign).

To overturn the extant ITQ system, the opponents require a majority vote in parliament. Hence, norm entrepreneurs have emerged for creating public outrage at the system and to turn the opposition into a broad political movement.[20] The general public usually is not very interested in industrial organization or competing forms of management and regulation, but a grossly illegitimate actions by the government are another matter. To explain why free quotas constitute theft, the intellectual leaders of the anti-ITQ movement have developed models of legitimate ownership, which they often put in historical context with links to familiar cultural symbols. Central to the argument is the idea of a "national commons" or "property of the nation," and for illustrating these concepts, reference is made to ownership of the ancient manuscripts of the Icelandic sagas (which the Danish government generously gave back to the Icelanders in the 1970s) or ownership of the national park at Thingvellir, the birthplace in 930 of the country's parliament. Attempts are also made to link national ownership of ocean resources to the country's ancient communal mountain pastures.[21] Various moral and practical arguments are both common and popular. Clergymen have preached in their Sunday sermons that it is immoral to buy and sell fish in the ocean before it is caught (although for generations Icelandic sport fishermen have bought licenses from farmers and other owners to fish for trout and salmon in the country's lakes and rivers). Another popular argument is that undeserving winners in the quota lottery, like all winners of big lottery prizes, will dissipate their wealth, sometimes with disruptive economic effects.

The social model of national ownership, which had a central role in the classic twentieth-century debate about private and public ownership, has returned in a new form and a new mode, now involving ownership of natural resources rather than ownership of factories. A 2000 report to the Icelandic parliament by a committee of high-level civil servants and experts on the subject of utilization of natural resources has recommended that the legislature claim national ownership over all natural resources in the country that currently are not strictly under exclusive ownership (including much of the highlands in central Iceland and the ocean) (Auðlindanefnd, Álitsgerð 2000). The report further recommends that the government put nonowned and currently abundant natural resources in custody of the nation to prevent surprise appropriation by private actors. It is recommended that the country's constitution be changed to explicitly recognize these two new forms of property. As a sign of the authors' preoccupation with their new ownership models, the report recommends that wind energy, notoriously abundant and bothersome in Iceland, be put in custody of the nation. Wind energy in Iceland will never be a scarce resource; therefore, the recommendation concerns the ethics of ownership. If private entrepreneurs decide to invest in windmills for generating electricity, they should pay the owners (the nation) for use of the resource: free use would be theft.[22]

At the beginning of the twenty-first century, outside observers may find it hard to understand why the debate about the free quotas is still alive. The original free allocation of groundfish quotas took place between 1985 and 1990. A great many of those who received the initial windfall gain have sold their quotas, and most current owners have received no windfall. Moreover, the industry's organization has changed dramatically: many of the biggest firms are now owned by large groups of stockholders. To an outsider, a proposal for recalling the quotas is an attempt to rewrite history. Yet the country's largest opposition party, the Social Democrats, makes recall and fishing fees a central theme of its platform. The proposal calls for a gradual rather than wholesale withdrawal of the rights, with a fixed percentage of the total quota recalled each year. The government would then rent individual quotas back to the industry.[23]

Earlier, I mentioned Lord Perry's question about regulatory overfishing and the manner in which pressures for overfishing manifest themselves in different management schemes. Fisheries economist Anthony Scott has speculated that the element of exclusive rights embedded in a system of individual quotas might gradually implant a sense of ownership in fishers and spontaneously give rise to self-management by the industry. In the same spirit, the government of New Zealand, which is the only country besides Iceland that uses an ITQ system to manage its fisheries nationwide, has gradually devolved certain management responsibilities to commercial stakeholder organizations. These organizations are usually composed of ITQ owners, who take some responsibility for managing the commercial fishery in which they are active (Yandle 2003). At the beginning of the twenty-first century, these transfers of management responsibility are still somewhat modest, and they supplement government regulation. In view of worldwide failures by governments in restoring fish stocks, building successful stakeholder organization is a major challenge and opportunity.

In Iceland, social modeling has not turned in this direction. The bitter debate over the consequences of structural reorganization and free transfers has crowded out the subtle issue contained in Lord Perry's question. Instead, the authorities focus on strengthening government monitoring and enforcement and aligning incentives on various margins.[24]

Notes

1. Whatever progress has been made in this difficult area owes much the pioneering work of Simon Kuznets. For a brief evaluation of Kuznets's various scholarly contributions, see Fogel 2000.

2. Nations that become temporarily rich as a result of random good fortune, such as the discovery of a valuable resource, are an exception to my statement. The ranking of nations also can change considerably when we measure national income per hour of work instead of per capita, but it is unlikely that the reordering will put poor countries in a high-income category.

3. Studies that estimate the world distribution of income by giving each individual one data point generally conclude that the income distribution between nations is a much greater source of inequality than the distribution within nations—accounting for some 70 percent of the variation (Sala-i-Martin 2002). Looking at 1970–98, Sala-i-Martin (2002) concludes that the world as a whole became richer during this period, that there was a sharp decline in the number of individuals below the poverty line of one (or two) U.S. dollar(s) per day, and that there was no dramatic increase in world inequality during the period (again if we give each individual one data point instead of treating nations as data points). Late-twentieth-century reversals in inequality depend on recent economic progress among the 1.2 billion Chinese individuals and 1 billion Indians. The declining fortunes of 700 million Africans pull in the opposite direction. These findings should be viewed with caution. The data for the world distribution of income are incomplete, and different estimating procedures can generate different outcomes. Recent worldwide trends in inequality are contested issues. For a different viewpoint, see United Nations 1999.

4. Environmentalists (and many others) argue that national product statistics overestimate economic growth because they ignore or underestimate important environmental cost categories, such as costs associated with depletion of natural resources or harmful spillover effects such as pollution. The criticism is valid, but the neglect of environmental costs and corresponding overestimates of net output and economic growth are at least partly offset by a propensity in official statistics to seriously underestimate growth by not fully registering improvement in the quality of goods and services (Advisory Commission 1996). Finally, by increasing income levels, growth creates public demand for a clean environment (when people are relatively well off, the income elasticity of environmental goods is high).

Furthermore, technical progress has previously introduced cheap substitutes for vanishing resources, new and relatively clean production processes, and new methods for measuring environmental damage and for cleaning up.

5. Cited in Rodrik, Subramanian, and Trebbi 2002, 1. Based on World Bank data adjusted for purchasing power parity (PPP) differences (caused by exchange-rate distortions). The richest country was Luxembourg and the poorest Sierra Leone.

6. The two main branches of (mainstream) economics are macroeconomics, which focuses on short-term fluctuations around the long-run productive capacity of an economy, and microeconomics, which studies the allocation of resources in a market system with secure exclusive property rights and some given level of production technology. Noneconomists might be interested to know that growth theory is the daughter of macroeconomics and that both fields make the national economy their main level of analysis. Development economics, which has close ties to applied microeconomics but also deals with macroeconomic issues, specializes in the economic problems of developing countries. Development economics emphasizes issues such as structural transformations from agriculture to industry, demographic transitions, and behavior of households and other economic units in preindustrial societies but also looks at social institutions and institutional change (Lin and Nugent 1995). Because development economics sometimes uses eclectic methods and violates the rhetorical norm of mainstream economics that only arguments stated in terms of (specific types of) mathematical models are valid, the field often receives the cold shoulder from orthodox economists: "Once upon a time there was a field called development economics—a branch of economics concerned with explaining why some countries are so much poorer than others, and with prescribing ways for poor countries to become rich. . . . That field no longer exists" (Krugman 1995, 6–7; see also Hirschman 1981).

7. In their graduate education, economists are led to believe that there is only one legitimate way to study society: the basic neoclassical approach, with its emphasis on rigorous mathematical modeling, equilibrium analysis, and explicit optimization by agents who have fixed preferences and neutral beliefs. Lurking behind this view is an idea of a general theory of social phenomena. In its field, physics has made good progress toward an increasingly more general theory, and physicists have been successful in using empirical tests to screen their theories. Similar progress in the study of economic systems has not occurred, although high theory in economics has reached comparable levels of mathematical sophistication to theoretical physics. Perhaps Brian Loasby (1989, 41) is right when he argues that physicists have specialized in studying problems where mathematical arguments map relatively easily onto empirical observations, whereas economists and other social scientists are left with more intractable types of problems.

8. This is true of closed economies. International trade allows countries to operate outside their production frontiers.

9. Endogenous growth theory sets high formal (mathematical) modeling standards, making it technically difficult to incorporate social institutions into the model and to do it in a sophisticated manner—for example, to allow for incomplete knowledge (rather than incomplete information).

10. New or endogenous growth theory also links technical change to economies of scale, as we shall see.

11. Although I do not discuss their theories here, classical economists beginning with Adam Smith were deeply interested in the sources of economic growth.

12. Ruttan 1998 provides an excellent discussion of the three waves of growth theory in modern economic thought and their lessons for development economics; see also Solow 1994; R. R. Nelson 1998.

13. Labor-saving technological change reduces the number of labor units required to produce a unit of output but leaves physical capital requirements unaffected.

14. The maximum rate of extensive growth per time period cannot exceed *(n + a)*, where *a* stands for the autonomous process of labor-saving technical change and *n* represents population (or workforce) growth. With a fixed ratio of capital to labor, the country's capital stock must also grow at rate *(n + a)* to accommodate the national workforce, but there is no mechanism that ensures that people's saving and investment activities will expand *K* exactly at the rate *(n + a)*. Balanced growth requires that the sum *(n + a)* be equal to the country's saving ratio, *s*, divided by the fixed capital-output ratio, *v*, or $(\frac{s}{v} = n + a)$. In Harrod-Domar terminology, a country that experiences extensive growth at rate *(n + a)* is growing at its natural rate, but if the growth rate falls short of *(n + a)* (because of a low saving and investment rate) the economy is growing at its warranted rate.

15. In the 1950s, Kaldor (1956) and others tried to make the saving ratio, *s*, endogenous, but their version did not catch on. Moreover, prior to the appearance of the Solow-Swan model, Kaldor already had described the properties of a neoclassical growth theory without formally presenting such a model.

16. Neoclassical growth theory has also developed multisector growth models with separate production functions for individual sectors of a national economy that add up to the aggregate function.

17. Neoclassical growth theory assumes perfect competition. Although various forms of inefficiency characterize all economies, they are not part of the neoclassical growth model.

18. According to Robert Solow (2001, 1–2), "growth theory was conceived as a model of the growth of an industrial economy. . . . So far as I can remember, I have never applied such a model to a developing economy, because I thought that the underlying machinery would apply mainly to a planned economy or a well-developed market economy. This is not a matter of principle, just wariness."

19. Constant returns to scale imply that large economies have no efficiency advantage over small economies or, in technical terms, that an increase in the use of both *K* and *L* by a given percentage always increases output by the same percentage.

20. Easterly 1999 assumes (a) that the countries channel all aid they receive into investment and (b) that an incremental capital-output ratio of 3.5 (which is the midpoint of the commonly cited range) effectively translates investments into outputs.

21. The reader should not take these tests of failed aid programs to imply that long-term growth is possible without investment.

22. "It is quite possible, without Solow's 1957 article which expressly grounded the empirical calculations in formal neoclassical growth theory, that the empirical work of Kendrick and Denison, which involved vastly more digging and calculating, would have received less attention" (R. R. Nelson 1998, 506). In a 1952 essay surveying growth theory, Moses Abramovitz discusses most of the major ideas (along with many others) that neoclassical and modern or endogenous growth theorists use in their models (R. R. Nelson 1998, 501–3).

23. Hulten 2000 provides a history and evaluation of the concept of total factor productivity.

24. Growth accounting has become a sophisticated activity involving complex theoretical and empirical issues. The topics studied include the theoretical justifications for using aggregate production functions, the implications of defining several categories of K and L and employing changing weights over time, the consequences of increasing returns to scale, the pros and cons of using econometric methods in growth accounting, and a host of other issues (Barro 1998; Hulten 2000).

25. The basic Solow model, augmented to allow for both human and physical capital, has been thoroughly tested. The determinants of the level of steady-state income are usually statistically significant and have the predicted signs, although the regressions typically explain only a small portion of the variation. The empirical evidence for endogenous or new growth theory is not as clear. According to Wacziarg (2002, 911), because of the multiplicity of models of endogenous growth, each with a specific emphasis and specific predictions, " 'Tests' of endogenous growth theory . . . are all over the place."

26. For references and greater detail concerning the origins and methods of new or endogenous growth theory, see *Journal of Economic Perspectives* 1994.

27. In the late 1980s and early 1990s, a wave of regression studies sought indirect support for new growth theory by testing the convergence hypothesis of neoclassical growth theory, but new growth theory, unlike neoclassical growth theory, does not predict convergence of per capita incomes. In retrospect, the convergence controversy was not a productive enterprise (Pack 1994; Romer 1994). A vast regression literature has recently emerged, exploring the sources of growth (Barro 1997). The ironic title of a paper by Sala-i-Martin (1997), "I Just Ran Two Million Regressions," captures the exploratory nature of those cross-country regression studies that informally include economic, political, and social variables. Brock and Durlauf (2000, 2) identify and offer solutions to "some general methodological problems which we believe explain the widespread mistrust of growth regressions." Clague et al. 1997 provides interesting cross-country tests of some of the propositions in the new institutional economics.

28. There were in fact isolated attempts to make technological change an endogenous part of neoclassical growth theory, but they did not catch on (Binswanger and Ruttan 1978). For a critical review, see Nordhaus 1973. With the arrival of new growth theory, these early contributions are now seen in a favorable light.

Chapter 2

1. Paul Krugman's Ohlin Lectures (1995) are dedicated to making the third point.

2. In my (somewhat arbitrary) terminology, a knowledge problem arises when actors do not know the basic structure of their choice set or the appropriate model, while an information problem arises when actors lack information about the distribution of the elements in a known choice set or a model. See Nakamura and Steinsson 2003.

3. Of the many attempts to modify the basic rational-choice approach, the work of Herbert Simon (1957, 1959) is best known. Simon analyzes choices in terms of the psychological principle of *satisficing,* which, in its applications in social science, is known as *bounded rationality.* According to this view, cognitive limitations compel people to follow routines and modify their behavior in small steps. A powerful, generally recognized theory has not emerged to explain and predict how routines are formed and how they change. In the new institutional economics, many studies do not explicitly deal with bounded rationality but emphasize the high transaction costs of making decisions, which these studies interpret as constraints. Transaction-cost analysis of such nature is actually a hybrid of Simon's bounded-rationality approach and neoclassical economics. Although decisions by agents are often formulated in terms of (weak) optimization, institutions have the cognitive role of coordinating decisions and simplifying choices (De Alessi 1983). The social-models approach, which I follow, complements the bounded-rationality/transaction-costs approaches and assumes that social actors, like social scientists, make sketchy models of their environments and then purposefully seek their goals in terms of these social models. The idea that incomplete causal theories and worldviews shape political action is well known in political science, although the origins and evolution of such models are not well understood (Goldstein and Keohane 1993).

4. Until 1600 or thereabouts, many new technologies came from China and the Middle East. The reason why these regions did not generate an industrial revolution comparable to that in the West is an important question for modern institutional analysis.

5. This argument includes the possibility that individual citizens of a poor country collectively possess full knowledge of modern production technologies but that various factors prevent effective pooling and application of such knowledge. In addition to commonly acknowledged economic, political, and social disincentives, the distribution of knowledge within the country can be a restricting factor.

6. Parente and Prescott (2000) take a similar but a narrower view than I do of the implications of new growth theory for developing countries. Their analysis is tied to traditional economic variables such as "market imperfections" and does not explore underlying social and political factors.

7. Like me, R. R. Nelson and Sampat (2000) employ the term *social technology,* but they use it to describe the production routines of actors in specific industries—for example, in the nineteenth-century German chemical industries. I use *social technology* to describe (incomplete) knowledge of the mechanisms whereby "social institutions" create specific outcomes, and I use the term *policy model* to describe individual strategies or routines. Policy models are often based on the actor's ideas about relevant social technologies, but some players may acquire their policy models (in certain areas) through conscious or subconscious imitation.

8. Figuratively, rules are the bones of institutions, enforcement mechanisms are the muscles, and social models are the brains.

9. North (1990) emphasizes the distinction between institutions and organizations. Coase (1937) offers an explanation based on transaction costs for the existence of firms (organizations). At one level of analysis, firms constitute social systems that are analytically comparable to larger systems such as nations, but the new institutional economics is still vague about the relationship between social systems at different levels.

10. Consider the complications of effectively transplanting U.S. corporate law to another country with no comparable legal tradition, hoping to reach a comparable level of legality to that of the United States. When the basic institutional structures of both source country and transplant country are compatible, the task of transplanting law requires relatively little knowledge of social technologies. The socially close Nordic countries (Denmark, Finland, Iceland, Norway, and Sweden) for decades have with relative ease harmonized their social institutions (legislation) in many areas.

11. See Alt and Shepsle 1990; Banks and Hanushek 1995. The *Journal of Institutional and Theoretical Economics* 1998 includes a special section with nine essays on "Views and Comments on the 'New Institutionalism' in Sociology, Political Science, and Anthropology." For the impact of economics on contemporary political science, see G. Miller 1997.

12. At the aggregate level, actual or realized transaction costs of operating a property rights regime such as Y or Z include the transaction costs of private actors as well as the costs of public agencies that support the system, such as courts and the police.

13. In this book I am concerned with institutional reforms—introduction of new social technologies—that raise a community's aggregate wealth. Institutional reforms in this sense are (almost) never Pareto improvements, which require that no one be made worse off by the change, but institutional reforms (as defined here) in principle meet the Kaldor-Hicks welfare criterion. A Kaldor-Hicks welfare improvement occurs when those who gain from institutional reforms are technically able to compensate the losers (ignoring the transaction costs of the compensation process) and still be better off than before.

14. Demand for reforms need not originate at the top of a social organization but may come from below. The actual changes in legislation, regulations, or private rules, however, are usually the prerogative of political or governing bodies. Even when the demand for new institutions comes from below, there is no guarantee that the proposals are backed by a workable knowledge of relevant social technologies.

15. The transition to markets in Eastern Europe has generated interest in these questions and considerable advances in knowledge. Roland 2000 provides a good summary of these findings.

16. Many scholars, including economists, have recently concluded that it is useful to distinguish between the immediate (or proximate) and underlying (or deeper) causes of economic growth. The basic growth determinants that the literature mentions most often are openness to trade, geography, and institutions (although openness, an economic policy variable, does not quite belong in this category). For example, Rodrik, Subramanian, and Trebbi (2002) estimate the direct effects on per capita income levels of these three factors in cross-country regres-

sions using recently developed instruments for openness and institutions. They conclude that the quality of institutions totally dominates the effects of geography, whereas openness is insignificant and has a negative sign. The study also uncovers both reverse causation and indirect effects. Geography influences the quality of institutions and thus has indirect effects on income levels.

17. As I discuss in chapter 11, massive institutional change, such as the introduction of a modern, well-functioning judicial system, puts huge resource demands on a poor country, which may not immediately be able to afford the necessary buildings, qualified legal professionals, and recording systems. My thesis, however, is that absence of credible commitment by key actors is more likely to undermine the new institutions in the early years than are limited material resources.

Chapter 3

1. The fourth section in this chapter, "Economic Institutions: The Modern History of Long Waves," draws on Eggertsson 1997b.

2. Full knowledge of coming decline and collapse, however, should have made younger members of Stalin's basic support group (and the population at large) disaffected and should have weakened their support.

3. The Weingast (1997) model actually focuses only on political equilibria. The model assumes explicitly that the country has set up effective economic structures (property rights) suitable for economic growth but that producers find it difficult to operate the economic system because of political instability and predatory behavior by the government. Olson's Stalin has done better than Weingast's rulers by initially combining a stable political equilibrium with an effective economic equilibrium.

4. As late as the 1980s, even some bitter critics of the Soviet regime were inclined to overestimate the country's economic performance. In the 1970s, standard American textbooks of economics seriously contemplated the possibility that living standards in the USSR might soon overtake those in the United States.

5. Rosa (1993, 1997) provides a political economy/public finance explanation of nationalization/denationalization cycles. In his view, the cycles reflect attempts by governments to lower the political cost of taxation. Rosa assumes (a) that social models are neutral and (b) that public enterprises and private enterprises are equally efficient. He then argues that at certain times it is politically expedient for governments to nationalize firms and raise tax revenue through their profits rather than to increase regular taxation. Later, when interest rates are high and the political cost of increasing taxes is also high, the best strategy for governments to increase their revenues is to sell the family jewels (the public enterprises). Rosa finds empirical support for his hypothesis in European data for the second half of the twentieth century. Institutional change in this instance can be seen as solely distributive (shifting the tax burden) because public and private firms are assumed to be equally efficient, but if we interpret the switches as attempts to minimize the cost of providing public services, the cycles have a remedial element. However, Rosa's key assumption about policymakers consistently believing that nationalization/denationalization has no implications for productivity is not convincing.

6. Of course, regulatory regimes also can initiate virtuous circles.

7. Comparison between jurisdictions often plays a large role in evaluating institutions. In the United States, the performance of unregulated intrastate airlines in Texas and California helped convince rule makers that the regime governing the national airlines should be abolished (Vietor 1990, 19). Comparisons across countries, of varying degrees of accuracy, often help align social models in entire regions. The mainstream of the British Conservative Party used examples of state-owned industries abroad to fight nationalization at home. In 1928 a Tory publication noted that "the state railways in Australia were reported to be at the mercy of voracious union leaders and their lazy overpaid members, while the government coal mines in Bulgaria were deemed to be hives of inefficiency" (as summarized by Singleton 1995, 19).

8. Regular long-term business cycles conceivably could drive systematic cycles of institutional change. If we believed that market economies regularly experience severe crashes—say, every 50 or 100 years—these crashes might give rise to long private-public cycles. However, the case for long business cycles, as put forth by Kitchin, Juglar, Kondratieff, and others, remains to be proven.

9. The Western industrial powers, often as part of their policies of imperialism, opened up trade with China, Japan, and other countries.

10. In Britain as late as 1831, the electorate was less than 500,000 in a population of 14 million. The Reform Act of 1832 opened Parliament to the business world, but the working class entered via the Reform Act of 1867, which gave the vote to two-thirds of adult males. Finally, a 1918 act opened the vote to males over twenty-one and women over thirty (Checkland 1989, 608–28).

11. At the time of this writing, in 2003, however, some of the successor states of the former Soviet Union still more or less follow the Soviet model.

12. In 2002 accounting scandals in the United States created a (mini) crisis of confidence in laissez-faire capitalism, which led to calls for new regulations.

Chapter 4

1. External shocks can also have positive effects by cracking poverty traps and creating support for institutional reform, as chapter 10 discusses.

2. The discussion in this section draws on the first sections of Eggertsson 1998b.

3. For an introduction to the literature on traditional systems of social security in developing countries, see Ahmad et al. 1991; see also de Janvry, Fafchamps, and Sadoulet 1991. Newbery (1989) combines the economics of risk and the information-transaction-costs perspective in a lucid survey of the theory of agricultural institutions for insurance and stabilization. Also using the transaction-cost framework, Binswanger and Rosenzweig (1986) lay out a general theory of economic institutions in traditional rural areas, Binswanger and McIntire (1987) explore the structure of land-abundant tropical agriculture, and Binswanger, McIntire, and Udry (1989) analyze institutions in semiarid African agriculture. Bromley and Chavas (1989) examine risk and transactions in semiarid tropics, and Fafchamps (1992; 1993) studies mutual insurance networks in preindustrial societies in terms

of information and transaction problems. Townsend (1992, 1993) applies general equilibrium analysis and contract economics in an empirical and theoretical study of Asian village communities, and Cheung (1969, 1970) pioneered the study of agricultural contracts in terms of risks and transaction costs.

4. If diversification of effort reduces expected wealth, then risk-neutral actors or actors in a risk-free world would avoid output-reducing diversification. If actors diversify in spite of expected reduction in wealth, their action can be interpreted as willingness to pay an implicit premium for more security.

5. "Although all studies find strong positive correlation between temperature and hay yield, there is only a weak correlation between temperature and output in the part-time fisheries (Ogilvie 1981)" (Eggertsson 1998b, 7). Chapter 7, "Why Iceland Starved," gives a fuller account of the peculiar history of the country's fisheries.

6. In 1281 the Icelandic parliament ratified a new law code, Jónsbók, that was modeled extensively on the Grágás and remained in use in the nineteenth century. (Even in the twenty-first century, a handful of Jónsbók laws remain in effect.)

7. In the census of 1703, some 90 percent of all male heads of farm households but only 2 percent of male farm laborers were married men or widowers. Illegitimacy was fairly low, and couples who had children out of wedlock often later married (Vasey 1996, 377).

8. For centuries, Iceland was under the Danish Crown. If the scope of risk management had included the entire Danish kingdom, general risks in Iceland caused by cold spells and volcanic activity would have been specific risks in the kingdom. If the royal administration in Copenhagen had operated a relief system for Iceland (which the Danish Crown did not), poor communications with Iceland would have required supplies to be stored mostly in Iceland rather than in Denmark. Storing the supplies in Iceland, however, would have solved only part of the problem, because poor communications within the country would have hampered the distribution of supplies, especially in winter. During the crises of the eighteenth century, sporadic attempts by Copenhagen to send supplies to Iceland floundered because of poor communications (Eggertsson 1998b, 26).

9. Rodrik (1998, 4), using data for 110 countries, regresses average growth rates in 1975–89 on average growth rates in 1960–75 and on a constant term. The regression yields an R^2 of only 0.12 (and a coefficient on lagged growth of 0.39). When Rodrik excludes 11 East Asian countries and Botswana from his sample, the coefficient on lagged growth becomes statistically insignificant and R^2 shrinks to 0.02.

10. Robert Solow (1994, 51) expresses doubts about international cross-section regressions using social variables: "A particular style of empirical work seems to have sprung from the conjunction of growth theory and the immensely valuable body of comparative national-accounts data compiled by Summers and Heston (1991). It rests on international-cross section regressions with the average growth-rates of different countries as the dependent variable and various politico-economic factors on the right-hand side that might easily affect the growth rate if the growth rate were easily affected. I had better admit that I do not find this a confidence-inspiring project. It seems altogether too vulnerable to bias from omit-

ted variables, to reverse causation, and above all to the recurrent suspicion that the experiences of very different national economies are not to be explained as if they represented different 'points' on some well-defined surface."

11. A reverse line of causation is also possible—economic outcomes often affect political outcomes.

12. Admittedly, we cannot rule out strategic knowledge falsification by the leaders.

Chapter 5

1. The discussion in this chapter is based on general assumptions concerning the nature of growth-friendly institutional environments. In particular, rulers or governments must (1) credibly commit to protecting capital assets against arbitrary seizure by private and public actors; (2) facilitate and tolerate institutions that lower transaction costs in productive activity; and (3) provide macroeconomic stability and essential public goods and encourage the production and importation of pure and applied knowledge.

2. For a formal analysis, see also Olson1993; McGuire and Olson 1996. See also North 1979, 1981; Levi 1988.

3. North (1979) also considers agency problems of autocrats who rely on a large number of representatives for supplying public goods and collecting taxes. Agency limits the rulers' effective power, while self-serving behavior by the agents may harm the economy.

4. In a one-period model, the optimal rate of taxation, s^*, is reached when an increase in the rate of taxation beyond s^* would, through negative supply effects, reduce the tax base (national income) by a larger proportion than the proportional increase in the tax rate. As for the provision of public goods, the ruler increases spending on public goods until a further increase in public goods expenditures by one dollar increases national income just enough to add one dollar to tax revenues. If the equilibrium tax rate is ½, the last dollar invested in growth-enhancing public goods must increase future national income by two dollars, yielding one dollar in additional tax revenues. See Olson 2000, 8–9.

5. We assume that the autocrat relies on a small band of supporters and finds it more effective to reward the supporters directly than to use public goods to increase supporters' incomes through the effect on economic growth.

6. This analysis of democracy ignores agency problems between elected leaders and the voters that support those leaders, including the role of powerful special interests.

7. Several countries have recently experimented with individual transferable shares or quotas (ITQs) in their fisheries. ITQs are a hybrid system of exclusive property rights and government regulation (see chapter 12).

8. The buying and selling of countries is not unknown in history. As late as 1917, the United States bought from Denmark three islands now known as the U.S. Virgin Islands.

9. For the definitive account of the selectorate model, see Bueno de Mesquita et al. 2003; see also Bueno de Mesquita 2000 and Buena de Mesquita et al. 2000.

10. The selectorate model takes some liberty with standard definitions of "private goods" and "public goods." For example, perverse economic regulations, such as granting of monopoly rights to supporters, are classified as private goods.

11. I owe this point to Timur Kuran.

12. Moreover, people also show loyalty to the current leader of a dictatorial regime because they fear that the next leader may be even worse. In a dictatorship where the likelihood of constitutional reforms is virtually zero, the alternative to a brutal dictator is another dictator. I owe this argument to Alastair Smith.

13. High rates of economic growth in the Soviet Union under Stalin, especially during the first five-year plans, seem to contradict the claim that a small winning coalition and a large selectorate are associated with policies of economic stagnation. Economic growth in the Soviet Union, however, was closely tied both to the rulers' personal taste for growth and to the perceived need to build a formidable army to meet real and imaginary external threats to survival. Private consumption in the country was minimized and held at the bare minimum required for maintaining the health and energy of the workforce. The leaders then allocated the surplus to projects intended to build economic and military might.

14. See chapter 4.

15. In the modern literature, North and Thomas (1973) were among the first to explain the rise of the Western world in terms of appropriate property rights.

16. Historians trace the economic emergence of northwestern Europe back to around 1500. The development of cities with direct access to the North Atlantic has been linked to redirection of trade routes brought about by new geographic discoveries. The seventeenth century saw the decline of many cities associated with the medieval trade routes, including Italian cities and cities of the Hanseatic League.

17. See Weingast 1997 for reference to the debate in political science about whether democratic values or limited government comes first.

18. For example, they are indifferent *ex ante* about which side of the road to drive on.

Chapter 6

1. See also *University of Pennsylvania Law Review* 1996.

2. See also Ehrenberg 1977.

3. According to the economics of transaction costs, experience goods disappear from the market unless producers make credible commitments to deliver the level of quality specified for the products (Eggertsson 1990, chapter 6). If producers invest large sums in developing a brand name for an experience good, in the long run they will lose their brand-name capital if consumers discover a lower quality in the product than was promised. Rational buyers will buy experience goods on trust (without being able immediately to measure their true quality) when their calculations show that a producer's gain from cheating is less than the associated loss of brand-name capital. The credible-commitment argument does not apply to afterlife consumption unless old buyers can pass their experience on to new buyers.

4. Wittman (1996) further boosts Demsetz's efficiency claim by arguing that democratic political processes are efficient. Wittman's argument, which goes against the thrust of the public-choice literature, rests on shaky empirical foundations.

5. Demsetz's (1967) influential study uses as illustration the case of the Indians of Labrador, who adopted norms of exclusive property rights in land when external demand for beaver furs had created incentives for individuals to wastefully exploit the region's beaver population. Eric Posner (1996a, 1712–13) maintains, however, that the data collected by Eleanor Leacock, which Demsetz uses, indicate that the new property rights emerged in the mid-1700s, whereas fur trading "had reached significant proportions by the middle of the 1500s. Thus efficient norms may have lagged by *two centuries.*"

6. A fundamental impetus for modifying neoclassical economics was a perceived lack of robust theory for analyzing the organization of firms and markets. The effort has produced a variety of theories that have strong, weak, or nonexisting ties to the standard economic paradigm (Coase 1937; Putterman 1988). In a survey of different approaches to business organization, Knudsen (1995) identifies the following lines of attack in addition to traditional microeconomics: modern industrial organization, managerialism, principal-agent models, behavioralism, the nexus of contract view, Williamson's transaction-costs economics, R. R. Nelson and Winter's evolutionary paradigm, and knowledge-based theories. Most of these approaches challenge with varying degrees of intensity the standard assumptions of rational egoistic actors and fixed preferences; introduce new theoretical tools, especially from psychology; and make new assumptions about the level of analysis, the information available to actors, and the ability of actors to process information and make optimal decisions. These alternative theories also present new methods for aggregating individual decisions and modeling the formation and evolution of knowledge, tastes, and preferences.

7. The theories of functionalism fall outside my classification, which refers only to theories that assume methodological individualism.

8. Katzenstein, Keohane, and Krasner (1998), in a thoughtful review of theoretical issues in international political economy, also discuss the basic dichotomy of static and dynamic analysis. International political economy emerged in the 1970s and introduced economic methods to the study of international politics (673). Static international political economy has been criticized for taking preferences and identities for granted while ignoring nationalism and other (partly) norm-driven concerns, such as increased interest in human rights and environmental issues (673–74). See *International Organization* 1998. Hechter and Kanazawa (1997), in a review of rational-choice sociology, also recognize a similar need for a dynamic theory.

9. Aoki (2001, 28) uses individual subjective game models to introduce a dynamic element: "By discussing how the agents cognitively revise their own subjective game models in response to external shocks or internal crises in a correlated manner, [the analysis] attempts to describe a possible mechanism of institutional change."

10. A local group, however, is capable of cooperating with other local groups when their interests overlap.

11. First-best solutions are found in perfect markets with full information and no transaction costs, but such markets are theoretical or imaginary constructs.

12. For more detail and references, see Eggertsson 1998b.

13. "According to the law, farmers who were short of hay could request public searches for surplus hay in their general area, both in their own and neighboring communes. Appointed agents (farmers) would then estimate whether any farmers in the area had stored more fodder than they required for the winter. Surplus hay was to be sold and first offered to farmers in the same commune as the source. The law prescribed severe punishment for those who refused to comply with the redistribution scheme: Their reserves were to be confiscated and the offenders receive a fine. The law permitted use of force to remove surplus hay, and farmers who received injury while defending their surplus could not claim compensation, but the crown would decide in each case whether compensation was justified if those resisting were killed. The law also created an incentive for people to expose stubborn neighbors who hid their reserves. If the neighbors refused to trade, those who first requested the hay could buy it at half price and also receive half the fine" (Eggertsson 1998b, 22).

14. A cold spell in 1800–1802 reduced the sheep population by three-fifths, or 171,000 animals. In the cold spell of 1881–83, the loss was 187,000 sheep, and for the period 1881–1908 the loss of grown sheep, lambs, and horses and reduction in quality of survivors was equivalent to 884,000 sheep, or an average of about 13 sheep for each person in the farm community (Eggertsson 1998b, 18–19).

15. There are two likely explanations why we have little evidence of advocacy for hay storing and livestock management prior to the seventeenth century: climate changes and the history of printing. Printing was first introduced in Iceland in the sixteenth century for publishing religious texts. In the late sixteenth century, a general cooling of temperatures occurred in the northern hemisphere, continuing into the nineteenth century. With these climate changes, the fodder crises in Icelandic farming presumably became more urgent, as did calls for reform.

16. Conditions in premodern Iceland did not make central storage of hay a good economic proposition. There were no scale advantages in storage that justified such an arrangement. Icelandic farms were not grouped into agricultural villages but were scattered throughout each district.

17. According to Bjarnason (1913, 198), the communes that experimented briefly with livestock planning used the unanimity rule to allocate public funds for administering the plan, giving each farmer in the district a veto. Apparently, virtually no funds were forthcoming and the short-lived experiment relied mostly on voluntary work. The experiments did not rely on coercion. Two or three times a year, appointed local inspectors visited all farms in the commune and advised the farmers about how to plan their fodder requirements. In one instance, the livestock management of all the farmers in the district was rated and made public, and those who took especially good care of their animals received special recognition.

18. I make the conventional assumption that the actors prefer greater rather than less wealth and security.

19. The idea that actors operate in subjective worlds is well established in the literature. Hofstede (1980, 1991, 1998) probably has done more than any other

scholar to make operational the idea of social models. Hofstede talks about the collective programming of the mind. Folta and Ferrier (1996) are a recent example of a Hofstede-type study that analyzes the relationship between business organization and national character. At a more abstract level, Vanberg (1998, 432), citing work by Hayek, Popper, Heiner, Holland, and Arthur, interprets rational behavior as follows: In a complex world, actors "do not, and cannot, respond to the full complexity of each and every particular problem situation they confront. Instead they rely on simplifying mental models that reflect past experience and are adjusted to new experience."

20. Timur Kuran (1998) suggests that antinorm measures of a given size may have unpredictable effects, either large or small. Kuran's results depend on unobservable tipping points, implying, for example, that small policy changes can have large behavioral effects, and vice versa. The chapter's final section discusses some of these issues.

21. E. A. Posner (1996a, 1736) points out that the authorities can assist norm violators and reduce the weight of sanctions by introducing measures that hide the circumvention of a norm. A government, for example, can provide legal support for actors who structure loans as sales or leases to avoid usury laws. Moreover, private norm entrepreneurs both in Christianity and Islam have historically provided social technologies for circumventing usury laws. E. A. Posner (1996a, 1735–36) interprets a market in tradable emission rights, which was authorized in the United States in 1990, as norm circumvention—circumvention of a norm that allows firms to pollute, but not too much. The old norm was inefficient because it did not distinguish between high-value and low-value polluters—between differences in the opportunity costs of firms of cleaning up. As for the Icelandic case, I have not found instances where the authorities sought to help violators of the hay-sharing norm to hide their circumventions.

22. Bendor and Swistak (2001) argue that third-party enforcement is the defining characteristic of social norms. Third-party enforcement refers to sanctions for deviating from social rules that are administered by people who are unaffected by the deviation but in position to punish the deviant. Dyadic enforcement and enforcement through internalization or self-sanctions may coexist with third-party enforcement. We are interested in all forms of informal enforcement.

23. Avner Greif, in an unpublished manuscript, proposes the following procedure: "First, using historical and comparative information, sort out what technological and institutional factors can be treated as 'exogenous' and what institutional factors are to be treated as 'endogenous,' that is, must be explained. Then, build a context-specific, game-theoretic model in which those exogenous factors define the exogenous rules of the game and solve for possible equilibria. Next, find out if some of these solutions are useful for understanding the nature of the institutional factors needing to be explained. Finally, examine what 'historical' factors can be considered responsible for the selection of that particular equilibrium solution to determine the role of history" (cited and paraphrased in Aoki 2001, 16–17).

24. Kuran (1998) formally derives the conditions that make an individual allocate more resources toward his or her ethnic activities when expecting an increase in overall levels of ethnic activities in society.

25. Multiple equilibria are not an inherent feature of the model. Single equilibrium at any level of ethnic activity is also possible.

26. One of the themes that the antimodernists initially emphasized was that people's characters would degenerate if they turned to full-time occupations other than farming. The following citation from the October 1838 Icelandic journal *Sunnanpósturinn*, in an article opposing modernization of the country's fishing fleet (which had consisted primarily of open rowboats), captures the spirit of the traditionalists: "That we somehow are more immune from the moral corruption and wretchedness of the sailors on decked vessels than we are from that of other fishermen, is against the nature of things" (cited in Hálfdanarson 1991, 148).

27. A variant of this social model still survives in certain circles both in America and Europe as the "family farm" ideal, which has had considerable policy influence.

28. The country's Marxist party apparently was not as divided as the other parties over the merits of farm-rural versus industrial-urban life, perhaps because the Marxists saw industrialization as an inevitable historical stage.

29. The country is still without railways.

30. Bayes's rule is a statistical formula for updating prior beliefs in light of new information. This rule is the formal rational way to update beliefs in a probabilistic environment.

Chapter 7

The epigraph to this chapter is cited in Cutting 1955, 126. This chapter is a revised version of Eggertsson 1996. Sections in chapters 4 and 6 use material from the economic history of Iceland as illustration and provide additional (but not essential) background material for this chapter.

1. The chapter's concluding section looks briefly at the knowledge problem involved in evaluating the consequences of structural change in historical Iceland. Although various cultural beliefs or social models doubtlessly helped reduce the transaction costs of operating traditional institutions in Iceland, I do not go as far as Hastrup (1990, 4), who concludes that "the Icelanders were actually imprisoned by their mentality." Hastrup does not explain how the Icelanders eventually passed from one mentality to another, which is the basic weakness in the mentalities (social model) approach (Burke 1986). In Iceland, a dynamic mentalities approach must explain the collapse of traditional institutional structures in the nineteenth century and the country's vigorous response to the opportunities offered by English and German interlopers in the fifteenth and sixteenth centuries.

2. During the commonwealth period, 930–1262, woolen cloth, *vaðmál,* was the country's most important export product, but after the union with Norway in 1262, dried fish, *skreið,* gradually replaced *vaðmál* as the basic export. By 1340, woolen products were no longer the country's major export. In 1361 the Crown assigned control of Iceland's exports to merchants in Bergen. Hanseatic merchants, who at the time controlled Bergen's trade with countries outside the Danish-Norwegian kingdom, reexported Icelandic *skreið* to their markets in Europe (Gelsinger 1981, 181–94). Thoroddsen (1924, 54) notes that already in the four-

teenth century, Icelandic stockfish had become a known quality product in Europe's Mediterranean region, and on contemporary maps Iceland was sometimes known as Stokkafixa.

3. The legal system of the commonwealth was based on self-enforcement of the law (see, for example, Friedman 1979).

4. The apparently perverse social norms that prevented storage of hay and effective livestock management in premodern Iceland (see chapter 6) undermined the farm economy, but the norm of sharing was part of the country's relatively effective informal insurance system for coping with specific risks. The hay-sharing norm in itself, however, was not a critical factor in holding back the development of a strong independent fishing industry. The periodic crises provoked by poor livestock management, in effect, were an incentive to put more emphasis on the fisheries, which were held back by other factors, as we shall see.

5. Toward the end of the tenth century, the Icelanders established two colonies in southwestern Greenland, which suggests that Iceland was fully settled by the year 1000. It is not entirely clear why the commonwealth ended in a civil war, leading in 1262 to a union with the king of Norway, but population pressures and economic stagnation probably were contributing factors. Incursions by English fishing interests, which began around 1400, tilted the economy toward the fishing sector and, as the century wore on, created a boom in Iceland (discussed subsequently) that probably extended into the sixteenth century. Finally, the economy entered a period of steep decline during the period of Danish monopoly trade, 1602–1787. The first signs of recovery appeared in the early 1800s, although the premodern age continued until the last years of the nineteenth century.

6. The drop in temperatures "happened most frequently during the 13th and 14th centuries and during the so-called Little Ice Age in the period between 1600 and 1900" (Friðriksson 1986, 32). In these periods, a fall in average air temperature caused substantial drop in the primary production of grassland (Friðriksson 1986, 35). Icelandic farming depended on the yield of grassland.

7. During the eighteenth century, Danish authorities made several attempts to overcome objections from the local elite and allow wintering by Danish merchants (see the first section of chapter 3).

8. Crew size on an efficient contemporary fishing vessel, however, was not large enough to pose any problems of scale for the small Icelandic community.

9. European colonial powers—for example, the British—frequently did not maintain a strong presence in their overseas territories but depended on a handful of nationals who recruited a large number of loyal local agents. Denmark did not follow this practice in Iceland. A curious 1809 episode illuminates Denmark's informal reliance on cooperation from the local elite. An adventurer of Danish origin, Jörgen Jörgensen, arriving in Iceland on a British merchant ship, organized his shipmates to arrest the Danish governor and take over the country. At this time, Denmark, having sided with France, was at war with England. Jörgensen proclaimed himself king of Iceland and ruled the country unopposed for two months. A visit by a British navy ship dethroned Jörgensen, who ended his days as a journalist and writer in Tasmania (Þorsteinsson and Jónsson 1991, 261–64).

10. The new ships had two masts and several sails instead of the one mast that

had been typical of ships during the Viking period. With two masts, the ships were far more maneuverable (Þorsteinsson 1976, 9). Icelandic historical writing has been rather silent about the English era in Icelandic history, partly because relatively few documents of the period are available in Danish and Icelandic archives and libraries. Much of the recent interest in the period has resulted from research by the late historian Björn Þorsteinsson, who drew on British sources.

11. On 6 April 1491, Henry VII wrote to "John Ver, Erle of Oxynford, Gret Chambyrleyn and Admirale of Yngland," "in that ye desyer all the dogers of thos partes schuld have our licens to departe in the viage towardes Islond, as they have ben accustommyd to do yerly in tyme passyd . . . owr fully interly beloovyd cousyn the Kyng of Demarke hath . . . complaynyd . . . that our subjectes . . . stelle, robbe, and exstorte his subjectes there ageynse ryght and conciens" (Cutting 1955, 7). In 1423 English traders seized and brought to England the Danish Crown's highest representative in Iceland. In 1467 they killed the Danish king's deputy in the country, and during this era an Englishman became bishop over the northern half of Iceland (Þorsteinsson and Jónsson 1991, 149–77).

12. In 1523, Christian II of Denmark offered Iceland both in Amsterdam and England as collateral for a loan needed to defend his throne (Þorsteinsson and Jónsson 1991, 174).

13. The Hamburgers were free riding on the Hanseatic League, in which they were members. To avoid alienating the English, the league did not favor trade by its members with Iceland.

14. Aðils 1971 provides the classic historical account of Danish monopoly trade in Iceland. For the definitive modern analysis, see Gunnarsson 1983, which has created new perspectives on the economic history of Iceland. This chapter benefits extensively from his work. Gunnarsson has estimated the Crown's and merchants' income from the monopoly. Until 1662 the price of licenses to trade with Iceland was kept low, and the Crown relied on taxing the trade. After 1662, taxes and duties were abolished, and the price of licenses was raised, usually to what the market could bear.

15. The Crown had agents in Iceland who collected rent from farmsteads and income from fishing operations. For a brief account of how the Crown sought to deal with its agency problems in distant Iceland, see Gunnarsson 1983, 155–56.

16. The distribution of land (and wealth) in historical Iceland was remarkably unequal, more so than in many modern low-income countries.

17. Iceland's fishing season mostly took place in winter, when there was little demand for farm labor in the rural sector. The marginal cost of using farm servants in the winter fisheries was small, which made the arrangement attractive to landowners.

18. Grágás, the laws of the commonwealth of 930–1262, forbid nonfarm households except when members of a farming commune guaranteed their support (Karlsson, Sveinsson, and Árnason 1992, 104). The laws that took effect after the union with Norway (Jónsbók, from 1281) required a minimum size for farms, justifying the measure by referring to a shortage of farm workers (Halldórsson 1970, 234). Attempts to prevent overpopulation and starvation may originally have guided the creation of institutions for tying together land, marriage, and labor constraints.

19. Á. Jónsson 1994 provides (in Icelandic) an excellent analysis of the Icelandic economic system in the premodern period, including a discussion of the relations between the farming and fishing sectors, economic regulations, and the commercial system and prices.

20. Although premodern Iceland lacked a formal police force, individual offenders, such as thieves and murderers, received harsh punishments—sometimes death or slave labor in Denmark.

21. "Prices were fixed in this trade; bargaining was not allowed. From 1619, the crown decided which prices should exist and these changed very little till 1776, with the exception of the period 1684–1702, when the prices were made more favorable to the Icelanders. The monopoly trade price lists 1619–1776 corresponded well to the very old price lists in Iceland internal trade which had changed little since the High Middle Ages" (Gunnarsson 1983, 28).

22. Exchange in premodern Iceland used commodity-based but abstract units of value. Fish was the value unit most used in foreign trade, and ell (a unit of coarse cloth) was most common in domestic trade (Gunnarsson 1983, 19).

23. The ship was lost at sea, and the Crown ignored the message (Thoroddsen 1924, 74). The Protestant Reformation eroded the autonomy and wealth of the Icelandic bishops, and by the seventeenth century the sees were no longer the powerful independent entrepreneurial force they had once been.

24. The voyage of John Cabot occurred in 1497, and by December that year word had reached Italy "that this kingdom [England] would have no further need of Iceland, from which place there comes a great quantity of fish called stockfish" (Mitchell 1977, 155). The discovery of Newfoundland, however, did not put an end to England's Iceland fisheries. In Newfoundland, the English initially repressed agriculture, allowing only small plots (called gardens), a mirror image of the industrial organization of premodern Iceland (Sider 1980 cited in Gunnarsson 1983).

25. The French made their request for a land base in 1855, when free trade was introduced in Iceland. As a follow-up, in 1856 the French sent Prince Jerome Napoleon (a nephew of Napoleon Bonaparte) on a visit to Iceland. The request was denied (Þorsteinsson 1976, 147–54).

26. A large majority of Icelanders were not directly involved in the fisheries. Figures for the occupational structure of Iceland in 1703 suggest that 69 percent of all Icelanders were engaged in farming only, while another 15 percent (mostly in the northeastern region) were involved both in farming and fishing, but only during the critical summer months of hay harvesting, which suggests very limited engagement in the fisheries. The remaining 16 percent includes primarily households engaged both in farming and in the important winter fishing season (Magnússon 1985, 37–39).

27. In the 1750s, Skúli Magnússon and others, with financial support from the Crown, attempted to start light industries in Reykjavík as well as fishing operations with decked vessels. The attempt failed, partly because of opposition from merchants of the trade monopoly, who felt that their territory had been violated (Gunnlaugsson 1982).

28. Several valuable new studies of the transition became available toward the end of the twentieth century; see, for example, Magnússon 1985; Gunnlaugsson

1988; A. Kristjánsson and Gunnlaugsson 1990; Hálfdanarson 1991; G. Jónsson 1991.

29. Denmark lost both its navy and Norway by joining the losing side in the Napoleonic wars.

30. In the previous centuries, transportation constrains ruled out large-scale emigration from Iceland. After the country was opened fully to foreign trade in the mid–nineteenth century, immigration agents from North America quickly appeared.

31. It is also unlikely that the landlords contemplated whether an effective export industry in the fisheries with international contacts might transmit new inputs and new technologies to the moribund farm sector, with its Viking-age technology.

32. For example, McCloskey (1985, 167–70) uses the tools of general equilibrium analysis to explore in an elementary fashion how two decades (1730–50) of weather favorable to British agriculture affected the production of manufactures. The question there concerns whether a temporary increase in agricultural productivity helped or retarded the Industrial Revolution. Formal analysis cannot resolve the question because unspecified negative and positive effects are involved. Empirical studies indicate that the net effect was trivially small.

33. For example, around 1740 the Danish navy searched Dutch fishing vessels off Iceland in an effort to stop illegal Dutch trade with the Icelanders and found supplies of woolens that the Dutch had purchased from farmers in the northern region during the summer months (Gunnarsson 1987, 71–72).

34. Á Jónsson (1994) argues that the very low relative price of labor in the fisheries (virtually free services of farm laborers during the winter season), because of the restrictions in the labor market, made operators in Iceland substitute labor for capital in the fisheries, favoring small open boats with large crews. The price structure thus reinforced the poverty trap. Yet in the nineteenth century, when Denmark began liberalizing Iceland's foreign trade, a modern fishing industry emerged even though most of the labor market restrictions remained formally intact.

Chapter 8

This chapter draws substantially on Eggertsson 1997a, 1998a, 1999.

1. Tinbergen 1952, 1956. Frisch pioneered models designed explicitly for planning and policy purposes but published relatively little of this material internationally; see Johansen (1977, 22). Tinbergen 1952 recognizes his debt to Frisch's work on decision models.

2. In his later work, Johansen (1977), a Norwegian, went beyond the traditional planning mode and incorporated team theory, games, and pressure groups into his representation of the planning process.

3. Reported in Johansen ([1974] 1987, 227–33). Johansen tells us that Frisch first made the distinction between selection analysis and implementation in a 1944 University of Oslo memorandum.

4. Tinbergen's distinction between quantitative and qualitative or structural

policy is more blurred than it may appear because apparent quantitative policy initiatives—such as rent controls, increases in tax rates, or new welfare benefits—may unleash fundamental changes in the social system. Dixit (1966, 144) elaborates this point and argues that most policy acts lie somewhere between the two poles.

5. The idea is not new. In 1938 Norwegian economist Ragnar Frisch criticized Tinbergen for his stationary policy models and argued that model structures would shift when policy changed (Heckman 1992).

6. The Phillips curve is named for A. W. Phillips, an economist who discovered what he saw as a stable inverse relationship between inflation and the level of unemployment over extended periods in British modern economic history. His findings of a "tradable" Phillips curve indicated that governments could choose their favorite low rate of unemployment (inflation), albeit at the cost of high inflation (unemployment), by manipulating the level of aggregate demand. Subsequent work showed that a stable Phillips curve does not exists; the apparent relationship breaks down when governments attempt to trade less (more) inflation for more (less) unemployment.

7. Sargent (1993, 160–65) provides a fascinating summary of studies by Sims (1988) and Chung (1990), in which they model a private sector that knows its rational expectations economics and an "irrational" government that does not and erroneously believes in an exploitable Phillips curve. Using data for the United States, Chung estimates a model of the government's learning process where the government gradually corrects its policy model.

8. Political macroeconomics is a research program that spans a wide range of topics and attracts the interest of both economists and political scientists. Alesina (1995, 145) lists the following topics as among the examples of recent work in the field: political business cycles, the politics of the government budget, the political economy of growth, the politics of inflation and stabilization policies, problems of external debt and capital flight in less developed countries, the effects of different electoral systems on economic policy, and the performance of coalition and minority governments relative to single party governments.

9. The formulation $W = G(g, x)$ assumes that policymakers pursue both universally recognized economic goals and politically motivated economic goals involving special privileges for support groups. Many political economists see all economic decisions as shaped by political considerations. In their models, the target preference function would take the form $W = G(g)$.

Chapter 9

1. Compared to the ideal, a second-best solution can involve an inferior economic system, inferior operational economic policy, or both.

2. The Benham investigation probably underestimates the number of unconventional transition studies written by economists. Many mainstream journals would have refused to publish such studies, forcing authors to submit their work to other journals.

3. One can only speculate about how a reliable theory of institutional change, if it emerged, would affect the economic prospects of poor countries. The net effect

could be either negative or positive. On the positive side, a reliable and widely trusted theory should create a broad consensus on technical issues and reduce disagreements about how to reach specific goals. Moreover, new theoretical insights might supply policymakers with useful tools—for example, for improving the capacity to make credible commitments to investors about the future security of their assets. On the negative side, a powerful new theory might retard reforms by pulling aside Rawls's metaphysical veil of ignorance and making crystal clear to potential losers from reform (including perhaps members of the political elite) that their future under a new institutional regime would be bleak.

4. In neoclassical welfare economics, a state or outcome B is inefficient if there exists a state A where at least one actor is better off than in B and no one is worse off. If all actors optimize, including government leaders, rational actors would always choose state A over B, unless some cost, such as the cost of collective action, blocks the move to A; see Hettich and Weiner 1993.

5. To be consistent, we should also model experts as selfish maximizers with personal agendas. The following section touches on these issues when discussing the preferences of OECD policy advisers.

6. Critics sometimes claim that theories that derive social outcomes from the behavior of actors who maximize their utility are telling us that the outcomes are perfect or optimal. These are mistaken beliefs. Constrained maximization leads to the best of all worlds only in the narrow technical sense of "best choice under constraints"—for example, sometimes the best treatment for a wounded leg is to amputate it, although in general it is not optimal to lose a leg.

7. *Quantitative policies* and *qualitative policies* are terms that Tinbergen introduced; see chapter 8.

8. Even though quantitative policy measures do not threaten a stable polity, political preferences and political uncertainty may strictly limit quantitative policy, even routine fiscal and monetary policy, in an unstable political environment.

9. The determinacy paradox is also known as the Bhagwati paradox.

10. Olson (1965, 1982) made pioneering contributions to the micropolitical approach, which gives the initiative to interest groups rather than to the state. Vast derivative literature has emerged using various labels, such as the theory of rent seeking and the economics of regulation (Stigler 1971; Buchanan, Tollison, and Tullock 1980; Tollison 1982; Becker 1983).

11. In countries where the balance of power is fragile, the limits for reform also extend to standard macroeconomic policy (which belongs to what I have called quantitative policy). Mainstream economists are fairly uniform in condemning certain economic practices, such as overvalued exchange rates, import substitution, excessive supply of money, or credit rationing (Krueger 1993). Economists used to blame such policies on ignorant politicians but are now more likely to explain the pursuit of "counterproductive" macroeconomic policies as strategic behavior by rational political actors.

12. Monetarism was an intellectually powerful school of macroeconomics in the 1970s. Many elements of this approach survive at the beginning of the twenty-first century as elements of the New Keynesian research program. The two principal advocates of monetarism were Milton Friedman and the team of Karl Brunner

and Allan Meltzer. The main difference between the two approaches was primarily technical. Brunner and Meltzer explicitly rejected the so-called IS-LM model and presented an alternative formal model of monetary influences on the economy; see Bordo and Schwartz 2003.

13. See Denzau and North 1994. The idea that people rely on a series of schematic models finds support from scholars in cognitive psychology and evolutionary biology, who do not view the human mind as an integrated system for processing data or a general-purpose computer but as "a large and heterogeneous network of functionally specialized computational devices" (Cosmides and Tooby 1994, 329). Mainstream economics treats preferences as exogenous, but Cosmides and Tooby are hopeful that a union of evolutionary psychology and economics "might be able to create a science of preferences" (331).

14. DeNardo (1995) offers a survey of the cognitive and psychological approach to mental models with an emphasis on applications in political psychology. He recognizes that formal theorists are uncomfortable with the incompleteness of the models or belief systems that this literature reveals. Converse's (1964) study of belief systems in mass publics is a seminal contribution that has for decades framed the debate about political belief systems. Converse emphasizes the frequent lack of systematic thinking, but recent theorists have brought some order to this world by introducing schematic models that according to DeNardo "give local coherence to people's thinking without necessarily providing a globally integrated world view. . . . Schemas are mental prototypes, images, metaphors, 'scripts,' or categories that provide a frame of reference against which experience is compared and interpreted" (81). An interesting application of schema theory is found in Larson 1985.

15. Also significant is inertness of individual behavior caused by adjustment costs, including the time required to discover how to use or exploit a new system or to make adjustments such as changing jobs.

16. Lindbeck 1995a, 12–13, suggests that a policy of redistribution that substantially reduces income inequality need not lower the demand for further redistribution. Growing awareness of inequalities can make the topic salient among voters, who then continue to ask for more equality. The demand for redistribution may also increase if the public concludes that the distribution of income depends on political decisions, not on market forces rewarding actors for productive contributions.

Chapter 10

1. In terms of figure 4, we can say that the institutions necessary for growth are missing from the innermost circle, $X_{z,r,p}$, in the space labeled "resulting state of the economy." As we are here dealing with institutional policy (rather than macroeconomic policy), "resulting state of the economy" refers to the institutional environment.

2. The concerns of the landlords were not entirely without reason. Even in retrospect, modern social science is not able to predict with great accuracy the economic and political outcomes had the Danish Crown, say in the 1600s, encouraged

Iceland to set up a full-scale fishing industry with the help of foreigners. If the effort had succeeded, it is reasonable to expect that domestic and foreign investors collecting rent from the fisheries would have become the country's chief power brokers.

3. In sharp contrast to the vision of Stigler and many of his colleagues at the University of Chicago, Harberger (1993) describes his heroes as motivated only by public service and as not seeking personal gain of any kind. In any case, their role in the reforms did not hurt these policymakers' careers; they usually did well afterward, and one reformer became the president of his country.

4. This view contrasts with recent political economy studies that model switches in policy as being planned ahead by rational forward-looking politicians who design strategies that involve policy reversals in midstream; see Sturzenegger and Tommasi 1998.

5. The study does not examine the role of precolonial institutions.

6. A second-best version of Demsetz's theory of property rights may have a better empirical record than the first-best one. According to the second-best version, actors operating within imperfect political and cultural institutions have a propensity to create social structures that maximize their joint wealth, given the exogenous institutional environment. Assuming that actors are intendedly rational wealth seekers, one would expect to find second-best institutional arrangements in many areas, especially where the property rights structure does not depend on complex political processes representing conflicting interests.

7. In some instances, as Acemoglu, Johnson, and Robinson (2000) show, colonial institutions became the foundations for growth.

8. See, for example, North and Weingast's (1989) analysis of social transformations in seventeenth-century England, which, they believe, created an institutional environment enabling England to grow rich.

9. Similar arguments apply also to discoveries of valuable new markets for known natural resources.

10. The phrase *resource curse* refers to all growth-limiting forces that the discovery of abundant natural resources releases, including the so-called Dutch disease, which originally is associated with the Netherlands after the discovery of North Sea gas. In a Dutch disease scenario, the discovery of a valuable natural resource that is sold abroad raises the value of that nation's currency, making domestic goods less competitive with the products of other nations. In a sense, the natural resource industry chokes other domestic industries.

11. See Landes 1999, 175–81, for a sympathetic discussion of Weber's idea that the Protestant ethic was a driving force of early capitalism.

12. See Weingast 1993, 1995, 1996, 1997; Montinola, Qian, and Weingast 1995; Parikh and Weingast 1997; Careaga and Weingast 2000. For an alternative view of a federal system (the United States), see V. Ostrom 1987.

13. If the economic properties of market-preserving federalism, as Weingast and his coauthors describe them, had been well understood for 300 years, these scholars would not have attracted considerable attention in the 1990s by outlining these features in scholarly journals.

14. Entrepreneurs of the Industrial Revolution in England did not find a

friendly home in London and the southern regions but had the choice of starting up in northern England (Weingast 1995).

15. Dynamics comparable to market-preserving federalism could also emerge through interactions among independent countries that allow unrestricted trade in inputs (including labor) and outputs across their borders.

16. "A famous experiment started in Fengyang county of Anhui province where the households in the village began to contract with the local government for delivering a fixed quota of grain in exchange for farming on a household basis. The practice was later imitated by other regions and also promoted by the central government. By 1984 almost all farm households across China had adopted this method" (Roland 2000, 63).

17. "Indeed the state has attacked private enterprises during several general political crackdowns after the reform, which include the 'anti-spiritual pollution campaign' of 1983, the 'anti-bourgeois liberalization campaign' of 1987, and most recently, after the Tiananmen Square of 1989" (Qian 2002, 20).

18. Qian (2002) provides a detailed analysis of favorable incentive effects of the fiscal system in China, including explaining how the system constrains the government without reducing its revenue.

19. Party control of personnel in state-owned enterprises (SOEs) gives the enterprise party committee extraordinary power in making strategic decisions, which creates tension with recent plans by the government to introduce international corporate management practices to the SOEs.

20. At the outset of the twenty-first century, there are a few dark clouds on the horizon. Eckholm (2001) reports that "a startlingly frank new report from the [Chinese] Communist Party's inner sanctum describes a spreading pattern of collective protests and group incidents arising from economic, ethnic and religious conflicts in China and says relations between party officials and the masses are 'tense with conflicts on the rise.'"

21. The Soviet economy and its satellites were organized in functional ministries (branch organization), and similar activities were combined in gigantic factories. The Chinese economy was organized mainly along regional principles, which, unlike the Soviet economy, allowed regional initiative and experimentation (Roland 2000, 56–65; Qian and Xu 1993). The Eastern European system has been compared to U-form hierarchies, and the Chinese one to M-form hierarchies (Williamson 1975). Reform and experimentation from below were unlikely in Eastern Europe, and Soviet leaders probably felt more threatened by economic slowdown than did the Chinese leaders.

22. Easterly and Levine 1997 provides various data on economic decline in Africa.

23. Rodrik, Subramanian, and Trebbi 2002 provides a useful discussion of the problems of reverse causality as well as direct and indirect effects. Geography can affect income levels directly or can do so indirectly, through institutions or trade. Levels of income do not affect geography (the geography of a country does not change when it becomes rich). Therefore, we need not worry about reverse causal links from wealth to geography, whereas income levels can affect the quality of

institutions, which poses a problem in statistical studies of the influence of institutions on economic growth. Part of the measured effect of institutions on economic growth is actually the effect of growth on (the quality of) institutions. There exist, however, statistical methods that control for reverse causality.

24. The study uses survey responses by investors to measure the quality of institutions. The investors are asked whether their assets are safe from expropriation.

25. See Acemoglu and Robinson 2000 for a theory of the role of political losers in economic development.

26. Arguing that states are viable only when they control all the territory within their borders, Herbst (2000) focuses on various conditions that limit many African governments' ability to fully control their territory. Herbst argues that problems of state building often preceded colonialism and claims that "it is critical to understand the continuities in state consolidation over the centuries" (4).

27. Mistrust also made some newly independent countries in Africa (and elsewhere) reject the political and economic systems of their former rulers and instead experiment with control-and-command economies and seek help from Soviet, Cuban, and East German economic advisers.

28. See chapter 5.

29. Botswana has recently been hit particularly hard by the AIDS epidemic. Implications for long-term economic growth in the twenty-first century are uncertain.

30. We need to know more about the Botswana assemblies to understand their impact on modernization. Advisory assemblies in traditional societies—for example, *panchayats* in India and *shura* in Arabia—are often major sources of conservatism.

31. "Botswana's record in human development is equally impressive, with one important exception—HIV infection. Major emphasis has been placed on providing basic education and primary health care throughout the country. Primary school enrollment has gone from 66,100 in 1966 to 319,000 in 1995, representing an average compounded growth rate of 5.4 percent per annum. Further, in recent decades, the gender balance has consistently involved greater than 50 percent female enrollment. Meanwhile, secondary school and university enrolment, from a much lower base, both grew at double digit growth rates" (World Bank Group: Africa Region Findings, no. 161, "2000: Botswana: An Example of Prudent Economic Policy and Growth," 1, http://www.worldbank.org/afr/findings/english/find161.htm).

Chapter 11

1. The study measures the level of association by the density of sports clubs, choral societies, and similar associations. Civic engagement is reflected in newspaper readership and voting in referenda (Putnam with Leonardi and Nanetti 1993).

2. Committed rational-choice scholars sometimes argue that valued rules are instrumental rules that emerged in a former social equilibrium and persist in a new setting because actors are often slow to adjust their social models and strategies.

Even if this were true of all valued rules, a long adjustment lag could make such "irrational structures" an important social force.

3. "Although the line between judicial and legal reforms blurs at the margin, the core of a judicial reform program typically consists of measures to strengthen the judicial branch of government and such related entities as the public prosecutor and public defender offices, bar associations, and law schools" (Messick 1999, 118).

4. The U.S. Agency for International Development, the Ford Foundation, and other private American donors underwrote the program, which engaged professors from leading U.S. law schools (Messick 1999, 125).

5. Berkowitz, Pistor, and Richard (2000) identify only ten source countries— that is, countries with a modern legal order mostly developed at home. These countries are the United Kingdom, France, Germany, Austria, Switzerland, the United States, and the Nordic family (Denmark, Finland, Norway, and Sweden). The United States has developed its own legal order, but there is an early influence of English common law. The laws of Austria and Switzerland, although distinct, belong to the German legal family.

6. The transplant countries in the sample received their foreign legal systems during 1769–1945.

7. The transplant effect is estimated while controlling for type of legal family. German civil law partly offsets the transplant effect, reducing it to 24 percent, but English common law and French civil law do not offset the transplant effect. The finding by Berkowitz, Pistor, and Richard (2000) of a positive statistical relationship between the quality of property rights (legality) and per capita income is confirmed in many other studies; see, for example, Knack and Keefer 1995.

8. The authors find that the transplant effect influences economic development only indirectly through the impact on legality; there is no direct effect. "The estimated linear regression coefficient implies that a 1 percent increase in legality is associated with a 4.75 percent increase in GNP per capita" (Berkowitz, Pistor, and Richard 2000, 1).

9. The five proxies are efficiency of the judicial system, rule of law, corruption, risk of expropriation, and risk of contract repudiation.

10. In addition to 10 countries with original law, the sample contains "11 receptive transplants and 28 unreceptive transplants; 6 out of 11 of the receptive transplants are voluntary, and 14 of the 28 unreceptive transplants are voluntary" (Berkowitz, Pistor, and Richard 2000, 12–13).

11. Timur Kuran communicates to the author that Turkey adopted the French Commercial Code in full in 1850. It did not take seventy-seven years to transplant it. Also, it is more correct to say that adaptations were slow and tentative rather than to say that it "did not adapt." Numerous adaptations in fact occurred.

12. Ecuador received French law voluntarily from two other transplant countries, Spain and Venezuela (Berkowitz, Pistor, and Richard 2000, 21).

13. "Our basic argument is that for law to be effective, a demand for law must exist so that the law on the books will actually be used in practice and legal intermediaries responsible for developing the law are responsive to this demand. If the transplant [country] adapted the law to local conditions, or had a population

already familiar with basic legal principles of the transplanted law, then we would expect that the law would be used. Because the law would be used, a strong public demand for law would provide resources for legal change. Where these conditions are present we would expect the legal order to function just as effectively as in an origin country where the law was developed internally" (Berkowitz, Pistor, and Richard 2000, 2–3).

14. Rulers other than colonial masters followed a strategy of shielding traditional family law. Turkey adopted the French commercial code in 1850 but did not change family law until 1926. In both cases, Turkish rulers made the change—a monarch in the first case, Atatürk in the second. I owe this observation to Timur Kuran.

15. Moreover, reforming governments must avoid replacing well-functioning traditional ownership rights with new arrangements that malfunction. E. Ostrom (1997) observes that some newly independent states abolished traditional common property regimes that governed natural resources and instead nationalized the assets but did so without providing effective governance and enforcement. The change sometimes gave rise to open access and dissipation of the resources. According to Ostrom, central government reformers often lack full appreciation of the governance problem and the sophistication of traditional rights. Traditional common property regimes can be complex structures that involve rules and enforcement mechanisms, often located at several societal levels, that regulate exclusion of outsiders and (internal) governance. When an asset is under a well-defined common property regime, an easily identifiable group of insiders controls the use and management of the resource and holds exclusive user rights, which outsiders do not enjoy. The rights of insiders usually are formally recognized by the state, although in traditional societies rights of isolated groups sometimes are based only on local customary law and social norms.

16. See also McMillan and Naughton 1996.

Conclusion

1. At the beginning of the millennium, the new institutional economics is surging again. Employing game theory, Aoki (2001) and Greif (forthcoming) provide landmark studies. Acemoglu, Johnson, and Robinson (2000), examining the colonial origins of comparative development, have found striking evidence for long-term institutional path dependence, and Rodrik, Subramanian, and Trebbi (2002), controlling for reverse causation and indirect effects, find statistical support for the primacy of institutions over geography and integration in economic development. Leading scholars involved in international economic reform, including Sachs and Stiglitz, have reconsidered their earlier views, giving greater weight to institutions in the process of growth. Yet with continued and growing theoretical interest in institutions, opportunities and limits for institutional reform have not received thorough scrutiny in the literature.

2. See also Denzau and North 1994.

3. Regulating fisheries is a particularly difficult task. Gylfason and Weitzman (2002, 25) list four factors that complicate regulation in this area: (1) the high cost of

monitoring an industry offshore; (2) "the large number of outputs being jointly regulated or managed and the extreme degree of interdependence among their cost and production functions"; (3) the severe instability of these interdependent cost and production functions; and (4) the "technological inability of fishermen to control exactly the 'product mix' of jointly produced species caught." These four factors illustrate well the close interdependence between social technologies and production technologies and how discoveries in the natural sciences can transform social technologies—for example, by providing new measurement methods. Gylfason and Weitzman offer a new social technology for regulating deep-sea fisheries in which a government board would use prices (fees on landed fish) to create desired outcomes. Their proposal is a new entry in the competition of social models in this area.

4. My chief sources for the discussion of the new fisheries management system are reports commissioned by the Icelandic government, especially a report by Auðlindanefnd (2000), a committee on natural resources. These reports are available only in Icelandic.

5. At the beginning of the twenty-first century, per capita income in Iceland is among the highest in the world. Although the fisheries play a central role in the economy, only about 11 percent of the country's labor force is employed in fishing and processing, and the industry contributes about 15 percent of the country's gross domestic product. The share of fishing and processing in the economy fluctuates from year to year, but there is a long-term downward trend because other sectors now grow faster than the fisheries. For more information, see the Web page of the Census Bureau of Iceland, www.hagstofa.is.

6. A total moratorium on fishing for herring was imposed during 1972–75. The ban was lifted in 1976, when individual quotas were introduced. The quotas were tied to vessels with a history in the herring fisheries. In 1979 the individual quotas became transferable at the request of the industry. A few years later, ITQs were introduced in the capelin fisheries in a similar two-step manner.

7. Under a fishing-days regime, the government sets a target for total catch and then estimates how many days it will take the current fishing fleet to meet the catch target. Costly competition among the fishers usually forces the government to lower its estimates of total fishing days. The regime creates incentives to use more ships, more powerful engines, and more effort.

8. The government initially licensed only vessels with fishing histories prior to the introduction of the ITQ system. The country's supreme court invalidated these restrictions on trading rights. The government now licenses all domestic fishing vessels that are appropriately equipped.

9. More technically, the price equals the present value of the expected future net income from the resource.

10. Experts as well as the public usually rely on various "tragedy of the commons" models to explain the collapse of fish stocks. The "sustainable fisheries model" is a relatively sophisticated version of such interpretations. According to the model, fishing effort will increase continuously in an open access fishery until the level of sustainable stocks is reduced to a point where any further increase in effort yields zero rent—that is, the rent from the fishery is dissipated. Moreover, when fish stocks reach very low levels, it is possible that the stocks collapse for biological reasons, putting an end to the fishery, at least temporarily. The sustainable

fisheries model also explains how to maximize the rent from a fishery. Some party (the government or a monopoly) must control total effort and select the effort level and associated stock size that maximizes net income—in the model, the difference between the total revenue and the total cost curves (Scott 1955). The sustainable fisheries model usually holds organization constant, not allowing for profit-enhancing reorganization of the industry; any increase in industry profits is achieved by adjusting effort measured in some constant units.

11. On the positive side, herring and capelin, two surface species, have recovered, and Iceland has avoided the collapse of stocks such as cod and haddock that other nations have experienced.

12. When put under competitive pressure, the fishing industry in Iceland recognized that fresh fish often has the highest value on international markets; processing the product typically lowers its value.

13. Lord Perry's third explanation can also be seen as failure of government administrators to enforce the rules.

14. Eagle and Thompson (2003) do not provide conclusive answers but call for more data on scientific advice and management decisions. They believe, however, "that there is no one answer to Lord Perry's question, not even for a single fishery" (677).

15. Since the 1990s, the most serious failure of fisheries management in Iceland involves small fishing boats operating under their own complex system of regulations that is not part of the ITQ system. The small-boats system, which is a side payment necessary for getting support for the ITQ system, is a classic case of regulatory failure. Owners of small boats and their communities have strong representation in parliament.

16. One such theory claims that fish stocks are declining as a result of overcrowding and that the appropriate management response is to allow greater fishing effort. The theory is popular in fishing communities around the world.

17. With a population of about 300,000 individuals, oligopoly is the usual state of affairs in many or most Icelandic industries, but not in the fisheries industry, although the concentration recently has increased. The essential point is, however, that most Icelandic fisheries firms sell their output in competitive international markets, where the largest Icelandic firms are small compared with their leading international competitors. When evaluating competitive conditions, the first step should be to identify the relevant market.

18. Many of the critics believe that their home community would do relatively well under a fishing-days system.

19. Formal economic theory usually evaluates social arrangements in terms of their efficiency characteristics and lacks tools for comparing alternative distributions of wealth. In Iceland, some economists critical of the ITQ system, perhaps responding to this tradition in modeling, have presented formal mathematical models showing that a system where the quotas were initially sold or rented out is more efficient (and just) than the present ITQ system. Because the quota trade has worked smoothly, these models seek other explanations than high transaction costs.

20. In 2003, the government majority in parliament supports the present ITQ system, but many or most opposition members would like to change the system. It

is entirely possible that opponents of the system will form a government following the next national election, which will be held no later than in 2007.

21. In my view, the historical communal mountain pastures resemble the current ITQ system. Each farmer had a quota, based on farm size, for how many animals he or she could graze in the pastures, and the quotas could be rented out. The farmers did not pay any fee for use of the pastures. (Eggertsson 1992).

22. The report identifies three types of public property: state property that can be sold (such as banks) and property of the nation as well as resources in custody of the nation that cannot legitimately be sold.

23. To get support in parliament for major restructuring of the system, compromise would probably have to be made with those who altogether oppose free transfer of quotas. The compromises might involve putting various new limits on the transfer of quotas to protect needy localities.

24. In 2003, the Icelandic government responded to criticism about free quotas with a plan to charge the industry for the cost to taxpayers of managing the industry. The industry currently pays about half of these transaction costs, which arise from various monitoring and research activities.

Bibliography

Abramovitz, Moses. 1952. "Economics of Growth." In *A Survey of Contemporary Economics,* ed. B. Haley, 2:132–78. Homewood, Ill.: Richard D. Irwin for the American Economic Association.

Acemoglu, Daron, Simon Johnson, and James A. Robinson. 2000. *The Colonial Origins of Comparative Development: An Empirical Investigation.* Working Paper 00–22. Cambridge, Mass.: MIT Department of Economics.

Acemoglu, Daron, Simon Johnson, and James A. Robinson. 2001. *An African Success Story: Botswana.* Cambridge, Mass.: MIT Department of Economics.

Acemoglu, Daron, Simon Johnson, and James Robinson. 2002. *The Rise of Europe: Atlantic Trade, Institutional Change, and Economic Growth.* NBER Working Paper W9378. Cambridge, Mass.: National Bureau of Economic Research.

Acemoglu, Daron, and James Robinson. 2000. "Political Losers as a Barrier to Economic Development." Unpublished paper.

Aðils, Jón Jónsson. 1971 [1919]. *Einokunarverslun Dana á Íslandi 1602–1787* [Danish Monopoly Trade in Iceland 1602–1787]. Reykjavík: Heimskringla. (In Icelandic.)

Advisory Commission to Study the Consumer Price Index. 1996. *Toward a More Accurate Measure of the Cost of Living: Final Report to the Senate Finance Committee.* Washington, D.C.: U.S. Government Printing Office.

Ahmad, Ehtisham, Jean Drèze, John Hills, and Amartya Sen, eds. 1991. *Social Security in Developing Countries.* Oxford: Clarendon.

Alesina, Alberto. 1988. "Macroeconomics and Politics." In *NBER Macroeconomic Annual,* ed. S. Fisher, 13–52. Cambridge: MIT Press.

Alesina, Alberto. 1995. "Elections, Party Structure, and the Economy." In *Modern Political Economy: Old Topics, New Directions,* ed. J. S. Banks and E. A. Hanushek, 145–70. Cambridge: Cambridge University Press.

Allen, Douglas W. 1991. "What Are Transaction Costs?" *Research in Law and Economics* 14:1–18.

Almond, Gabriel A. 1988. "The Return to the State." *American Political Science Review* 82:853–74. Reprinted in Almond, *A Discipline Divided: Schools and Sects in Political Science,* 189–218. Newbury Park, Calif.: Sage, 1990.

Alt, James E., and Kenneth A. Shepsle, eds. 1990. *Perspectives on Positive Political Economy.* Cambridge: Cambridge University Press.

Aoki, Masahiko. 2001. *Toward a Comparative Institutional Analysis.* Cambridge: MIT Press.

Arnott, Richard, and Joseph E. Stiglitz. 1991. "Moral Hazard and Nonmarket Institutions: Dysfunctional Crowding Out or Peer Monitoring?" *American Economic Review* 81:179–90.

Arrow, Kenneth J. 1956. "Statistics and Economic Policy." *Econometrica* 25:523–31.

Ásgeirsson, Ólafur. 1988. *Iðnbylting hugarfarsins, 1900–1940: Átök un atvinnuþróun á Íslandi* [The Industrial Revolution of the Mind, 1900–1940: Struggle over Economic Development in Iceland]. Reykjavík: Menningarsjóður. (In Icelandic.)

Auðlindanefnd, Álitsgerð. 2000. Report to Parliament by the Committee on Natural Resources. Reykjavík: Parliament.

Axelrod, Robert. 1984. *The Evolution of Cooperation.* New York: Basic Books.

Azzi, Corry, and Ronald D. Ehrenberg. 1975. "Household Allocation of Time and Church Attendance." *Journal of Political Economy* 83:27–56.

Bairoch, P. 1989. "European Trade Policy, 1815–1914." In *The Cambridge Economic History of Europe,* ed. P. Mathias and S. Pollard, 8:1–160. Cambridge: Cambridge University Press.

Banerjee, Abhijit. 2002. *The Uses of Economic Theory: Against a Purely Positive Interpretation of Theoretical Results.* Working Paper 02–24. Cambridge: MIT Department of Economics.

Banks, Jeffrey S., and Eric A. Hanushek, eds. 1995. *Modern Political Economy: Old Topics, New Directions.* Cambridge: Cambridge University Press.

Bardhan, Pranab. 1983. "Labor Tying in Poor Agrarian Economy: A Theoretical and Empirical Analysis." *Quarterly Journal of Economics* 98:501–14.

Bardhan, Pranab. 1989. "A Note on Interlinked Rural Economic Arrangements." In *The Economic Theory of Agrarian Institutions,* ed. Pranab Bardhan, 237–42. New York: Oxford University Press.

Barro, Robert J. 1997. *Determinants of Economic Growth: A Cross-Country Empirical Study.* Cambridge: MIT Press.

Barro, Robert J. 1998. *Notes on Growth Accounting.* NBER Working Paper 6654. Cambridge, Mass.: National Bureau of Economic Research.

Barzel, Yoram. 1997. *Economic Analysis of Property Rights.* 2d ed. Cambridge: Cambridge University Press.

Bates, Robert H. 1981. *Markets and States in Tropical Africa.* Berkeley: University of California Press.

Bates, Robert H. 1990. "Macropolitical Economy in the Field of Development." In *Perspectives on Positive Political Economy,* ed. J. Alt and K. Shepsle, 31–54. Cambridge: Cambridge University Press.

Bates, Robert H., Rui J. P. de Figueiredo Jr., and Barry R. Weingast. 1998. "The Politics of Interpretation: Rationality, Culture, and Transition." *Politics and Society* 26:603–42.

Bates, Robert H., A. Greif, M. Levi, J.-L. Rosenthal, and B. R. Weingast. 1998. *Analytic Narratives.* Princeton: Princeton University Press.

Bates, Robert H., and Anne Krueger, eds. 1993. *Political and Economic Interactions in Economic Policy Reform: Evidence from Eight Countries.* Oxford: Blackwell.

Bawn, Kathleen. 1996. *Constructing "US": Coalition Politics as the Foundation of Ideology, Identity, and Empathy.* Los Angeles: Department of Political Science, UCLA.

Becker, Gary S. 1983. "A Theory of Competition among Pressure Groups for Political Influence." *Quarterly Journal of Economics* 98:371–400.

Bendor, Jonathan, and Piotr Swistak. 2001. "The Evolution of Norms." *American Journal of Sociology* 106:1493–545.

Benham, Alexandra, Lee Benham, and M. Merithew. 1995. *Institutional Reforms in Central and Eastern Europe: Altering Paths with Incentives and Information.* New York: International Center for Economic Growth.

Ben-Ner, Avner, and Louis Putterman, eds. 1998. *Economics, Values, and Organization.* Cambridge: Cambridge University Press.

Bergson, A. 1938. "A Reformulation of Certain Aspects of Welfare Economics." *Quarterly Journal of Economics* 52:310–34.

Berkowitz, Daniel, Katharina Pistor, and Jean-François Richard. 2000. *Economic Development, Legality, and the Transplant Effect.* Working Paper 39. Cambridge: Center for International Development, Harvard University.

Bernstein, Lisa. 1992. "Opting Out of the Legal System: Extralegal Contractual Relations in the Diamond Industry." *Journal of Legal Studies* 21:115–57.

Bhagwati, Jagdish. 1978. *Anatomy and Consequences of Exchange Control Regimes.* Cambridge, Mass.: Ballinger.

Bhagwati, Jagdish, Richard Brecher, and T. N. Srinivasan. 1984. "DUP Activities and Economic Theory." In *Neoclassical Political Economy,* ed. David Colander, 17–32. Cambridge, Mass.: Ballinger.

Biberaj, Elez. 1991. "Albania's Bumpy Road to Markets." *Transition* 2(2): 9–10.

Binmore, Ken. 1994. *Game Theory and the Social Contract: Playing Fair.* Vol. 1. Cambridge: MIT Press.

Binswanger, Hans P., and John McIntire. 1987. "Behavioral and Material Determinants of Production Relations in Land-Abundant Tropical Agriculture." *Economic Development and Cultural Change* 36:73–99.

Binswanger, Hans P., John McIntire, and Chris Udry. 1989. "Production Relations in Semi-Arid Africa." In *The Economic Theory of Agrarian Institutions,* ed. Pranab Bardhan, 122–44. New York: Oxford University Press.

Binswanger, Hans P., and Mark R. Rosenzweig. 1986. "Behavioral and Material Determinants of Production Relations in Agriculture." *Journal of Development Studies* 22:503–39.

Binswanger, Hans P., and Vernon W. Ruttan, eds. 1978. *Induced Innovation: Technology, Institutions, and Development.* Baltimore: Johns Hopkins University Press.

Bjarnason, Torfi. 1913. "Enn um heyásetning" [Further Thoughts on Balancing Livestock and Hay]. *Búnaðarrit* 27:182–213. (In Icelandic.)

Björnsson, Lýður. 1979. *Saga sveitarstjórnar á Íslandi II* [History of Local Government in Iceland]. Reykjavík: Almenna bókafélagið. (In Icelandic.)

Bloom, David E., and Jeffrey Sachs. 1998. "Geography, Demography, and Economic Growth in Africa." *Brookings Papers on Economic Activity* 2:207–95.

Bordo, Michael D., and Anna Schwartz. 2003. *IS-LM and Monetarism.* NBER

Working Paper W9713. Cambridge, Mass.: National Bureau of Economic Research.

Broad, William J., and Andrew C. Revkin. 2003. "Has the Sea Given Up Its Bounty?" *New York Times,* July 29, sec. F, p. 1.

Brock, William A., and Steven Durlauf. 2000. *Growth Economics and Reality.* Working Paper. Madison: Department of Economics, University of Wisconsin.

Bromley, Daniel W., and Jean Paul Chavas. 1989. "On Risk, Transactions, and Economic Development in Semiarid Tropic." *Economic Development and Cultural Change* 37:719–36.

Buchanan, James M. 1975. "A Contractarian Paradigm for Applying Economic Theory." *American Economic Review* 65:225–30.

Buchanan, James M. 1987. "The Constitution of Economic Policy." *American Economic Review* 77:243–50.

Buchanan, James M., Robert D. Tollison, and Gordon Tullock, eds. 1980. *Toward a Theory of the Rent-Seeking Society.* College Station: Texas A & M University Press.

Bueno de Mesquita, Bruce. 2000. *Principles of International Politics: People's Power, Preferences, and Perceptions.* Washington, D.C.: CQ Press.

Bueno de Mesquita, Bruce, James D. Morrow, Randolph M. Sivertson, and Alastair Smith. 2000. "Political Institutions, Political Survival, and Policy Success." In *Governing for Prosperity,* ed. Bruce Bueno de Mesquita and Hilton L. Root, 59–84. New Haven: Yale University Press.

Bueno de Mesquita, Bruce, and Hilton L. Root, eds. 2000. *Governing for Prosperity.* New Haven: Yale University Press.

Bueno de Mesquita, Bruce, Alastair Smith, Randolph Siverson, and James Morrow. 2003. *The Logic of Political Survival.* Cambridge: MIT Press.

Burke, Peter. 1986. "Strengths and Weaknesses of the History of Mentalities." *History of European Ideas* 7:439–51.

Byock, Jesse L. 1988. *Medieval Iceland: Society, Sagas, and Power.* Los Angeles: University of California Press.

Careaga, Maite, and Barry R. Weingast. 2000. *Institutions, Incentives and Good Governance: A Positive Approach to Fiscal Federalism in Developing Countries with an Application to Mexico.* Working Paper. Stanford, Calif.: Hoover Institution, Stanford University.

Chai, S. K. 1998. "Endogenous Ideology Formation and Economic Policy in Former Colonies." *Economic Development and Cultural Change* 46:263–90.

Checkland, S. G. 1989. "British Public Policy, 1776–1939." In *The Cambridge Economic History of Europe,* ed. P. Mathias and S. Pollard, 8:607–40. Cambridge: Cambridge University Press.

Cheung, Steven N. S. 1969. "Transaction Costs, Risk Aversion, and the Choice of Contractual Arrangement." *Journal of Law and Economics* 12:23–42.

Cheung, Steven N. S. 1970. "The Structure of a Contract and the Theory of a Non-Exclusive Resource." *Journal of Law and Economics* 13:23–42.

Cheung, Steven N. S. 1975. "Roofs or Stars: The Stated Intents and Actual Effects of Rent Ordinance." *Economic Inquiry* 13:1–21.

Cheung, Steven N. S. 1976. "Rent Control and Housing Reconstruction: The Postwar Experience of Prewar Premises in Hong Kong." *Journal of Law and Economics* 17:27–53.

Chung, Heetaik. 1990. "Did Policy Makers Really Believe in the Phillips Curve? An Econometric Test." Ph.D. diss., University of Minnesota.

Clague, Christopher, Philip Keefer, Stephen Knack, and Mancur Olson. 1997. "Institutions and Economic Performance: Property Rights and Contract Enforcement." In *Institutions and Economic Development,* ed. Christopher Clague, 67–90. Baltimore: Johns Hopkins University Press.

Clark, Andy. 1998. *Being There: Putting Brain, Body, and the World Together Again.* Cambridge: MIT Press.

Coase, Ronald H. 1937. "The Nature of the Firm." *Economica* 4:386–405.

Coase, Ronald H. 1960. "The Problem of Social Cost." *Journal of Law and Economics* 3:1–44.

Coase, Ronald H. 1992 [1991]. "The Institutional Structure of Production: Nobel Memorial Prize Lecture." *American Economic Review* 82(4):713–19.

Converse, Philip E. 1964. "The Nature of Belief Systems in Mass Publics." In *Ideology and Discontent,* ed. D. Apter, 206–61. New York: Free Press.

Cooter, Robert D. 1996. "Decentralized Law for a Complex Economy: The Structural Approach to Adjudicating the New Law Merchant." *University of Pennsylvania Law Review* 144:1643–96.

Cosmides, L., and J. Tooby. 1994. "Better Than Rational: Evolutionary Psychology and the Invisible Hand." *American Economic Review* 84:327–32.

Cutting, Charles L. 1955. *Fish Saving: A History of Fish Processing from Ancient to Modern Times.* London: Leonard Hill.

Davies, R. W. 1989. "Economic and Social Policy in the USSR, 1917–1941." In *The Cambridge Economic History of Europe,* ed. P. Mathias and S. Pollard, 8:984–1047. Cambridge: Cambridge University Press.

De Alessi, Louis. 1983. "Property Rights, Transaction Costs, and X-Efficiency: An Essay in Economic Theory." *American Economic Review* 73:64–81.

De Janvry, Alain, Marcel Fafchamps, and Elisabeth Sadoulet. 1991. "Peasant Household Behavior with Missing Markets: Some Paradoxes Explained." *Economic Journal* 101:1400–1417.

DeLong, Bradford J. 2000. *The Shape of Twentieth Century Economic History.* NBER Working Paper 7569. Cambridge, Mass.: National Bureau of Economic Research.

Demsetz, Harold H. 1967. "Toward a Theory of Property Rights." *American Economic Review* 57:347–59.

Demsetz, Harold H. 1980. *Economic, Legal, and Political Dimensions of Competition.* Amsterdam: North-Holland.

DeNardo, James. 1995. *The Amateur Strategist: Intuitive Deterrence Theories and the Politics of the Nuclear Arms Race.* Cambridge: Cambridge University Press.

Denzau, Arthur, and Douglass C. North. 1994. "Shared Mental Models: Ideologies and Institutions." *Kyklos* 47:3–31.

De Soto, Hernando. 1989. *The Other Path. The Invisible Revolution in the Third World.* New York: Harper and Row.

Dewatripont, Mathias, and Gérard Roland. 1995. "The Design of Reform Packages under Uncertainty." *American Economic Review* 85:1207–23.

Diamond, Larry J., and M. F. Plattner, eds. 1996. *The Global Resurgence of Democracy.* 2d ed. Baltimore: Johns Hopkins University Press.

Dixit, Avinash K. 1996. *The Making of Economic Policy: A Transaction-Cost Politics.* Cambridge: MIT Press.

Domar, Evsey. 1946. "Capital Expansion, Rate of Growth, and Employment." *Econometrica* 14:137–47.

Drobak, John N., and John V. C. Nye, eds. 1997. *The Frontiers of the New Institutional Economics.* San Diego: Academic Press.

Eagle, Josh, and Barton H. Thompson Jr. 2003. "Answering Lord Perry's Question: Dissecting Regulatory Overfishing." *Ocean and Coastal Management* 46:649–79.

Easterly, William. 1999. "The Ghost of Financing Gap: Testing the Growth Model Used in the International Financial Institutions." *Journal of Development Economics* 60:423–38.

Easterly, William, Michael Kremer, Lant Pritchett, and Larry Summers. 1993. "Good Policy or Good Luck? Country Growth Performance and Temporary Shocks." *Journal of Monetary Economics* 32:459–83.

Easterly, William, and Ross Levine. 1997. "Africa's Growth Tragedy: Policies and Ethnic Divisions." *Quarterly Journal of Economics* 112:1203–50.

Eckholm, Erik. 2001. "China's Inner Circle Reveals Big Unrest." *New York Times,* June 3, sec. 1, p. 14.

Eggertsson, Thráinn. 1990. *Economic Behavior and Institutions.* New York: Cambridge University Press.

Eggertsson, Thráinn. 1992. "Analyzing Institutional Successes and Failures: A Millennium of Common Mountain Pastures in Iceland." *International Review of Law and Economics* 12:423–37.

Eggertsson, Thráinn. 1996. "No Experiments, Monumental Disasters: Why It Took a Thousand Years to Develop a Specialized Fishing Industry in Iceland." *Journal of Economic Behavior and Organization* 30:1–23.

Eggertsson, Thráinn. 1997a. "The Old Theory of Economic Policy and the New Institutionalism." *World Development* 18:1187–1204.

Eggertsson, Thráinn. 1997b. "When the State Changes Its Mind: Discontinuity in State Control of Economic Activity." *In Privatization at the Turn of the Century,* ed. Herbert Giersch, 76–104. Berlin: Springer-Verlag.

Eggertsson, Thráinn. 1998a. "Limits to Institutional Reforms." *Scandinavian Journal of Economics* 100:335–57.

Eggertsson, Thráinn. 1998b. "Sources of Risk, Institutions for Survival, and a Game against Nature in Premodern Iceland." *Explorations in Economic History* 35:1–30.

Eggertsson, Thráinn. 1999. "State Reform and the Theory of Institutional Policy." *Revista de Economica Política* 19:49–62.

Eggertsson, Thráinn. 2001. "Social Norms with Special Reference to Economic Development." In *Social Norms,* ed. Michael Hechter and Karl-Dieter Opp, 76–104. New York: Sage.

Eggertsson, Thráinn. 2003. *The Subtle Art of Major Institutional Reform: Intro-ducing Property Rights in the Iceland Fisheries.* Working Paper. Reykjavik: University of Iceland, Faculty of Business and Economics.

Ehrenberg, Ronald G. 1977. "Household Allocation of Time and Religiosity: Replication and Extension." *Journal of Political Economy* 85:415–23.

Ellickson, Robert C. 1991. *Order without Law: How Neighbors Settle Disputes.* Cambridge: Harvard University Press.

Ellickson, Robert C. 1994. "The Aim of Order without Law." *Journal of Institutional and Theoretical Economics* 150:97–100.

Elster, Jon. 1989. *The Cement of Society: A Study of Social Order.* Cambridge: Cambridge University Press.

Fafchamps, Marcel. 1992. "Solidarity Networks in Pre-Industrial Societies: Rational Peasants with a Moral Economy." *Economic Development and Cultural Change* 41:147–74.

Fafchamps, Marcel. 1993. "The Rural Community, Mutual Assistance, and Structural Adjustment." Mimeo. Stanford University.

Fernandez, Raquel, and Dani Rorik. 1991. "Resistance to Reform." *American Economic Review 91:*1146–55.

Fishlow, Albert. 1989. "Alexander Gerschenkron." In *The New Palgrave: Economic Development,* ed. John Eatwell, Murray Milgate, and Peter Newman, 145–47. New York: Norton.

Fogel, Robert W. 2000. *Simon Kusnetz: April 30, 1901–July 9, 1985.* NBER Working Paper 7787. Cambridge, Mass.: National Bureau of Economic Research.

Folta, Timothy B., and Walter J. Ferrier. 1996. "International Expansion through Sequential Investment: The Effects of National Culture on Buyouts and Dissolutions in Biotechnology Relationships." Unpublished paper. Lexington: University of Kentucky.

Ford, A. C. 1989. "International Financial Policy and the Gold Standard, 1870–1914." In *The Cambridge Economic History of Europe,* ed. P. Mathias and S. Pollard, 8:197–249. Cambridge: Cambridge University Press.

Frankel, Jeffrey, and David Romer. 1999. "Does Trade Cause Growth?" *American Economic Review* 89:379–99.

Fratianni, Michele, and John C. Pattison. 1976. "The Economics of the OECD." In *Institutions, Policies, and Economic Performance,* ed. K. Brunner and A. Meltzer, 75–140. Amsterdam: North-Holland.

Friðriksson, Sturla. 1986. "Factors Affecting Productivity and Stability of Northern Ecosystems." In *Grazing Research at Northern Latitudes,* ed. Ó. Guðmundsson. New York: Plenum.

Friedman, David. 1979. "Private Enforcement and Creation of Law: A Historical Case." *Journal of Legal Studies* 8:399–415.

Furubotn, Eirik G., and Rudolf Richter. 1997. *Institutions and Economic Theory: The Contribution of the New Institutional Economics.* Ann Arbor: University of Michigan Press.

Gallup, John L., Andrew D. Mellinger, and Jeffrey D. Sachs. 1998. *Geography and Economic Development.* NBER Working Paper 6849. Cambridge, Mass.: National Bureau of Economic Research.

Gelsinger, Bruce E. 1981. *Icelandic Enterprise, Commerce, and Economy in the Middle Ages.* Columbia: University of South Carolina Press.

Gerschenkron, Alexander. 1962. *Economic Backwardness in Historical Perspective.* Cambridge: Harvard University Press.

Goldstein, Judith, and Robert O. Keohane. 1993. *Ideas and Foreign Policy: Beliefs, Institutions, and Political Change.* Ithaca: Cornell University Press.

Gordon, H. S. 1954. "The Economic Theory of a Common Property Resource: The Fishery." *Journal of Political Economy* 62:124–42.

Granick, D. 1990. *Chinese State Enterprises: A Regional Property Rights Analysis.* Chicago: University of Chicago Press.

Greif, Avner. 1994. "Cultural Beliefs and the Organization of Society: A Historical and Theoretical Reflection of Collectivist and Individualist Societies." *Journal of Political Economy* 102:912–50.

Greif, Avner. 1995. *Institutional Structure and Economic Development: Economic History and the New Institutionalism.* Working Paper. Stanford, Calif.: Department of Economics, Stanford University.

Greif, Avner. Forthcoming. *Institutional Theory and History: Comparative and Historical Analysis.* New York: Cambridge University Press.

Gunnarsson, Gísli. 1980. *A Study of Causal Relations in Climate and History.* Lund: Ekonomisk-Historiska Institutionen.

Gunnarsson, Gísli. 1983. *Monopoly Trade and Economic Stagnation: Studies in the Foreign Trade of Iceland, 1602–1787.* Lund: Ekonomisk-Historiska Föreningen.

Gunnarsson, Gísli. 1987. *Upp er boðið Ísaland: Einokunarverslun og íslenskt samfélag, 1602–1787* [Iceland on the Block: Monopoly Trade and Icelandic Society, 1602–1787]. Reykjavík: Örn og Örlygur. (In Icelandic.)

Gunnlaugsson, Gísli Ágúst. 1982. "The Granting of Privileges to Industry in Eighteenth Century Iceland." *Scandinavian Journal of Economic History* 7:195–204.

Gunnlaugsson, Gísli Ágúst. 1988. *Family and Household in Iceland 1801–1930: Studies in the Relationship between Demographic and Socio-Economic Development, Social Legislation, and Family and Household Structures.* Stockholm: Almqvist and Wiksell.

Gustafsson, Harald. 1981. "Fiskveiðiáætlunin 1762: Athuganir á ákvarðatökunni" [The Fisheries Regulation of 1762: A Study of the Decision Making]. *Saga* 19:107–21. (In Icelandic.)

Gustafsson, Harald. 1985. *Mellan kung och allmoge—ämbedsmän, beslutsprocess och inflytande på 1700-talets Island* [Between the Crown and the Public: Civil Servants, the Decision Process, and Influence in Eighteenth Century Iceland]. Stockholm: Almqvist and Wiksell. (In Swedish.)

Gylfason, Thorvaldur. 2001. "Natural Resources, Education, and Economic Development." *European Economic Review* 45:847–60.

Gylfason, Thorvaldur, Tryggvi Thor Herbertsson, and Gylfi Zoega. 1999. "A Mixed Blessing: Natural Resources and Economic Growth." *Macroeconomic Dynamics* 3:204–25.

Gylfason, Thorvaldur, and Martin L. Weitzman. 2002. "Icelandic Fisheries Management: Fees versus Quotas." Paper presented at the Small Island Economies Conference, Center for International Development, Harvard University.

Haber, Stephen, Armando Razo, and Noel Maurer. 2003. *The Politics of Property Rights: Political Instability, Credible Commitments, and Economic Growth in Mexico, 1876–1929.* New York: Cambridge University Press.

Hálfdanarson, Guðmundur. 1991. "Old Provinces, Modern Nations: Political Responses to State Independence in Late Nineteenth- and Early Twentieth-Century Iceland and Brittany." Ph.D. diss., Cornell University.

Hall, P. A. 1986. *Governing the Economy: The Politics of State Intervention in Britain and France.* Cambridge: Polity.

Halldórsson, Ólafur, ed., 1970. *Jónsbók.* Odense: Odense University Press. (In Icelandic.)

Hansen, Bent. 1963. *Lectures in Economic Theory.* Part 3, *The Theory of Economic Policy.* Cairo: Institute of Planning.

Hansen, Bent. 1976. "The Economics of the OECD: A Comment." In *Institutions, Policies, and Economic Performance,* ed. K. Brunner and A. H. Meltzer, 141–53. Amsterdam: New-Holland.

Harberger, Arnold C. 1993. "Secrets of Success: A Handful of Heroes." *American Economic Review* 83:343–50.

Hardin, Russell. 1997. "The Economics of Religious Belief." *Journal of Institutional and Theoretical Economics* 153:259–78.

Harrod, Roy F. 1939. "An Essay in Dynamic Theory." *Economic Journal* 49:14–33.

Hastrup, Kirsten. 1990. *Nature and Policy in Iceland, 1400–1800: An Anthropological Analysis of History and Mentality.* Oxford: Clarendon.

Hay, Jonathan R., Andrei Shleifer, and Robert W. Vishny. 1996. "Toward a Theory of Legal Reform." *European Economic Review* 40:559–67.

Hayek, Friedrich A. von. 1945. "The Use of Knowledge in Society." *American Economic Review* 35:519–30.

Hayek, Friedrich A. von. 1960. *The Constitution of Liberty.* Chicago: University of Chicago Press.

Hechter, Michael, and S. Kanazawa. 1997. "Sociological Rational Choice Theory." *Annual Review of Sociology* 23:191–214.

Hechter, Michael, and Karl-Dieter Opp, eds. 2001. *Social Norms.* New York: Sage.

Heckman, J. J. 1992. "Haavelmo and the Birth of Modern Econometrics: A Review of the History of Econometric Ideas by Mary Morgan." *Journal of Economic Literature* 30:876–86.

Henning, Christian, and Xiaobo Lu. 2000. "The Political Foundations of Chinese Style Gradualism." *Journal of Institutional and Theoretical Economics* 156:35–59.

Herbst, Jeffrey. 2000. *States and Power in Africa: Comparative Lessons in Authority and Control.* Princeton: Princeton University Press.

Hettich, W., and S. L. Weiner. 1993. "Economic Efficiency, Policy Institutions, and Policy Analysis." *Kyklos* 46:3–25.

Higgs, R. 1982. "Legally Induced Technical Regress in the Washington State

Salmon Fishery." *Research in Law and Economics* 7:55–86. Reprinted in L. Alston, T. Eggertsson, and D. C. North, eds., *Empirical Studies in Institutional Change,* 247–79. Cambridge: Cambridge University Press, 1996.

Hinich, Melvin, and Michael Munger. 1992. "A Spatial Theory of Ideology." *Journal of Theoretical Politics* 4:5–30.

Hirschman, Albert O. 1981. "The Rise and Decline of Development Economics." In Hirschman, *Essays in Trespassing: Economics to Politics and Beyond.* Cambridge: Cambridge University Press.

Hirschman, Albert O. 1982. *Shifting Involvements: Private Interest and Public Action.* Princeton: Princeton University Press.

Hoff, Karla. 2000. *Beyond Rosenstein-Rodan: The Modern Theory of Underdevelopment Traps.* Working Paper. Washington, D.C.: World Bank.

Hofstede, Geert. 1980. *Culture's Consequences: International Differences in Work-Related Values.* Beverly Hills, Calif.: Sage.

Hofstede, Geert. 1991. *Cultures and Organizations: Software of the Mind.* London: McGraw-Hill.

Hofstede, Geert. 1998. "Attitudes, Values, and Organizational Culture: Disentangling the Concepts." *Organizational Studies* 19:477–92.

Hollander, Paul. 1999. *Political Will and Personal Belief: The Decline and Fall of Soviet Communism.* New Haven: Yale University Press.

Hull, Brooks B., and Frederick Bold. 1994. "Hell, Religion, and Cultural Change." *Journal of Institutional and Theoretical Economics* 150:447–64.

Hulten, Charles. 2000. *Total Factor Productivity: A Short Biography.* NBER Working Paper 7471. Cambridge, Mass.: National Bureau of Economic Research.

Huntington, Samuel P. 1987. "The Goals of Development." In *Understanding Political Development,* ed. Myron Weiner and Samuel P. Huntington, 3–32. Boston: Little, Brown.

Iannaccone, Laurence R. 1998. "Introduction to the Economics of Religion." *Journal of Economic Literature* 36:1465–95.

International Organization. 1998. Vol. 52, no. 4. Special Issue on Research in International Political Economy.

Jóhannesson, Jón. 1974. *A History of the Icelandic Commonwealth.* Trans. Haraldur Bessason. Winnipeg: Manitoba Press.

Jóhannesson, Þorkell. 1948. *Alþingi og atvinnumálin: Landbúnaður og útvegsmál: Höfuðþættir* [Parliament and the Economy: Agriculture and Fisheries: Main Issues]. Reykjavík: Alþingissögunefnd. (In Icelandic.)

Jóhannesson, Þorkell. 1950. *Saga Íslendinga, VII, 1770–1830* [History of the Icelanders, VII, 1770–1830]. Reykjavík: Menntamálaráðuneytið og Þjóðvinafélag. (In Icelandic.)

Johansen, Leif. 1974. "Establishing Preference Functions for Macroeconomic Decision Models: Some Observations on Ragnar Frisch's Contributions." *European Economic Review* 5:41–66. Reprinted in *Collected Works of Leif Johansen,* ed. F. Försund, 2:541–66. Amsterdam: North-Holland, 1987.

Johansen, Leif. 1977. *Lectures on Macroeconomic Planning.* Vol. 1, *General Aspects.* Amsterdam: North-Holland.

Johansen, Leif. 1979. "The Report of the Committee on Policy Optimization—UK." *Journal of Economic Dynamics and Control* 1. Reprinted in *Collected Works of Leif Johansen,* ed. F. Försund, 2:567–76. Amsterdam: North-Holland, 1987.

Johnson, Simon, John McMillan, and Christopher Woodruff. 1999. *Property Rights, Finance, and Entrepreneurship.* CESifo Working Paper 212. Munich: CESifo.

Jónsson, Ásgeir. 1994. "Siglt gegn vindi" [Sailing against the Wind]. *Fjármálatíðindi* 2:236–64. (In Icelandic.)

Jónsson, Guðmundur. 1991. "The State and the Icelandic Economy, 1870–1930." Ph.D. diss., London School of Economics.

Journal of Economic Perspectives. 1994. Vol. 8, no. 1. Special section on new growth theory.

Journal of Institutional and Theoretical Economics. 1998. Vol. 154, no. 4. Special section with nine essays on "Views and Comments on the 'New Institutionalism' in Sociology, Political Science, and Anthropology."

Jovannovic, Boyan. 2000. *Growth Theory.* NBER Working Paper 7468. Cambridge, Mass.: National Bureau of Economic Research.

Kaldor, Nicholas. 1956. "Alternative Theories of Distribution." *Review of Economic Studies* 23:83–100.

Karlsson, Gunnar, Kristján Sveinsson, and Mörður Árnason, eds. 1992. *Grágás: Lagasafn íslenska Þjóðveldisins* [Grágás: The Laws of the Icelandic Commonwealth]. Reykjavík: Mál og menning. (In Icelandic.)

Katz, Avery. 1996. "Taking Private Ordering Seriously." *University of Pennsylvania Law Review* 144:1745–64.

Katzenstein, Peter J., Robert O. Keohane, and Stephen D. Krasner. 1998. "International Organization and the Study of World Politics." *International Organization* 52:645–85.

Keynes, J. Maynard. 1936. *The General Theory of Employment, Interest, and Money.* London: Macmillan.

Killick, T., ed. 1995. *The Flexible Economy: Causes and Consequences of the Adaptability of National Economies.* London: Routledge.

Kindleberger, Charles P. 1958. *Economic Development.* New York: McGraw-Hill.

Klaes, Matthias. 2000. "The Birth of the Concept of Transaction Costs: Issues and Controversies." *Industrial and Corporate Change* 9:567–93.

Knack, Stephen, and Philip Keefer. 1995. "Institutions and Economic Performance: Cross-Country Tests Using Alternative Institutional Measures." *Economics and Politics* 7:207–27.

Knudsen, Christian. 1995. "Theories of the Firm, Strategic Management, and Leadership." In *Resource-Based and Evolutionary Theories of the Firm: Towards a Synthesis,* ed. Cynthia A. Montgomery, 179–218. Boston: Kluwer.

Kornai, János. 1992. *The Socialist System: The Political Economy of Communism.* Princeton: Princeton University Press.

Kranton, Rachel E. 1996. "Reciprocal Exchange: A Self-Sustaining System." *American Economic Review* 86:830–51.

Kreps, David. 1990. "Corporate Culture and Economic Theory." In *Perspectives* on *Positive Political Economy,* ed. J. Alt and K. Shepsle, 90–143. Cambridge: Cambridge University Press.

Kristjánsson, Aðalgeir. 1977. "Álitsgerð Skúla Magnússonar 1784 um brottflutning Íslendinga vegna Móðuharðindanna" [Report by Skúli Magnússon from 1784 concerning expatriation of Icelanders Following the Famine of the Mist.] *Saga* 15:29–40. (In Icelandic.)

Kristjánsson, Aðalgeir, and Gísli Ágúst Gunnlaugsson. 1990. "Félags-og hagþróun á Íslandi á fyrri hluta 19du aldar" [Social and Economic Development in Iceland during the First Half of the Nineteenth Century.] *Saga* 28:7–62. (In Icelandic.)

Kristjánsson, Lúðvík. 1980–86. *Íslenskir sjávarhættir* [The Icelandic Fisheries]. Vols. 1–5. Reykjavík: Menningarsjóður. (In Icelandic.)

Krueger, Anne O. 1978. *Foreign Trade Regimes and Economic Development: Liberalization Attempts and Consequences.* Cambridge, Mass.: Ballinger.

Krueger, Anne O. 1990. "The Political Economy of Controls: American Sugar." In *Public Policy and Development: Essays in Honour of Ian Little,* ed. M. Scott and D. Lal. Oxford: Oxford University Press.

Krueger, Anne O. 1993. *Political Economy of Policy Reform in Developing Countries.* Cambridge: MIT Press.

Krugman, Paul. 1995. *Development, Geography, and Economic Theory.* Cambridge: MIT Press.

Kuran, Timur. 1995. *Private Truths, Public Lies: The Social Consequences of Preference Falsification.* Cambridge: Harvard University Press.

Kuran, Timur. 1998. "Ethnic Norms and Their Transformation through Reputational Cascades." *Journal of Legal Studies* 27:623–60.

Landa, Janet T. 1994. *Trust, Ethnicity, and Identity: Beyond the New Institutional Economics of Ethnic Trading Networks, Contract Law, and Gift-Exchange.* Ann Arbor: University of Michigan Press.

Landes, David S. 1999. *The Wealth and Poverty of Nations: Why Some Are So Rich and Some Are So Poor.* New York: Norton.

Larson, Deborah W. 1985. *Origins of Containment: A Psychological Explanation.* Princeton: Princeton University Press.

Lárusson, Björn. 1967. *The Old Icelandic Land Registers.* Lund: Glerup.

Lárusson, Ólafur. 1958. *Lög og Saga* [Law and History]. Reykjavík: Hlaðbúð. (In Icelandic.)

Letwin, W. 1989. "American Economic Policy, 1865–1939." In *The Cambridge Economic History of Europe,* ed. P. Mathias and S. Pollard, 8:641–90. Cambridge: Cambridge University Press.

Levi, Margaret. 1988. *Of Rule and Revenue.* Berkeley: University of California Press.

Lewis, W. Arthur. 1954. "Economic Development with Unlimited Supplies of Labor." *Manchester School* 22:139–91.

Lewis, W. Arthur. 1955. *The Theory of Economic Growth.* London: Allen and Unwin.

Libecap, Gary D. 1989. *Contracting for Property Rights.* Cambridge: Cambridge University Press.

Lin, Justin Yifu, and Jeffrey B. Nugent. 1995. "Institutions and Economic Development." In *Handbook of Development Economics,* ed. J. Behrman and T. N. Srinivasan, 3A:2303–70. Amsterdam: Elsevier Science.

Lindbeck, Assar. 1994. "Overshooting, Reform, and Retreat of the Welfare State." *De Economist* 104:1–19.

Lindbeck, Assar. 1995a. "Hazardous Welfare-State Dynamics." *American Economic Review* 85:9–15.

Lindbeck, Assar. 1995b. "Welfare State Disincentives with Endogenous Habits and Norms." *Scandinavian Journal of Economics* 97:477–94.

Lindbeck, Assar. 1997. "Incentives and Social Norms in Household Behavior." *American Economic Review* 87:370–77.

Lindbeck, Assar, Sten Nyberg, and Jörgen W. Weibull. 2003. *Social Norms and Welfare State Dynamics.* CESifo Working Paper 931. Munich: CESifo.

Loasby, Brian J. 1989. *The Mind and Method of the Economist.* Aldershot: Elgar.

Lucas, Robert E., Jr. 1976. "Econometric Policy Evaluation: A Critique." *Journal of Monetary Economics,* supp. ser. 1(2): 19–46.

Lucas, Robert E., Jr. 1986. "Adaptive Behavior and Economic Theory." *Journal of Business* 59:401–26.

Lucas, Robert E., Jr. 1988. "On the Mechanics of Economic Development." *Journal of Monetary Economics* 22:3–42.

Lucas, Robert E., Jr. 1990. "Supply-Side Economics: An Analytical Review." *Oxford Economic Papers* 42:293–316.

Macmillan, Harold. 1938. *The Middle Way: A Study in the Problem of Economic and Social Progress in a Free and Democratic Society.* London: Macmillan.

Maddison, Agnus. 1982. *Phases of Capitalistic Development.* Oxford: Oxford University Press.

Magnússon, Magnús S. 1985. *Iceland in Transition: Labor and Socio-Economic Change before 1940.* Lund: Ekonomisk-Historiska Föreningen.

Mathias, P., and S. Pollard, eds. 1989. *The Cambridge Economic History of Europe.* Vol. 8, *The Industrial Economies: The Development of Economic and Social Policies.* Cambridge: Cambridge University Press.

McCloskey, Donald N. 1985. *The Applied Theory of Price.* 2d ed. New York: Macmillan.

McCloskey, Donald N., and J. R. Zecher. 1976. "How the Gold Standard Worked, 1880–1913." In *The Monetary Approach to the Balance of Payments,* ed. J. A. Frenkel and H. G. Johnson, 357–85. London: Allen and Unwin.

McGuire, Martin C., and Mancur Olson Jr. 1996. "The Economics of Autocracy and Majority Rule: The Invisible Hand and the Use of Force." *Journal of Economic Literature* 34:72–96.

McKinnon, Ronald. 1991. *The Order of Economic Liberalization.* Baltimore: Johns Hopkins University Press.

McMillan, John, and Barry Naughton, eds. 1996. *Reforming Asian Socialism: The Growth of Market Institutions.* Ann Arbor: University of Michigan Press.

McMillan, John, and Christopher Woodruff. 2000. *Private Order under Dysfunctional Public Order.* Working Paper 189. Stanford, Calif.: Stanford Law School, John M. Olin Program in Law and Economics.

Messick, Richard E. 1999. "Judicial Reform and Economic Development: A Survey of the Issues." *World Bank Research Observer* 14:117–36.

Milgrom, Paul R., Douglass C. North, and Barry R. Weingast. 1990. "The Role of Institutions in the Revival of Trade: The Law Merchant, Private Judges, and the Champagne Fairs." *Economics and Politics* 2:1–21.

Miller, Gary J. 1997. "The Impact of Economics on Contemporary Political Science." *Journal of Economic Literature* 35:1173–1204.

Miller, William Ian. 1990. *Bloodtaking and Peacemaking: Feud, Law, and Society in Saga Iceland.* Chicago: University of Chicago Press.

Mitchell, A. R. 1977. "The European Fisheries in Early-Modern History." In *Cambridge Economic History of Europe,* ed. E. E. Rich and C. H. Wilson, 5:133–84. Cambridge: Cambridge University Press.

Moggridge, D. E. 1989. "The Gold Standard and National Financial Policies, 1913–1939." In *The Cambridge Economic History of Europe,* ed. P. Mathias and S. Pollard, 8:250–314. Cambridge: Cambridge University Press.

Mokyr, Joel. 1990. *The Lever of Riches: Technological Creativity and Economic Progress.* New York: Oxford University Press.

Montinola, Gabriella, Yingyi Qian, and Barry R. Weingast. 1995. "Federalism Chinese Style: The Political Basis for Economic Success in China." *World Politics* 48:50–81.

Mowery, David C., and Richard R. Nelson, eds. 1999. *Sources of Industrial Leadership: Studies of Seven Industries.* Cambridge: Cambridge University Press.

Murrell, Peter. 1995. "The Transition According to Cambridge, Mass." *Journal of Economic Literature* 33:164–78.

Nakamura, Emi, and Jón Steinsson. 2003. *Econometric Learning.* Working Paper, Harvard University.

Ndulu, Benno, and Nicolas van de Walle. 1996. "Africa's Economic Renewal: From Consensus to Strategy." In *Agenda for Africa's Economic Renewal,* ed. Benno Ndulu and Nicolas van de Walle, 3–32. Washington, D.C.: Overseas Development Council.

Nelson, Phillip. 1970. "Information and Consumer Behavior." *Journal of Political Economy* 78:311–29.

Nelson, Richard R. 1996. *The Sources of Economic Growth.* Cambridge: Harvard University Press.

Nelson, Richard R. 1998. "The Agenda for Growth Theory: A Different Point of View." *Cambridge Journal of Economics* 22:497–520.

Nelson, Richard R., and Bhaven N. Sampat. 2000. "Making Sense of Institutions as a Factor Shaping Economic Performance." *Journal of Economic Behavior and Organization* 44:31–54.

Nelson, Richard R., and Sidney A. Winter. 1982. *An Evolutionary Theory of Economic Change.* Cambridge: Harvard University Press.

Newbery, David M. G. 1989. "Agrarian Institutions for Insurance and Stabilization." In *The Economic Theory of Agrarian Institutions,* ed. Pranab Bardhan, 267–96. New York: Oxford University Press.

Noll, Roger G., and B. M. Owen. 1983. "Conclusions: Economics, Politics, and Deregulation." In *The Political Economy of Deregulation: Interest Groups in the*

Regulatory Process, ed. Noll and Owen. Washington, D.C.: American Enterprise Institute.

Nordhaus, William D. 1973. "Some Skeptical Thoughts on the Theory of Induced Innovation." *Quarterly Journal of Economics* 87:208–19.

North, Douglass C. 1979. "A Framework for Analyzing the State in Economic History." *Explorations in Economic History* 16:249–59.

North, Douglass C. 1981. *Structure and Change in Economic History.* New York: Norton.

North, Douglass C. 1990. *Institutions, Institutional Change, and Economic Performance.* Cambridge: Cambridge University Press.

North, Douglass C. 1993. "Institutions and Credible Commitment." *Journal of Institutional and Theoretical Economics* 149:11–23.

North, Douglass C., William Summerhill, and Barry R. Weingast. 2000. "Order, Disorder, and Economic Change: Latin America versus North America." In *Governing for Prosperity,* ed. Bruce Bueno de Mesquita and Hilton L. Root, 17–58. New Haven: Yale University Press.

North, Douglass C, and Robert P. Thomas. 1973. *The Rise of the Western World: A New Economic History.* Cambridge: Cambridge University Press.

North, Douglass C., and Barry R. Weingast. 1989. "Constitutions and Commitment: The Institutions Governing Public Choice in Seventeenth-Century England." *Journal of Economic History* 44:803–32. Reprinted in L. J. Alston, T. Eggertsson, and D. C. North, eds., *Empirical Studies in Institutional Change,* 134–65. Cambridge: Cambridge University Press, 1996.

Nove, Alec. 1986. *The Soviet Economic System.* Boston: Allen and Unwin.

Nove, Alec. 1992. *An Economic History of the USSR.* 3d ed. London: Penguin.

Ogilvie, Astrid E. J. 1981. "Climate and Society in Iceland from the Medieval Period to the Late Eighteenth Century." Ph.D. diss., University of East Anglia, School of Environmental Science.

Olson, Mancur. 1965. *The Logic of Collective Action.* Cambridge: Harvard University Press.

Olson, Mancur. 1982. *The Rise and Decline of Nations: Economic Growth, Stagflation, and Social Rigidities.* New Haven: Yale University Press.

Olson, Mancur. 1993. "Dictatorship, Democracy, and Development." *American Political Science Review* 87:567–76.

Olson, Mancur. 1996. "Big Bills Left on the Sidewalk: Why Some Nations Are Poor and Others Are Rich. Distinguished Lecture on Economics in Government." *Journal of Economic Perspectives* 10:3–24.

Olson, Mancur. 2000. *Power and Prosperity: Outgrowing Communist and Capitalist Dictatorships.* New York: Basic Books.

Ostrom, Elinor. 1990. *Governing the Commons: The Evolution of Institutions for Collective Action.* Cambridge: Cambridge University Press.

Ostrom, Elinor. 1997. "Private and Common Property Rights." *Encyclopedia of Law and Economics.* http://encyclo.findlaw.com/lit/2000.art.htm

Ostrom, Vincent. 1987. *The Theory of a Compound Republic.* Lincoln: University of Nebraska Press.

Ostrom, Vincent. 1993. *Great Experiments and the Welfare State: Paradigmatic*

Challenges. Working Paper. Bloomington: Indiana University Workshop in Political Theory and Policy Analysis.

Ostrom, Vincent. 1997. *The Meaning of Democracy and the Vulnerability of Democracies: A Response to Tocqueville's Challenge.* Ann Arbor: University of Michigan Press.

Pack, Howard. 1994. "Endogenous Growth Theory: Intellectual Appeal and Empirical Shortcomings." *Journal of Economic Perspectives* 8:55–72.

Parente, Steven L., and Edward C. Prescott. 2000. *Barriers to Riches.* Cambridge: MIT Press.

Parikh, Sunnita, and Barry R. Weingast. 1997. "A Comparative Theory of Federalism: India." *Virginia Law Review* 83:1593–1615.

Posner, Eric A. 1996a. "Law, Economics, and Inefficient Norms." *University of Pennsylvania Law Review* 144:1697–1744.

Posner, Eric A. 1996b. "The Regulation of Groups: The Influence of Legal and Nonlegal Sanctions on Collective Action." *University of Chicago Law Review* 63:133–97.

Posner, Eric A. 2002. *Law and Social Norms.* Cambridge: Harvard University Press.

Posner, Richard A. 1986. *Economic Analysis of Law.* Boston: Little Brown.

Posner, Richard A. 1998. "Creating a Legal Framework for Economic Development." *World Bank Research Observer* 13:1–11.

Putnam, Robert D., with Robert Leonardi and Raffaella Y. Nanetti. 1993. *Making Democracy Work: Civic Traditions in Modern Italy.* Princeton: Princeton University Press.

Putterman, Louis, ed. 1988. *The Economic Nature of the Firm: A Reader.* Cambridge: Cambridge University Press.

Qian, Yingyi. 2000a. "The Institutional Foundations of China's Market Transition." In *Proceedings of the World Bank's Annual Conference on Development Economics, 1999,* ed. B. Pleskovic and J. Stiglitz, 289–310. Washington, D.C.: World Bank.

Qian, Yingyi. 2000b. "The Process of China's Market Transition (1978–98): The Evolutionary, Historical, and Comparative Perspective." *Journal of Institutional and Theoretical Economics* 156:151–71.

Qian, Yingyi. 2002. *How Reform Worked in China.* Working Paper. Berkeley: University of California, Department of Economics.

Qian, Yingyi, and Chenggang Xu. 1993. "Why China's Economic Reforms Differ: The M-Form Hierarchy and Entry/Expansion of the Non-State Sector." *Economics of Transition* 1:135–70.

Rafnsson, Sveinbjörn. 1983. "Um matarhætti Íslendinga á 18. öld" [The Icelandic Diet in the Eighteenth Century]. *Saga* 21:73–87.

Rawls, John. 1971. *A Theory of Justice.* Cambridge: Harvard University Press.

Rebelo, Sergio. 1998. *The Role of Knowledge and Capital in Economic Growth.* Working Paper. Evanston: Northwestern University.

Roberts, J. M. 1997. *A Short History of the World.* Oxford: Oxford University Press.

Rodrik, Dani. 1996. "Understanding Economy Policy Reform." *Journal of Economic Literature* 34:9–41.

Rodrik, Dani. 1998. *Where Did All the Growth Go? External Shocks, Social Conflict, and Growth Collapses.* Working Paper. Cambridge: Harvard University.

Rodrik, Dani, Arvind Subramanian, and Francesco Trebbi. 2002. *Institutions Rule: The Primacy of Institutions over Geography and Integration in Economic Development.* NBER Working Paper 9305. Cambridge, Mass.: National Bureau of Economic Research.

Roland, Gérard. 2000. *Transition and Economics: Politics, Markets, and Firms.* Cambridge: MIT Press.

Romer, Paul M. 1986. "Increasing Returns and Long-Run Growth." *Journal of Political Economy* 94:1002–37.

Romer, Paul M. 1994. "The Origins of Endogenous Growth." *Journal of Economic Perspectives* 8:3–22.

Rosa, Jean-Jacques. 1993. "Nationalization, Privatization, and the Allocation of Financial Property Rights." *Public Choice* 75:317–37.

Rosa, Jean-Jacques. 1997. "Public Choice Aspects of Privatization Policies: Driving Forces and Obstacles." In *Privatization at the Turn of the Century,* ed. Herbert Giersch. Berlin: Springer.

Rosenberg, Nathan, and L. E. Birdzell. 1986. *How the West Grew Rich: The Economic Transformation of the Western World.* New York: Basic Books.

Rosenstein-Rodan, Paul. 1943. "Problems of Industrialization of Eastern and South Eastern Europe." *Economic Journal* 53:202–11.

Ruttan, Vernon W. 1991. "What Happened to Political Development?" *Economic Development and Cultural Change* 39:265–92.

Ruttan, Vernon W. 1998. "The New Growth Theory and Development Economics: A Survey." *Journal of Developmental Studies* 35:1–26.

Sachs, Jeffrey D. 2001. *Tropical Underdevelopment.* NBER Working Paper 8119. Cambridge, Mass.: National Bureau of Economic Research.

Sachs, Jeffrey D., and Andrew M. Warner. 1995. *Natural Resource Abundance and Economic Growth.* NBER Working Paper 5398. Cambridge, Mass.: National Bureau of Economic Research.

Sachs, Jeffrey D., and Wing Thye Woo. 1997. *Understanding China's Economic Performance.* Working Paper 5935. Cambridge, Mass.: National Bureau of Economic Research.

Sala-i-Martin, Xavier. 1997. "I Just Ran Two Million Regressions." *American Economic Review* 87:178–83.

Sala-i-Martin, Xavier. 2002. *The Disturbing "Rise" of Global Income Inequality.* NBER Working Paper 8904. Cambridge, Mass.: National Bureau of Economic Research.

Samuelson, Paul A. 1947. *Foundations of Economic Analysis.* Cambridge: Harvard University Press.

Sargent, Thomas J. 1993. *Bounded Rationality Macroeconomics.* Oxford: Oxford University Press.

Schremmer, D. E. 1989. "Taxation and Public Finance: Britain, France, and Germany." In *The Cambridge Economic History of Europe,* ed. P. Mathias and S. Pollard, 8:315–494. Cambridge: Cambridge University Press.

Scott, Anthony. 1955. "The Fishery: The Objectives of Sole Ownership." *Journal of Political Economy* 63:116–24.

Sider, Gerald M. 1980. "The Ties That Bind: Culture and Agriculture, Property, and Propriety in the Newfoundland Fishing Village." *Social History* 5:1–39.

Siegmund, Uwe. 1996. *Are There Nationalization-Privatization Cycles? A Theoretical-Survey and First Empirical Evidence.* Working Paper 757. Kiel: Institute of World Economics.

Simon, Herbert A. 1953. "Causal Ordering and Identifiability." In *Studies in Econometric Methods, by Cowels Commission Research Staff Members,* ed. William C. Hood and Tjalling C. Koopmans, 49–74. New York: Wiley.

Simon, Herbert A. 1957. *Models of Man.* New York: Wiley.

Simon, Herbert A. 1959. "Theories of Decision Making in Economics and Behavioral Science." *American Economic Review* 49:253–58.

Sims, Christopher A. 1988. "Projecting Policy Effects with Statistical Models." *Revista de Analisis Economico* 3:3–20.

Singleton, J. 1995. "Labour, the Conservatives, and Nationalization." In *The Political Economy of Nationalization in Britain, 1920–1950,* ed. R. Millward and J. Singleton, 13–33. Cambridge: Cambridge University Press.

Skidelsky, Robert. 1994. *John Maynard Keynes.* Vol. 2, *The Economist as Savior, 1920–1937.* New York: Penguin.

Solow, Robert M. 1956. "A Contribution to the Theory of Economic Growth." *Quarterly Journal of Economics* 70:65–94.

Solow, Robert M. 1957. "Technical Change and the Aggregate Production Function." *Review of Economic Statistics* 39:214–31.

Solow, Robert M. 1994. "Perspectives on Growth Theory." *Journal of Economic Perspectives* 8:45–54.

Solow, Robert M. 2001. "What Have We Learned from a Decade of Research on Growth? Applying Growth Theory across Countries." *World Bank Economic Review* 15:283–88.

Statistical Abstracts of Iceland. 1984. Reykjavík: Statistical Bureau of Iceland.

Steffensen, Jón, 1958. "Stature as Criterion of the Nutritional Level of Viking Age Icelanders." In *Árbók Hins íslenska fornleifafélags, fylgirit* [Yearbook of the Icelandic Archeological Society, Supplement], ed. Kristján Eldjárn. Reykjavík: Hið íslenska fornleifafélag.

Stephenson, Matthew C. 2000. *A Trojan Horse behind Chinese Walls? Problems and Prospects of U.S.-Sponsored "Rule of Law" Reform Projects in the People's Republic of China.* Working Paper 47. Cambridge: Center for International Development, Harvard University.

Stigler, George J. 1971. "The Economic Theory of Regulation." *Bell Journal of Economics and Management Science* 2:3–21.

Stigler, George J. 1986. "The Theory of Economic Regulation." In *The Essence of Stigler,* ed. Kurt Leube and Thomas Moore, 243–64. Stanford, Calif.: Hoover Institution Press.

Stiglitz, Joseph E. 1994. *Whither Socialism?* Cambridge: MIT Press.

Stiglitz, Joseph E. 1999. "Whither Reform? Ten Years of the Transition." Paper presented at the Annual World Bank Conference on Development Economics.

Stiglitz, Joseph E., and Shahid Yusuf, eds. 2001. *Rethinking the East Asian Miracle*. Oxford: Oxford University Press.

Sturzenegger, Federico, and Mariano Tommasi, eds. 1998. *The Political Economy of Reform*. Cambridge: MIT Press.

Summers, Robert, and Alan Heston. 1988. "A New Set of International Comparisons of Real Product and Price Levels Estimates for 130 Countries, 1950–1985." *Review of Income and Wealth* 34:1–25.

Summers, Robert, and Allan Heston. 1991. "The Penn World Table (Mark 5): An Expanded Set of International Comparisons, 1950–1988." *Quarterly Journal of Economics* 106:327–68.

Svensson, Jakob. 1998. "Investment, Property Rights, and Political Stability: Theory and Evidence." *European Economic Review* 42:1317–41.

Svensson, L. E. O. 1996. "The Scientific Contributions of Robert E. Lucas, Jr." *Scandinavian Journal of Economics* 98:1–10.

Swan, Trevor. 1956. "Economic Growth and Capital Accumulation." *Economic Record* 32:334–61.

Tarrow, Sidney. 1996. "Making Social Science Work across Space and Time: A Critical Reflection on Robert Putnam's Making Democracy Work." *American Political Science Review* 90:389–97.

Thoroddsen, Þorvaldur. 1919, 1921. *Lýsing Íslands: Landbúnaður á Íslandi I–II* [Portrait of Iceland: Agriculture I–II]. Copenhagen: Hið íslenska bókmenntafélag. (In Icelandic.)

Thoroddsen, Þorvaldur. 1924. "Saga fiskveiðanna við Ísland" [The History of the Icelandic Fisheries]. In Hið íslenska fræðafélag í Kaupmannahöfn, eds., *Safn fræðafélagsins um Ísland og Íslendinga, III: Þorvaldur Thoroddsen: Fjórar ritgjörðir*. Copenhagen: Hið íslenska froðafélag. (In Icelandic.)

Þorsteinsson, Björn. 1976. *Tíu þorskastríð, 1415–1976* [Ten Cod Wars, 1415–1976]. Reykjavík: Sögufélagið (In Icelandic.)

Þorsteinsson, Björn. 1980. *Íslensk miðaldasaga* [The Middle Ages in Iceland]. 2d ed. Reykjavík: Sögufélagið. (In Icelandic.)

Þorsteinsson, Björn, and Bergsteinn Jónsson. 1991. *Íslands saga til okkar daga* [History of Iceland to the Present]. Reykjavík: Sögufélagið. (In Icelandic.)

Tiebout, Charles. 1956. "A Pure Theory of Local Expenditures." *Journal of Political Economy* 64:416–24.

Tinbergen, Jan. 1952. *On the Theory of Economic Policy*. Amsterdam: North-Holland.

Tinbergen, Jan. 1956. *Economic Policy: Principles and Design*. Amsterdam: North-Holland.

Tinbergen, Jan. 1959. "The Theory of the Optimum Regime." In Tinbergen, *Selected Papers*, ed. L. H. Klassen, L. M. Koyck, and H. J. Witteveen, 264–304. Amsterdam: North-Holland.

Tollison, Robert D. 1982. "Rent Seeking: A Survey." *Kyklos* 35:575–602.

Tooby, J., and L. Cosmides. 1992. "The Psychological Foundations of Culture." In *The Adaptive Mind: Evolutionary Psychology and The Generation of Culture*, ed. J. Barkow, L. Cosmides, and J. Tooby, 19–136. New York: Oxford University Press.

Tornell, Aaron. 1998. *Reform from Within.* NBER Working Paper 6497. Cambridge, Mass.: National Bureau of Economic Research.

Townsend, Robert M. 1992. "Understanding the Structure of Village and Regional Economies." In *Contract Economics,* ed. Lars Werin and Hans Wijkander, 114–38. Oxford: Blackwell.

Townsend, Robert M. 1993. *The Medieval Village Economy: A Study of the Pareto Mapping in General Equilibrium Models.* Princeton: Princeton University Press.

United Kingdom. Parliament. 1918. *First Interim Report of the Committee on Currency and Foreign Exchange after the War.* Cmnd 9182. London: HMSO.

United Nations Development Programme. 1999. *Human Development Report.* New York: Oxford University Press.

University of Pennsylvania Law Review. 1996. Vol. 144, no. 4. Special issue on law, economics, and norms.

Vanberg, Viktor J. 1998. "Rule Following." In *The Handbook of Economic Methodology,* ed. John B. Davis, Wade D. Hands, Uskali Mäki, 432–35. Cheltenham: Elgar.

Vasey, Daniel E. 1991. "Population, Agriculture, Famine: Iceland, 1784–1785.*" Human Ecology* 19:323–50.

Vasey, Daniel E. 1996. "Population Regulation, Ecology, and Political Economy in Preindustrial Iceland." *American Ethnologist* 23:366–92.

Vietor, R. H. K. 1990. "Regulation and Competition in America, 1920s–1980s." In *Governments, Industries, and Markets: Aspects of Government-Industry Relations in the UK, Japan, West Germany, and the USA since 1945,* ed. M. Chick, 10–35. Aldershot: Elgar.

Vietor, R. H. K. 1994. "Contrived Competition: Economic Regulation and Deregulation, 1920s–1980s." *Business History* 36:1–32.

Wacziarg, Romain. 2002. "Review of Easterly's *The Elusive Quest for Growth.*" *Journal of Economic Literature* 40:907–18.

Weingast, Barry R. 1993. "Constitutions as Governance Structure: The Political Foundations of Secure Market." *Journal of Institutional and Theoretical Economics* 149:286–311.

Weingast, Barry R. 1994. *The Political Impediment to Economic Reform: Political Risk and Enduring Gridlock.* Working Paper. Stanford, Calif.: Hoover Institution, Stanford University.

Weingast, Barry R. 1995. "The Economic Role of Political Institutions—Market-Preserving Federalism and Economic Development." *Journal of Law, Economics, and Organization* 11:1–31.

Weingast, Barry R. 1997. "The Political Foundations of Democracy and the Rule of Law." *American Political Science Review* 91:245–63.

Williamson, Oliver E. 1975. *Markets and Hierarchies.* New York: Free Press.

Williamson, Oliver E. 1985. *The Economic Institutions of Capitalism: Firms, Markets, Relational Contracting.* New York: Free Press.

Winiecki, Jan. 1986. "Are Soviet-Type Economies Entering an Era of Long-Term Decline?" *Soviet Studies* 38(3):325–48.

Winiecki, Jan. 1990. "Why Economic Reforms Fail in the Soviet System? A Property Rights–Based Approach." *Economic Inquiry* 28:195–221. Reprinted in *Empirical Studies in Institutional Change,* ed. Lee Alston, Thráinn Eggertsson, and Douglass C. North, 63–91. New York: Cambridge University Press, 1996.

Wittman, Donald A. 1996. *The Myth of Democratic Failure: Why Political Institutions Are Efficient.* Chicago: University of Chicago Press.

Woo-Cumings, Meredith. 2001. "Miracle as a Prologue: The State and Reform of the Corporate Sector in Korea." In *Rethinking the East Asia Miracle,* ed. Joseph E. Stiglitz and Shahid Yusuf, 343–78. Washington, D.C.: World Bank; New York: Oxford University Press.

Yandle, Tracy. 2003. "The Challenge of Building Successful Stakeholder Organizations: New Zealand's Experience in Developing a Fisheries Co-Management Regime." *Marine Policy* 27:179–92.

Author Index

Subject Index

Africa: Botswana growth miracle, 171–73, 227; economic decline, causes of, 170–72, 227
Albania, socialist, growth problems of, 186
antinorm policy, cooperation-defection differential, 75, 88–90

Bayes's rule, and updating of beliefs, 95
Botswana, modern growth, sources of, 171–73, 227

China: dual-track approach, 165–66; future developments, 166–67, 227; legal reforms, 177, 182; modern economic growth, 163–67, 227
contracts: definition, 27; linked employment contracts, 51, 111–12, 219; private order and growth, 186–89
convergence hypothesis, 131

decentralization/centralization, long waves in modern history, 42–46, 210
decision theory, mathematical, 128, 130
determinacy (Bhagwati's) paradox. *See* endogenous policy
development economics, 204
divide-and-rule equilibrium, 68–73

economic growth: and democracy/autocracy, 59–73, 212–13; extensive, 10, 205; historical roots, seventeenth-century England, 68–69; intensive, 10; modern experi-

ence of, 10–11, 42–46; punctuated, 47, 53–58, 211; rise of the West, role of Atlantic trade, 69–70, 213
economic policy, theory of, 4, 128–37, 221–22; basic assumptions, 129; convergence, 131; instruments, rules of thumb, 131–32; policy models, defined, 129–30, 136; role of economists, 130
Ecuador, legal transplant, 179, 228
endogenous policy, 5, 142–45; and coalition politics, 144–45; degrees of freedom, 145–48; and optimality, 223; and rent seeking, 144, 223; and social norms, 145; and theory of economic policy, 142
ethnicity: diversity and growth, 56–57; ethnic animosity, theory of, 91–93, 95

failed social models, durability of, 41–43, 210

game theory: evolutionary games and norms, 90–91; repeated games and norms, 79–80
Grágás, law code of Icelandic Commonwealth, 51, 211, 219
growth-friendly institutional environments: diverse foundations of, 183–90; general,182, 212; private order, limits of, 186–89; stability and endogenous dynamics, 184–85; and a strong or weak state, 185–86
growth regressions, international cross-country, 20, 170, 206, 211–12